Triumphant
Warrior

A Soul Survivor
Of The Wilmington Ten

Triumphant Warrior

A Soul Survivor
Of The Wilmington Ten

A Memoir

WAYNE MOORE

WARRIOR PRESS

Triumphant Warrior:
A Soul Survivor of the Wilmington Ten

By Wayne Moore

Published by Warrior Press
Ann Arbor, Michigan

For more information contact:
Warrior Press
Email: wmportcity@gmail.com
Website: www.wilmtenfoundation.org

ISBN-13: 978-0615978154 (Custom Universal)
ISBN-10: 0615978150
Library of Congress Control Number: 2014903974

Book cover and interior design: Audria Wooster
designbyindigo.com

DEDICATED TO MY MOTHER

This memoir is dedicated to my mother, civil rights activist Dolores Foy Moore. She was a direct descendant of my great-great grandfather Nathanial Foy, who was sold into slavery on the Poplar Grove Plantation. On January 3, 1857, plantation owner Joseph Foy purchased my great-great-grandfather Nathaniel, his brother Daniel, and their mother Nancy, for the sum of one thousand and ten dollars.

Poplar Grove Plantation is located just outside of Wilmington on Highway 17 near Scotts Hill. Poplar Grove was once one of the largest plantations in the area, covering over one hundred acres, from Market Street to Masonboro Sound.

On the next page is the original purchase agreement for my great-great-grandfather, Nathaniel Foy, his mother Nancy and his brother Daniel.

Wilmington N.C. Jany 3d 1857

Received of Jas. M. Foy One Thousand and Ten Dollars being in full for the purchase of a negro Slave named *Nancy* with her two Children *Daniel* and *Nathaniel* belonging to the Estate of A. J. Washburn Deced the right and title of Said Slaves I warrant and defend So far as I am authorized to do as Administrator of A. J. Washburn Decd and no further as witness my hand and Seal Signed Sealed and Delivered in presence of

M. Crowley

Nicholas Nixon
Admr

CONTENTS

ACKNOWLEDGMENTS

The idea to write a book about this saga began years ago during my imprisonment. Marilyn Moore of the former Commission for Racial Justice of the United Church of Christ convinced me that it was important that I chronicle my experience. Still I would not have taken this challenge seriously without the inspiration of my cousin Joe Wood.

Thanks to my family for supporting me every step of the way. Thanks to my friends, especially Jean Marie Gailliard, for providing the spiritual as well as moral support I needed throughout this process.

Thanks to my literary agent Faith Childs who compiled twelve pages of handwritten notes to guide me in the right direction after reading my rough draft. I will be forever grateful for the many hours Faith Childs, Karen Simpson, Dr. Liz Hines and Bertha Boykin Todd spent going over my manuscript, helping me to make sense of my scrambled thoughts. However my scrambled thoughts could not have taken the shape of a readable memoir without the expertise of Michel Marriot, my literary consultant. Special thanks to Karen Clay Beatty, Marion Morris and Ellie Mays for proof-reading page by page, correcting grammatical and syntactical errors.

From the outset my goal was to write a compelling memoir that embraced the importance of an accurate historical account of my life and experiences. That could not have been accomplished without the dedicated research assistance of people like the now retired Beverly Tetterton at the New Hanover County

Library; Jerry Parnell, Coordinator, Library Special Collections Department, Special Collections, Randall Library, University of North Carolina-Wilmington; Christina Jones, Archivist at the National Archives II College Park, MD, and Katie Nash Archivist/Special Collections Librarian at Elon University-Belk Library.

Many thanks to Amnesty International who pointed to the *Wilmington Ten* being held as political prisoners in the U.S., at a time when the Carter Administration was pressuring the Soviet Union to free its political prisoners. The Wilmington Ten became the first group of prisoners in the United States to be officially declared political prisoners by Amnesty International in 1978. This unanimous decision by Amnesty International received worldwide attention in light of President Carter's relentless demands on the Soviet Union to free its political prisoners. Before all was said and done, Presidents Nixon, Ford, Carter, and Reagan all had to address a tremendous national and international campaign to free the Wilmington Ten.

In addition to Amnesty International, there were millions of supporters of the Wilmington Ten during the 1970s and early 1980s. Most notably was the strong support from the Commission for Racial Justice of the United Church of Christ under the leadership of Reverend Dr. Charles E. Cobb, Sr. In fact, the majority of the 1.7 million members of the United Church of Christ denomination supported the campaign to free the Wilmington Ten.

Many thanks to Angela Davis, Charlene Mitchell, Maria Ramos and the National Alliance Against Racist and Political Repression whose relentless support helped to galvanize a worldwide campaign to free the Wilmington Ten. Many thanks also to Imani Kazana and the National Wilmington Ten Defense Committee who worked tirelessly to help free the Wilmington Ten. Many thanks to Attorney James E. Ferguson, Sr., and the entire Julius Chambers Law Firm in Charlotte, NC, supported by

Attorney Margaret Burnham, Attorney Reginald F. Lewis, and a host of other civil rights attorneys, including Charles Becton, Frank Ballance, John Harmon, Irv. Joyner, and Travis Francis. Many thanks to the National Council of Churches in the USA and the World Council of Churches who both supported the freedom of the Wilmington Ten.

Many thanks to Charles Rangel (D.,NY), John Conyers (D.,MI) Don Edwards (D.,CA), Walter Fauntroy (D.,DC), Fortney Stark (D.,CA), George Miller (D.,CA), Robert Drinan, and Ron Dellums (D.,CA) for visiting us in prison. These fearless warriors were also among 55 members of the Congress of the United States, who on January 23, 1980, filed an *Amici Curiae* brief before the United States Court of Appeals for the Fourth Circuit on behalf of the Wilmington Ten. Many thanks to God for teaching me strength through struggle. Thanks to George E. Curry of the National News Paper Association. Thanks to Mary Alice Jervay Thatch, Cash Michaels, Irv Joyner, and Sonya Bennetone for their hard work and dedication to the Wilmington Ten Pardon of Innocence Project. Thanks to Susie Edwards and William Winters at change.org who gathered over 100,000 signatures of support. Thanks to Rev. Barber and the NAACP for their support and the many signatures they gathered. Thank you Melissa Harris-Perry for your letter to the governor. And last but certainly not least, I would like to thank Beverly Perdue for listening to us and taking a stand for the cause of justice.

PROLOGUE

The air that blew lightly over Wilmington—salted and spiced with the sea that first gave this city meaning and purpose—had been strangely charged for days.

It was like all the air that had been breathed in and out of black chests and white chests, during those days on this coastal chunk of North Carolina, had picked up the fear, the suspicion, the anxiety, and the hatred that stirred inside too many for too long. There had been threats of racial violence in this place that had been shared, sometimes uneasily, by blacks and whites. There had been lots of talk about settling scores, how black folk had forgotten their rightful place beneath whites, who had simply been born superior. Some of the super-heated words evoked Biblical redemption. Other, cooler words called out bravely for reason and calm.

The press had been fanning the embers of racial ignorance for weeks, helping to spread the notion that trouble was on the wind, and that groups like the Ku Klux Klan might consider Wilmington a choice stop on their tour of terror. And their kind came. Lots of them, homegrown, didn't have to come from very far at all.

The *Wilmington Messenger*, *Raleigh News and Observer*, and *Charlotte Observer* all played their parts in dehumanizing black people and devaluing black life in their newspapers.

Against this backdrop, some prayed that a delicate peace might hold. Others armed themselves and built any barricade in any place that might stand against what was widely believed to be a coming storm of fists, fire and bullets.

Then, my hometown exploded.

Blood, mostly black blood, ran wild like the cowards who had unleashed it. The air, ashy and bitter, tasted like death. The fires could be heard crackling and loudly exhaling ugly clouds of what were once dear possessions, the sum total of ages of hard work, and of a community's longings and aspirations. There was the crash of window glass, the muffled thuds of walls falling in on themselves, and the jeers and cheers of mobs alive with a lethal lust for black destruction. There were also the wails of worry and weeping, and of firefighters struggling to save what was already lost.

When the smoke cleared, and the sun rose over the city again, it was a new day in more ways than one. Wilmington, once a commercial hub of the Confederacy and an emerging beacon for a multiracial America, would never be the same. The heart of black Wilmington, known as Brooklyn, was gone.

An unknown number of black men had been killed in the massacre. Some had been shot down in the streets like rabid dogs. Some barely escaped the lynch men's noose. Noted historians believe that the actual black death toll exceeded sixty, maybe in the hundreds. But no one would ever know the full truth, because police and hospital records of the dead and injured were either lost or criminally incomplete. No one will ever know how many black bodies were dumped like trash into the Cape Fear River that runs fast through my city to the Atlantic Ocean.

What is known is that no whites perished that day, nor were any ever charged. On the other hand, thousands of blacks fled Wilmington to never return. Much of its black political, financial and professional classes swept out across the country like unfortunates on shores overcome by a tsunami.

Wilmington never fully recovered from that day. I know because I was swept up some seventy-three years later in its echo, in a kind of historical aftershock of the Wilmington Race Riot of 1898. This is the legacy I was born to. History seldom, if ever, is set down in a straight line. Yet, the epicenter for a small group of activists—mostly black, mostly young and mostly men—standing up for black Wilmington's equal justice and dignity—were holed up in a church barely a block away from the intersection of Seventh and Nun Streets.

In 1898 a black-owned newspaper, the *Wilmington Daily Record*, proudly stood in that spot in a two-story, wood-frame building called Love and Charity Hall. It was the first physical victim of that November 10, when hundreds of armed whites rampaged into its office, tearing up anything that could be torn up. What couldn't be destroyed by hand was destroyed by fire.

It was a fire that on February 6, 1971, burned down Mike's Grocery. It was a modest, nondescript store owned by a local Greek family, located across the street from Gregory Congregational Church, an institution with roots to the first legal school for blacks in the city. I and nine others would be charged and convicted of destroying Mike's Grocery and, for good measure, shooting at firefighters who struggled to put the fire out. We did none of these things

We came to be known worldwide as the *Wilmington Ten,* in a stubborn era of hair-trigger injustice stretching from the Chicago Seven of the late 1960s to reverberations more recent, like the Central Park Five of the 1990s, and beyond.

Among the Ten was Benjamin Franklin Chavis, a twenty-three-year-old, yet-to-be-well-known civil rights activist and United Church of Christ minister, who led us. Forty years later, and after nearly fifteen-hundred days in prison, we remain friends.

At the time Mike's Grocery was going up in smoke, I was about a mile away at my sister Stephanie's apartment in the Hillcrest public housing project. My nephews were real young then, one and two years old. My sister and her husband were going to the movies, which is a rare treat when you have little kids. I was happy to babysit. There had been violence in the city all week. I knew, deep inside where you know things before your brain does, that something was going to happen. I could almost sense those words churning in my belly.

I had left the church in the middle of the night because there was so much stuff going on in there; it was getting out of hand. I thought things were getting too hot. The scene was so crazy and chaotic. White people were shooting at the church, and the mayor and police were refusing our requests for a curfew at night to help protect us.

The thing was that people had brought guns into Gregory Church. When you grow up in the Baptist church, you're brought up to know that the church is supposed to be a sanctuary. But I also understood that the guns were there strictly for defense. I had slipped out the night before disappearing into a back alley and walking the twenty minutes or so to my home with my mother on South Fourth Street, a low income section of the city. Far away, I could hear sirens and see the amber glow that big fires make when they are pushing back the night. Fires were raging all over the city. I wanted to hear what my mother, Dolores Foy Moore, had to say about all of this. She was an activist and the finest person I have ever known. I had been in Gregory Church since Monday. People had brought food in for us to eat, since many of us did not leave the church for days. We had made it kind of our new home. But *home* was home. I needed home. I needed my family that Friday night. Someone had tried to set fire to Mike's, but it didn't work. The next night, Stephen Mitchell was shot and killed by police. He was a student just like me. I knew him. We were the same age: seventeen.

I found out about it on the televised news at home alone in a darkened living room. The police said there was sniper fire coming from around the church. They said they returned fire, and Steve was killed. Just like that. When we began to organize our protests, we had no idea that things were going to escalate to the point that they did. People were dying.

When the fire started at Mike's the following day, I didn't return to the church. Instead, I walked several blocks from where I lived on South Fourth Street, and then on to my sister's place in Hillcrest. I got there around 7 p.m. that evening. Late that night, I returned home...

I had never been involved with Mike's Grocery more than to occasionally buy a dime's worth of loose butter and oatmeal cookies. We—nine black men, mostly high school juniors and seniors, and a thirty-five-year-old white woman—were collectively given 282 years behind prison bars.

I was handed a twenty-nine-year sentence. By then, I was nineteen years old, facing a future that had no relationship at all to my personal history. To me, I was a product of a close and loving family. Prison was not anything I, or anyone who knew me, ever imagined would be my destiny. I had my scrapes here and there, for example skipping school, taking a few under-age sips of cheap wine, or things of that nature. But I was a good kid with a good heart. I was a kid with a big afro and a keen eye for a pretty girl. In many ways, I was an all-American black boy fixed on being a man my mama would be proud of.

Wayne Moore? Firebombing a grocery store?

No one believed that except the members of the stacked jury that decidedly stacked the odds against me and my co-defendants.

In essence, the Wilmington Ten was a case in which state and some federal officials unjustly arrested, tried, convicted, imprisoned, and repressed us. As Willie Earl Vereen, one of my fellow Ten members told a newspaper late last year, "We were conspired against. We weren't the conspirators."

In the fall of 1968, most of us were just students caught up in the court-ordered desegregation of the public school system in New Hanover County, which included Wilmington. It was the county's largest and most urban city, with a population back then of just more than 57,000. With little or no preparation on the part of our Board of Education, our much beloved Williston Senior High School, which was all black, was closed. This came in the tense times after the assassination of Dr. Martin Luther King, Jr., in Memphis, another Southern town with a dubious racial history.

Williston's teachers and administration were transferred or retired, and its 1,100 students were assigned to two majority-white high schools. This was even more painful for a community in which Williston was always much more than its brick and mortar. For years, even while attending Williston's junior high, I had dreamed of wearing its colors—maroon and gold—and taking my place among the generations of black Wilmington who had gone there, learning at the feet of the best and the brightest of our community. These were teachers and coaches and principals who not only knew us, but *cared* about us.

Instead, I was, like all of my Williston classmates, cast into a student body that was resistant and unwelcoming to us. It was, to say the least, a bad fit.

Inspired by activists like Malcolm X, Huey P. Newton and Dr. King, a bunch of us black students stood up. We began actively protesting what we clearly saw as institutionalized racial discrimination and hostilities surrounding the desegregation of the public school system there. There would be marches and demands for justice.

And did I mention that all of this racial conflict drew the Ku Klux Klan and white supremacist groups to Wilmington? They seemed immune to police, openly riding around in their cars and shooting, seemingly whenever they wanted, at the Gregory Church where we regularly organized, strategized and operated a makeshift school in an adjoining church building, after more than 500 students joined a boycott of the county's public schools.

By 1971, there had been several months of violent clashes between white and black students, disorderly conduct arrests, protests and student suspensions and expulsions. When New Hanover County school administrators refused our requests for a memorial service for Dr. King, seventy students staged a civil rights style sit-in, in the cafeteria of Hoggard High School. Fifteen students were identified as the sit-in's leaders, including me, and were promptly expelled. That was January 15, 1971.

Less than two weeks later, Ben Chavis, who came to us as a field organizer for the United Church of Christ Commission for Racial Justice, held a press conference at Gregory Church. We detailed our grievances and demanded that the student leaders expelled from Hoggard and New Hanover High schools be reinstated—right away. We weren't. In fact, pleas to reinstate us went unheeded. I would have to attend an alternative night school to graduate high school at all.

Despite a hard winter, Wilmington, North Carolina, was literally heating up in early 1971, and it would remain so for much of the year. You could feel the tension, taste it on your tongue like black Wilmington must have experienced in 1898. Remember, history seldom, if ever, is set down in a straight line.

Basically, all we wanted was to be able to celebrate Dr. Martin Luther King's birthday, have more black cheerleaders, and see more of our talented athletes on the various sports teams. We were teenagers. Really, we were just kids. We quickly realized and decided that the only way the Board of Education would hear us was to shut the schools down. That meant a black boycott of all public schools in Wilmington and New Hanover County, but with an emphasis on Hoggard High and its sister school, New Hanover High.

Most of us had a combination of fear and anticipation, and anger too, swirling in our guts. There were all kinds of emotions. This was serious business and we knew it. At the same time, there were factions of white Wilmington that moved to take advantage of all the racial turmoil. These people didn't want to see black students bussed into their suburban schools. You couldn't read their minds, but you could read their lips: "We don't want you here, anyway."

Honestly, near the end of that first week of February 1971, we had no idea that things were going to escalate to the point they did. We did ask the mayor to grant a curfew that would help protect us from street attacks. But the mayor, Luther Cromartie, and his police chief refused, saying "there was no evidence that violence was being directed at the church" where we were staying. Besides, Cromartie said, a curfew would be "expensive."

Memories are long. Blacks marched on City Hall demanding that the city better protect its black neighborhoods. Suddenly, it didn't feel like 1898 was that long ago. Still no curfew. Sporadic fires blazed, claiming, among others, a local furniture store and restaurant. A black minister was shot just outside Gregory Church by whites. Then Mike's Grocery burned down and Stephen Mitchell was killed. The next day a fifty-seven-year-old vigilante was killed when he drove through barricades set up at Gregory Church, firing shots. Authorities alleged the fatal shot came from the church barricades.

Finally, two months later, after Ben and a group of my fellow students and Anne Sheppard, a VISTA volunteer, were charged with the grocery store fire, they came for me. It was the first day of May in 1971. My life imploded. I was the last to join the Wilmington Ten, ensnared in a joyless circus of injustice.

We all went to prison innocent of all charges. It would take almost a decade before the case brought against us would unravel like all lies eventually do. In 1980, the United States Court of

Appeals for the Fourth Circuit overturned the convictions of the Wilmington Ten, citing prosecutorial misconduct and perjury. Yes, three key witnesses recanted their stories, that ended up crudely rewriting ours.

And, on the last day of 2012, at 2:10 p.m., Eastern Standard Time, North Carolina's outgoing governor, Beverly Eaves Perdue, issued and signed a "Pardon of Innocence" for the Wilmington Ten. The pardon did not come without pressure, first and foremost from the black press. The NAACP took up the cause many months later. But also near year's end, pressure came from mainstream media like the *New York Times* and an "open letter" from Melissa Harris-Perry of MSNBC.

Petitions signed by more than 130,000 people calling for our pardon also landed on the desk of a Democratic governor of a red state. I never stopped believing what I learned from Dr. King: "The arc of the moral universe is long, but it bends toward justice." Perdue only helped to confirm it.

Today, four of the Wilmington Ten are no longer with us in body. But in so many ways they, like all of us, will live on as witnesses, as well as markers in the road to better intersections toward the just and the humane.

I hope this memoir can be a map to such a place where truth is everlasting and always liberating. Writing it over these years—starting as little more than scribbles to myself while I sat lost, at first, in a prison cell—has helped me regain a life in which so much was stolen.

I hold no bitterness.

Someone recently told me that my eyes still laugh. I don't know about all that. What I do know, as sure as my name, is that I still dream for myself; I still dream for my children; and always I dream for people who ceaselessly strive to be free, and are willing to fight to be free.

1

STRAINING TO LIFT
THE WEIGHT OF INJUSTICE

The violence that erupted over Wilmington, North Carolina, from 1968 to 1971, and, for that matter, throughout America during that time, was a direct result of pent-up rage. It was a collective straightening of a backbone long stooped. For me, and practically everybody who shared my skin's hue, that rage began with the Trans-Atlantic Slave Trade. This voracious cannibalization of fellow human beings came to American shores in the seventeenth century. Yes, it was a long time ago. But the spiritual stench of African slavery is still very much with us today.

That is definitely true for me, a sixty-one-year-old, great-great grandson of a North Carolina slave doing my best to live on the right side of the future.

Even with human physics, there are causes and effects.

Once, when I was a teenager, I sat on a huge rock at Fort Fisher, a state park with sugary sand beaches, squawking seagulls and keyhole urchins, all about thirty miles south of Wilmington. During the Civil War, this out-stretched earthen and brick fortress was, as one historical reference put it, "the South's most powerful bastion." But on this sunny afternoon, I wasn't thinking much about the Confederacy and the bulging buckets of blood, referring to the union and rebel blood that had soaked this ground. My gaze was fixed on the vast Atlantic Ocean that restlessly rippled and rolled against the shimmering horizon. I was thinking of a mighty carnage, of mass murdering and kidnapping on a global scale.

Before I fully realized it, I was reflecting on what the journey across the Atlantic must have been for my ancestors. I was lost in thought thinking about the Middle Passage. The roar of the waves as they pounded the shore gave due and timely notice of the destructive forces that most certainly confronted any vessel of that time on the high seas. It would have been hard enough for a seaman on some creaking, sea-slickened deck of a slave ship. But what about below, in the bowels of such ships? There, in a dark, dank, stink of a waking nightmare, I contemplated what it must have been like to be captured, chained, innocent of no crime other than being seen as inhuman in the cold eyes of those who captured you. Little did I know that I would, years later, get a glimpse of an answer, experiencing a twentieth-century version of the slave ship in which I was captured and locked away—confined—for no other reason than the color of my skin.

In the darkest days of my incarceration behind the "Wall" of Central Prison in Raleigh, NC, I reached into the not-so-deep recesses of my mind for ancestral memory. I would revisit where I had actually never been, the way lots of African Americans making their first trip to Africa talk about "going back." I daydreamed, *nightmared* really, of the ship and felt a real connection between my now and my people's then. I experienced a kind of inner vision, seeing myself lying on my back in manacles, as the ship groaned all around me in a horror hold of others just like me, chained.

I could hear the dying, the sick and the able bodies unable to do anything more than rattle their shackles, and beg their gods for freedom now stolen. I'd live these atrocities in my head, even experiencing enslaved Africans giving birth to the first African Americans in those ships, and I would appreciate, that much more, being a black American. Sometimes, during my incarceration, I would open my eyes and convince myself that I didn't have it so bad behind bars compared to their struggle.

Back then behind bars, I'd tell myself an unshakable truth: I come from people who have endured much worse, like slaves, lynch mobs and the likes of the Wilmington Massacre of 1898. With that, my pain would lessen for a while, and I'd feel my shoulders begin to square and my backbone stiffen.

I wish I had known all of that, the great record of black people's relentless courage, strength and faith, when I was a little black boy growing up in Wilmington, North Carolina.

* — *

It was an ordinary Thursday.

The weekend was coming fast, meaning no school and more time to play some basketball at the community center downtown on Second Street, and to hang out at Locke's Pool Room not far away. But on this particular Thursday late afternoon, I was thinking about my girlfriend, Ronette Washington, a brown-eyed, brown teen beauty I had met while we attended Williston Junior High. At the time, I didn't know that she was two-timing me and a buddy—a guy who had a flashy '55 Chevy when I had nothing more than the rubber soles laced to my feet.

They say ignorance is bliss, and I was blissful as could be as I walked along Castle Street on my way to Ronette's house. I had a little extra bounce in my long skinny-legged strides as I thought nothing could be wrong in the world. The sky was as blue as the bluest piece of stained glass in the great pointed-arch windows of Gregory Congregational Church close by on Seventh Street. I was never really into flowers, still I couldn't help to inhale with eyes as much as with my nose, all the azaleas around me that were in full bloom and full effect.

It was April, and no showers were in sight.

I turned a corner and slowed, suddenly hearing all these car horns blaring. At first, I thought maybe somebody just got married. It was, after all, a great spring day for new beginnings. I kept walking without a care I knew about. The horns got louder, closer. Must be some kind of celebration, I thought, like the way people do in Atlanta when the Braves win the pennant.

Then the words as sharp and bloody as butchers' blades tore open my heart.

"That nigger King is dead! That nigger King is dead! That nigger King is dead!

My legs and arms seemed to pump on their own as I found myself running home, fast. I felt confused, and empty inside, except for the crusty wheel of fear that was turning in my gut. Minutes later, I slammed through the front door of our house. The first thing I saw was my mother's face. The tears streaming down her cheeks told me everything I needed to know.

Yet, I flopped down in front of our television set for more.

Walter Cronkite was talking in that low, even way he talked. "Dr. Martin Luther King, Jr., the apostle of nonviolence in the civil rights movement, has been shot to death in Memphis, Tennessee. Police have issued an all-points bulletin for a well-dressed, young white man seen running from the scene."

No one spoke a word, not my mother, not me, nor any of my brothers or sisters. The earth had not flung its oceans into space. Our planet had not collided with the moon, nor had the world spun into a million pieces. But on that day, April 4, 1968, none of us seemed to know the difference.

As poor as we were back then—eight children crammed into a two-bedroom house, no daddy, and mama struggling to at least to get ends acquainted—we proudly displayed two possessions. Mounted prominently on the living room wall was a framed print of a white Jesus and right next to his blue-eyed, heavenly gaze was an over-sized portrait of Dr. Martin Luther King, Jr.

For most black people in the 1960s, especially those of my mother's generation, Dr. King was a messiah, if not in the Biblical way, certainly in the secular way, as in being a deliverer of us out of America's hellish determination to keep black people down. I'll never forget my mother being enthralled by Dr. King's prophetic words and the eloquence in which he spoke them. She had long been sick and tired of how black men in the movies and on TV were portrayed as shuffling, eye-popping buffoons, as Stepin Fecthit and Amos 'n' Andy.

Dr. King, so aptly named, was a man who stood up and whose grace and intelligence could not be denied.

Dr. King wasn't supposed to be in Memphis the day he was killed. He had been scheduled to speak in Wilmington on April 4, in fact, at Williston Senior High School. But his work with the sanitation workers strike, especially in the aftermath of a demonstration that had turned violent, held him in Tennessee. He had to cancel his speech at the city's only black high school, my school. Because of this twist of history, because of a feeling that if he had spoken to us that day he would have lived decades more, black Wilmington felt a special connection to Dr. King's death, as well as to his life.

Numb. That's the best way I could describe the way I felt in the immediate aftermath of Dr. King's death. I was just a kid, trying to be a kid. But the aching weight of the world, of my skin history from slave ship to plantation to the massacre of 1898 and then April 4, 1968, pressed hard on my young, bony shoulders. I realized that I was also standing on the shoulders of my ancestors, and I couldn't just live, like so many others, simply for myself. I owed my people more than that.

Later, not much later, days after Dr. King's assassination, I was filled with anger. And there was fear, too, fear for the future of black people in America.

It would be a long, long time before I could appreciate an azalea again.

❋ ——— ❋

There had been no preparation or premeditation for violence that April day. But as if on cue, as word of Dr. King's murder spread over Wilmington, so did a black rage. It spilled clumsily into and over the streets like unthinking lava, black on the outside, red and super-heated on the inside. Dangerous.

It was the very thing that contradicted everything that Dr. King was about. It was also in high contrast to centuries of history in which blacks had not responded en masse to physical and spiritual violence that fell over their lives, like a shadow strangely too heavy to lift or escape. When I was growing up, I often watched with disgust and anger how black protesters were beaten and scorned by white people. This was a time when figures like Theophilus Eugene "Bull" Connor became an international symbol for bull-headed racism. As commissioner of Public Safety for Birmingham, Alabama, Connor dedicated himself to enforcing racial segregation and injustice during the civil rights movement.

On television, I watched the result of his order to use fire hoses and police attack dogs against peaceful right-to-vote demonstrators, including children. On "Bloody Sunday," March 7, 1965, some six-hundred civil rights marchers headed east out of Selma on US Route 80. They got only as far as the Edmund Pettus Bridge six blocks away, where state and local lawmen attacked them with billy clubs and tear gas. The marchers were driven back into Selma.

I watched with a knot in my stomach. I sat there watching people who looked like me, children who could be my siblings, women who could be my teachers, my mother, and young men, who could... be me. It gave me a sinking feeling. It was the kind of outright wrong that in the movies John Wayne would ride in and right, or Tarzan would swing in and rout the evil, or on TV when Superman would stand up to those savage fire hoses, and sweep away the snarling dogs. Then I realized that these "heroes" looked more like the villains than me, and you think, maybe they were never intended to be our heroes. You watch and realize that we, black people, will have to be our own heroes.

Even as a thirteen-year-old boy, I wanted to stand up, join the protesters in some sort of way. But all the while I could feel fear blowing cold through my chest, through the place where my heart was supposed to be. I watched and I came to know just what white folks were capable of when you demanded no more than to be treated like them.

My mother had watched too, and realized all of these years before I ever did. She knew that the sharp, white blade of racial violence was never too far outside our front door. On the day that Dr. King was killed, Mom would not let me leave the house. The television droned on, broadcasting dispatches like from the front line of a war. I peered out from the safety of my upstairs window. Off in the distance, I could see fires lighting up the night sky. I understood the pain and madness that was stoking those flames.

I wanted to do something, but I didn't know what. I was in shock. We were all in shock. Dr. King was the hero of black people everywhere. For so many of us he was our only hope. Lots of us looked at Dr. King as if he was some kind of a messiah, our Moses, someone to lead us to the Promised Land, as he had said he glimpsed the night before he was slain. One question was never far from my thoughts that day, and for much of the horrible week that followed: "What do we do now?"

I had never been drawn to violence of any kind. It wasn't my nature. Back in junior high school, I had a reputation for running to school yard fights not to watch, but to break them up. I was a foot short of six feet and weighed no more than 140 pounds. Yet there I was, skin 'n' bones, pushing combatants apart and doing my best to be the cooler head. Long before Michael Jackson famously coined the phrase, "I was a lover, not a fighter."

It was as simple as that. When I had gotten old enough to think about things like that, I considered myself a disciple of Martin Luther King, Jr.; I still do. Then and now, I subscribe wholeheartedly to his belief in nonviolence. But on the hot April nights in Wilmington, I wanted to be in the streets. Suddenly, I wanted to be a part of the destruction of anything white. I wanted to be a part of the black struggle. I desperately wanted to be part of an answer, even if it wasn't the best answer.

I wanted to sneak out of the house. But I decided against it.

Still, without me fully realizing it, I had just begun a life-changing journey. The night that Dr. King died, so did a part of me.

Despite the uprising the night before, Wilmington and New Hanover County schools opened the following day—on time. At Williston Senior High, two-hundred students left classes at 8:30 a.m. and marched downtown to the courthouse. There, they prayed for peace, the way Dr. King would have done. I was going to Williston Junior High back then, and so only watched as the big kids stood up and acted with all the purpose and dignity grown people might.

I was a good boy and did my best to respect the wishes of my mother; I didn't get involved. I knew my mother was afraid for her children, all seven of us. She didn't venture onto the streets either when the trouble came. And that frightened me even more because my mother was a tough lady when she had to be.

In April 1968, my mother made a living by working at a sewing machine factory in Wilmington and making money on the side as a domestic. My father had disappeared years ago and provided no help that I knew about. My mother had such remarkable strength, even in the face of raw racism. When I was a little boy, she took me to the movies in Wilmington. When the white movie theater manager directed us to a set of stairs leading to segregated black seating in the theater's balcony, my mother shook her head and spoke up, telling the manager that "you know this isn't right."

She was always a community activist, always looking for new ways to right old wrongs. I loved her. Later, when Williston Senior High School was closed, she spoke out against it. She realized that whites, starting with their riot of 1898, had destroyed black Wilmington's political power, its financial power, and now with the closing of the only black high school in town, whites were destroying the black community's will power.

So, to please Mama, I watched as a group of Williston Senior High students marched to the predominately white New Hanover High School and lowered its flag to half-mast in honor of Dr. King. Despite the many calls for peace, when night fell over the city that night, the violence resumed, and so did my feelings to join the fiery fray.

But again, I didn't.

By late Saturday night, the mayor, O.O. Allsbrook, ordered a curfew that would stay in effect until after Dr. King's funeral in Atlanta on on April 9. That went Ok. The next day, a school day, groups of students held their own memorial services in Wilmington.

But during some of these memorials, groups of students started marching down Fourth Street, through downtown Wilmington on the Northside, then down Castle Street on the Southside. Lots of them lashed out and starting throwing rocks and bricks through store windows. Shooting, vandalism and looting went on for hours in the "Brooklyn" section of the city. And there were fire bombings. A state of emergency was declared and stay-off-the-streets curfew was ordered from 6:00 p.m. to 6:00 a.m. That night, the old pent-up rage that had flared up sporadically went full flame.

If the night Dr. King was killed sounded like a war zone, the new few days leading to his funeral definitely felt like one. There were even reports that snipers were firing on first responders.

I remember the panic. No one knew what was going to happen next. It must have been a lot like how local black folk felt huddled in their houses or shivering in terror hiding in the Wilmington swamps in 1898.

The National Guard was called in. Suddenly, Wilmington was occupied by two platoons of armed troops. The violence cooled—and a torrential downpour didn't hurt—but black anger and resentment still simmered.

By this time, Wilmington Police reported 198 arrests, 21 injuries and over $200,000 worth of damage to property. Though I had not participated in the violence, I felt very much connected to it.

By April 16, the city-wide curfew was officially lifted. Wilmington seemed to be returning to its normal abnormal, located firmly in a state of racial denial. But when the new school year started in September, we started hearing of black and white students fighting, and incidents of related racial confrontations. This time, as a student packed off to a white school, I was right in the middle of this mess.

For blacks all over America, the late 1960s were a time of racial awakening, a mighty moment in the midst of a radical transformation. And again, I was right in the middle of it. I was not only becoming a man, but a black man. When my shop instructor asked the class to do a woodworking project, I carved a black power fist.

* — *

In 1971—seven years after the Civil Rights Act of 1964, after the lives of Dr. King and Robert F. Kennedy had been spilled— Wilmington shared the lingering racism of other Southern cities where black people could do very little without the approval of white people. Much like in the rest of the South, blacks in Wilmington basically went along with the long established program of not bucking the system that oppressed them, accepting little more than crumbs from white people's table of status and opportunity.

This is the way it had been for decades. This didn't make everything alright, but it created an illusion that whites and blacks got along in Wilmington. It was like a mirror riddled with cracks and imperfections that were ignored by mutual agreement for the sake of agreement. To me, it didn't make sense.

This kind of mindset made change very difficult. A majority of Wilmington's older blacks were especially afraid to buck the system that crushed them. For them it was simple: if you bucked the system you would have to answer to "the man." That could be a policeman, a boss, or really any white person, male or female. White people controlled everything in town: the government, the commercial activity, the jobs, the news, and the transportation. They also controlled where blacks could live, work, eat, and play.

That's just the way it was.

Every neighborhood was segregated in a way that left no doubt about who could live where. Even the public spaces, like parks and waterfronts, were segregated so that one's place in society was forever fixed, and there was no question about who was doing the assigning of place, or who was in charge.

White rule was harsh and inflexible.

Although the Atlantic Ocean was only a few miles from the inner city, blacks were not welcome at local beaches and seldom got a chance to enjoy their majestic beauty. We could only dream of what it would be like to live in a beachfront cottage, or climb aboard one of the hundreds of yachts and sailboats docked and gently bobbing at the many marinas along the Intra-Coastal Waterway. All we had was Sea Breeze, an ocean front recreational area for blacks that flourished from the 1920s through the 1960s. But by 1971, when I was nineteen and growing weary of the confinement of never-distant horizons, I wondered why Sea Breeze was the best we could hope for. The place had been hard hit by Hurricane Hazel in 1954. The city fathers had not seen fit to do much to restore it. When I was a young man, it was badly deteriorated and was little more than a weekend party spot, with a broken down boardwalk and a couple of dinky night clubs. *Good enough for niggers* is what every missing plank, every warped floor, every dingy, unpainted wall and missing light bulb loudly whispered to me.

In Wilmington proper, white and black neighborhoods were almost totally segregated and most of them were also sorted by class. Poor white neighborhoods were usually in close proximity to black neighborhoods and both looked a lot alike. Without seeing people on the streets, a visitor to Wilmington might have had difficulty distinguishing between the two. Like poor blacks, poor whites usually lived in some form of federally subsidized public housing, most often, housing projects.

Several were built in the 1950s, like Taylor Homes on the north side of town, and from the start were intended for blacks. Others, like Nesbitt Court on the south side, were built for whites. Over the next decade or so, many other "projects" followed. While middle- and upper-class whites shunned poor whites, often calling them "poor white trash," well-to-do blacks relished living among poor blacks. Part of this phenomenon was that the city's black upper classes, unlike their white counterparts, had few other options. Another reason was that well off blacks experienced a sort of immediate upgrade in their social status when they lived near their much poorer, and often less educated, black neighborhoods. It was the first law of relativity that I learned.

For whites of that era, blacks, no matter what their social stripe might be, were the same. Ironically, this was especially true for poor whites. Black was black and white was white, and Jim Crow was still standing on our heads and shitting on our shoulders.

As a teenager, I did yard work for a Mrs. Whedbee in Forest Hills. She was a nearly middle-aged, white woman soon to be a widow when I started going out to her house to earn some extra money. I mostly worked to buy school clothes (too cool or too expensive for my mother to get me) and to afford the movies once in a while. My mother did domestic work for Mrs. Whedbee. Neither of us acted like we knew her first name. We never used it, not even when my mother and I were alone.

I can't say that Mrs. Whedbee was unkind to us. It just seemed that everything that animated her—her manner, her dress, the pronounced drawl in her speech, and, of course, her perspective about people, white and black—was set down by Southern Tradition, the kind you can find on almost any page of *Gone With the Wind*. She had gotten much of her money by way of her husband, Mr. Whedbee, who owned and operated Wilmington Hospital Supply. He died in the late 1960s and left everything to her. I never got to meet him. He was always away from the house when I was there.

The house itself was relatively modest for the area. It was a ranch-style, brick on an acre by a stream among several palatial homes in this old, established, upper-middle-class stretch of Wilmington. It, like its mistress, had a kind of new money quality, and maybe that helped to explain Mrs. Whedbee's fondness for Cadillacs. Back then, most white people who could afford a Cadillac shunned them, associating the luxury cars with black tastes and as symbols of have-nots trying to convince everyone, and themselves, that they were have-toos.

My mother and I didn't have a car of any kind, which added to our low-income-status-on-sight there. It was understood that any black person seen in this shiny white enclave was most likely a yard boy or a housekeeper. And it was understood among many of the whites who hired us that we not only sold our time and labor to them (for me, minimum wage, about a buck sixty cents an hour), but also a measure of our value as full human beings.

This is one of those hard meanings to press into words on a page, but so easily read by the heart when it cracks a little under the burden of unearned, low regard, even when it hides under the artificial fabric of affection.

I will never forget Mrs. Whedbee, for calling my mother "my *niggra* girl" or "Deelorees," when she very well knew that my mother's name was Dolores. Damn, my mother hated that. Yet, my mother loved Mrs. Whedbee... and Mrs. Whedbee, she loved herself some *Deelorees*. She even came to my mother's funeral in the spring of 2007 and mourned her loss like any dear friend would. They had remained close friends for over forty years.

I often wondered how black folk could manage to find some good in a bad situation. Maybe it helped us survive in times that were bad beyond my comprehension. And, then again, maybe women like my mother were just better than the Mrs. Whedbee's of the world.

Mom once told me, "Wayne, if Mrs. Whedbee knew better, she would do better."

She read the skepticism in the eyes that she gave me, but said nothing.

I seriously doubt, that if the slipper was on the white foot, Mrs. Whedbee would have been so generously forgiving. All of this, I told myself was part of the cost of working in places like Forrest Hills. It kept me tense, never knowing when the next insult—intended or not, real or not—was coming and from whom and where. I thought about what Bigger Thomas had said in Richard Wright's *Native Son*, when answering his own question, "You know where white folks live? Right down here in my stomach... Every time I think of 'em, I feel 'em... That's when I think something awful is about to happen to me."

For me, the immediate impact of working there also brought on recognition of the glaring disparity of wealth and privilege between their world and mine. Mrs. Whedbee was always well-dressed, plainly someone who didn't buy clothes in bags, but bought garments that came in boxes, boxes with the names of the best stores in town written all over them in big, fancy letters. My mother would often delight when Mrs. Whedbee would give her clothes that she had recently bought, but had decided she didn't want. And I couldn't help but appreciate the blinding beauty of these kinds of leafy, country club suburbs. At the same time, I began to appreciate the near downtown inner city. Here were older, white neighborhoods situated in what is now known as the historic district. There you saw magnificent antebellum mansions, bathed in the summer shade and filtered green light of magnificent magnolia trees. And even they were clothed in Spanish moss and accented by oleanders and azaleas.

I didn't need a history book to tell me that all I surveyed there was built by slave sweat, and it all paid tribute to Wilmington's unspoken (in polite society) past, when the plantation mentality prevailed and agricultural and urban slavery made this kind of wealth possible—and impossible for me to dream, at that time, of making a home there someday, of someday raising a family there.

I realized, with crystal clarity, that my hometown was doing its best to make me feel homeless and hopeless, and that would have to change. More important, I realized that I would have to be part of that change.

Wilmington was as much mine as it was their's.

2

WILLISTON FOREVER

There was always Williston, or at least we thought so until we couldn't continue attending there.

If this book had a million pages, it still wouldn't be enough to completely convey the bone-deep, heart-deep, pride-deep—love-deep—place Williston Senior High School occupied for generations of us in Wilmington's African-American community. This stately, high-walled institution of education and elucidation on how to live a purposeful life was a primary protector and projector of our community. And over the decades, as Williston lived and morphed in different buildings, took on variations of its name, this school was never, not for us, just brick, steel and mortar.

Williston was, like the modern columns that graced its facade, a pillar of black Wilmington. This was especially true after our community lost nearly everything else, political and economic power chief among them, in the Wilmington Race Riot of 1898. Yes, of course, we found solace and inspiration in our historically black institutions, like our churches. Our black achievers, in their own way, became institutions too; and these included our black doctors, teachers and community leaders. But black pride paramount, the kind that lifts over-burdened heads and soothes worry-wrinkled brows, was reserved for Williston Senior High School.

It was the only black high school in Wilmington and surrounding New Hanover County.

For as long as anyone I've ever known could remember, if you grew up black in Wilmington and went to high school, then it was very, very likely that you went to Williston. These sort of black public schools were not so unusual, especially in the South (if black students had a local high school at all). There was, for example, Central High School in Louisville, Kentucky. This school, founded in 1870, was boldly black and proud for most of its history. Muhammad Ali was among its graduates. These sorts of schools created enormous cohesion in black communities that sent their children to them in much the same way wealthier white families send their progeny to fancy boarding schools, finishing schools and ivy-covered universities where dear old dad and granddad—and their friends and associates—went. Only in our case, our tradition didn't start off as a choice.

The idea of a black school for Wilmington had its origins in 1865 with the close of the Civil War and the arrival of the American Missionary Association (AMA). The AMA committed itself to teaching free blacks to read and write. Its members were driven by a belief that it was God's will that every human being be able to read and understand the Scriptures. This went for black human beings, too, even if they were barred from white schools. So, classes for blacks were held in local churches until late 1866. That changed when Samuel Williston, a white philanthropist from Massachusetts, acquired land in town for a "colored" school.

It was named the Williston Academy, and located in the throbbing heart of the city's large black community on South Seventh Street near the city's first black newspaper, *The Daily Record*. At that time, the school's staff and administrators were Northern white progressives. By 1873, the school was turned over to the city's Board of Education and became the city's first public school for blacks. And like black dominoes falling from the first white nudge, black school buildings and education policies cascaded until there was the Williston Senior High School that stood until 1968.

For most of the twentieth-century, Wilmington was a de facto apartheid city. Everything was segregated, cleaved by race. I mean everything. That included schools, theaters, hospitals, lunch counters, public beaches and swimming pools, and most neighborhoods. If you were black and in Wilmington, Jim Crow segregation seemed to beat its filthy feathers everywhere, doing its damnedest to relegate generations of us to second-class citizenship from our first breath to our last. Even the Bibles in the courthouse were segregated for blacks and whites, but more on that later.

Yet, even in this hell-storm of limitations, Williston became an icon for black excellence, a stubborn rejoinder to considerable forces that preached on almost every wind that we, black people, were less than and would never be more than what white Wilmington would permit, would stomach. In our community, Williston's black teachers and administrators were given the same sort of high regard and soaring esteem a college professor might be given. Many moonlighted as our leaders, sponsored lectures and concerts open to everyone. Academic standards were high at Williston. Lots of students went on to college. It was not unusual for Williston graduates to attend and excel at Ivy League colleges and universities.

At one point, the SAT scores of Williston students were so high that the county's superintendent of schools, a white man, forced some Williston students to retake the test. Guess what? Their scores were still high the second time around. That's Williston for you. Every day there was like being part of a quiet revolution. Instead of hurling shouts and bricks, Williston's best and brightest hurled smarts and books at the fortress gates of racism and imposed segregation.

The school's mascot was a pouncing tiger.

Williston always felt like home to me even though I spent most of my time outside its walls dreaming about attending the school of my mother. In 1967, I was fifteen and went to Williston Junior High School. But I was itching to walk across the ramp that separated the two schools, into Williston Senior's gleaming, broad halls heading to classes where I knew I could continue to achieve.

The school had a legacy of high expectations. In many cases those expectations were met, and the result was remarkable men and women through the nurturing of caring teachers and administrators who emphasized strong moral character. I knew I would not find indifference there, or even worse, open hostility, because I was black. If there would be limitations, they would be those I imposed on myself, issues I could do something about. They would not be shortcomings imposed on me because of the color of my skin, something I could do absolutely nothing about.

The difference matters. It's a lot like riding in the backseat of someone else's car (knowing all the time that its owner would rather your ass was walking than riding) and driving your own car, head up, top down.

Oh boy! Homecomings at Williston Senior High. I still think about those amazing October days. Even when I was a little guy, I found a way to mainline Williston's celebratory spirit. I lived five blocks from my school, Gregory Elementary. But Gregory Elementary, Williston Senior High School and Williston Junior High were all adjacent to one another, a cluster of black schools. On my way to school, I passed a huge fenced-in area that included a field house, a baseball diamond and a practice field, all belonging to the predominantly white New Hanover High School. Right next to that facility was Williston Stadium, the epicenter of Williston's Homecomings.

My brother Harold, our friend Russell, and I were among several young guys who would sometimes scale Williston's ten-foot, cinder block-brick wall during home football games.

We would make it over the wall just in time for the playing of the National Anthem and melt into the huge crowd. We had the perfect place to see the half-time shows when the Marching Tigers took the field.

We could almost see the sparks of electricity on our skin when the stadium shook with thousands of Williston students and supporters chanting from the deepest recesses of their souls: "I would not be a Gold Bull; I'll tell you the reason why. I've been a Tiger all my life. I'll be a Tiger till I die." I never told my mother that Harold and I used to sneak into Williston games. I know if she had ever found out, she would have beaten our butts (but, hey, it would have been worth it).

Williston homecomings were not just for its students and recent graduates. Alumni and their families returned to Williston, too, for these weeklong affairs of good eating, good cheer and grand pageantry. Not just a few of the alumni took advantage of these gatherings to showcase their own success. Despite Wilmington's mild autumn weather, some of the ladies strolled Homecoming wearing full mink coats, the kind complete with heads and tails of the poor animals sacrificed more for status than warmth. There were also some of the coolest cuts of pre-Shaft leather coats and jackets you'd ever want to see. And afros... like fields of huge black dandelions.

Folks were clean. People looked good, and they were not afraid among friends and family to show it. People felt good, and they were not afraid to express that either. You hardly ever heard an ill word, not a note of profanity. Grown folks were there, even grown folks' moms and daddies, and grands were there, so everybody strove for their best behavior. What you mostly heard were people bragging about how well they were doing, how good their jobs were, or how good their kids were. You heard a lot of happy reminiscing. I pictured me one day with a touch of gray at my temples, being one of the old guys, returning to tell good-natured stories about my glory days at Williston. But that would never happen.

Most of the festivities took place in and around Williston's football stadium. Its parking lot looked almost like a Cadillac dealership with all the hand-waxed Caddies whispering loudly through the chrome contours and white-walled tires, about their owners' success or aspirations of success. And remember, this was when Cadillacs were big cars with backseats as lush and large as a living room sofa. I loved it.

Everything started with the naming of the Homecoming King and Queen and their courts. It was all taken very seriously with crowns, scepters, capes and speeches. Then came the day of the Big Game. They were truly heart-wrenching, hand-wringing competitions that pitted Williston against other all-black high schools from around the state, like Fayetteville's E.E. Smith, Durham Hillside and Wilson Darden. These gridiron clashes were as intense for the fans as they were for the players.

Throughout the rest of the week, there would be all kinds of events and parties hosted by Williston's various social clubs and organizations. You could be sure to find great music and dancing at them. And the food? Whew! I can almost smell and taste the collard greens, corn bread, sweet potatoes and, oh yes, pork chitterlings, as I recall those mouth-watering old days. Sometimes I think taste buds have longer memories than brain cells.

In the school's auditorium, the Williston Concert Band would put on brilliant performances of classic and popular music for its annual Homecoming concert. Everywhere you looked you saw Williston's colors of maroon and gold, in flags, in flower arrangements, on posters, in foods, and incorporated in all kinds of outfits. Many were bought or made for this special occasion. Like a page torn from some feel-good battle plan, those colors just so happened to compliment brown skin. The school even had its own "Williston bun." It was a cinnamon pastry created by one of the school's teachers, Irene Mack, and sold at lunchtime and often used to raise money for Williston. You would definitely find them being munched by the dozens at homecomings.

Everything came to a close on Friday night with a parade around the stadium's football field. It started with the Marching Tigers, complete with floats representing every campus organization. This was really something. I was always blown away by Williston's marching band, a city-wide favorite since it started performing at the city's Azalea Festival Parade in 1953. The Marching Tigers, like all things Williston, exemplified the fact that we were, indeed, a proud, unique and glorious people. It was an antidote to the poisonous insistence of so many whites hell bent on portraying us as a race of the conniving, lazy, shiftless, and always wanting something for nothing.

I was struck by the way each band member marched with their heads to the sky. And they didn't just step. No, they strutted their stuff as if saying to world, *We are here! No matter how hard you try, you can't stop us now. Yes, we're black, and we couldn't be more proud to be black. Can't you see it? Feel it?*

There must have been fifty to sixty members, each looking as good in their maroon and gold uniforms as they were skilled and graceful, performing their high-stepping dance routines at the last Williston Homecoming in 1967. And when they performed you could hear them from a mile away, blowing and banging out tunes in brass and drums like "Tighten Up" by Archie Bell and the Drells, or the theme from Batman, the old, original television series, not the movies. It might sound crazy now, but back then in the mid-to-late 1960s, that was the jam.

The Marching Tigers always played with a kind of confident groove, flash and style that was unmistakably and foot-stompingly black. The Marching Tigers were special and we all knew it. *Ain't going to get that at New Hanover High,* I'd think with mischievous delight most times I saw them.

Much the same thing could be said about Williston's football, baseball and basketball teams. I always looked up to the athletes who seemed to me able to out run, out leap, out tackle Jim Crow—or I wanted to believe they could. For years, segregation prevented North Carolina's black schools from competing with teams from white high schools. Nonetheless, Williston was a proven athletic powerhouse. As far back as 1956, it won the segregated state football championship, one of many victories that packed the school's trophy cases. In that same year, in fact, E. A. "Spike" Corbin, who started his coaching career at Williston, went on to lead the school to state championships in not only football, but basketball and baseball, too. It was this sort of demonstration of excellence that prompted its fans to crow that Williston was "the greatest school under the sun."

During the same era, in 1954 when I was still a toddler in New York City, a reporter from NBC's Wilmington affiliate, WECT-TV, contacted Constance O'Dell. She was Williston's Glee Club's concert choir director. Moved by what he had heard, he asked her if the Williston choir could perform for a live Christmas performance on television. For decades until the end, Williston's choir was featured each year in local television appearances at Thanksgiving and Christmas.

Mrs. O'Dell went on to mentor many Williston students. One of the most successful was my brother, Thomas. He went on to attend the Winston Salem School of the Arts, St. Paul University, and the Manhattan School of the Arts. After graduation in 1966, Thomas had an outstanding career as a professional opera singer and performed his initial recital at Carnegie Hall under the mentorship of the great Leontyne Price.

In testimony to the unique ability of Williston to transcend racial repression, Wayne Jackson, the WECT-TV reporter, recalled that baseball star and pioneer, Jackie Robinson, visited Williston in 1955.

"In those days, the *Star News* would not print the picture of a black person. And Jackie Robinson came to town and the sports writers might go talk to him, but they couldn't put his picture in the paper," Jackson recalled in a 2002 interview, drawing a contrast to how the Williston choir was treated in the media at the time. "The Williston Choir was so good, that even a town that would not allow the face of the great Jackie Robinson to appear in print, looked forward to seeing the Williston concert choir on television every year."

White churches and civic groups, eager to be entertained, readily patronized the choirs' local appearances, and the Williston choir traveled to those appearances on a rusty old bus the students nicknamed the "Bumblebee." The Bumblebee would also transport the choir to several music festivals held at predominately black campuses across the state where they performed a wide range of musical genres from classical to show tunes to Negro Spirituals. In part because of the exposure WECT gave the choir, the Glee Club was invited to make appearances from New York to Florida, and Wilmington's annual Christmas concert was broadcast on radio throughout the country. Still under the direction of Mrs. Odell, the Williston Alumni Choir performed at the White House on December 11, 1994.

That was part of the irony of forced segregation. We had to create our own quite separate institutions and traditions, our own clubs and symbols of pride and expression. Yet at the same time, we were taught in brutally overt and subtly covert ways to think of what we created and maintained to be inferior to their white counterparts. And the primary reason for this inferiority was that it was exclusively ours.

It was some hideous joke on us, a straight razor turn on the old Groucho Marx line that he wouldn't belong to any club that would accept him.

I wholesale rejected that.

By the time I was approaching my own high school years, I had come to think of racism as an enemy that had to be defeated. I saw it steal and cripple lives, cutting down those I loved and so many I would never know by name, but by common experience. Racism was out there, the tension on a sniper's trigger finger, the BOOM in the bomb that blew up bridges of opportunities for black people practically everywhere. But at Williston, I felt comfortable and safe behind its solid, heavy walls of black traditions and morals. I felt comfortable and safe there among people who looked like me, and with whom I shared a common historical bond and culture.

When talk about integrating Wilmington and New Hanover County schools began to seriously percolate in the mid-1960s, I never imagined that integration would result in more than giving Wilmington's black community a choice. Really. Who wouldn't like a choice to live, work, travel, vacation and go to school where they wanted?

My choice, as far as going to school was concerned, was to go to Williston.

In 1955, a year after the U.S. Supreme Court's historic ruling that struck down the separate-but-equal doctrine that was the basis for racial segregation in the nation's public schools, Zora Neale Hurston struck her own contrarian note. The great African-American woman of letters wrote in a letter to the editor of the Orlando Sentinel that she regarded the high court's ruling as "insulting rather than honoring my race." She wrote, disparagingly, that there had been "no greater delight to Negroes than physical association with whites."

Her greater point, one I subscribed to as I dreamed of attending Williston, was that forcing us to go to white schools, for example, "if there are adequate Negro schools and prepared instructors and instruction, then there is nothing different except the presence of white people." I have nothing against most white people. But I had to ask myself would the Board of Education, given a choice, close one of its white schools to help integrate our school? It would be years later that I discovered the writings of Derrick Bell, the late brilliant legal mind.

Like Hurston, he saw something else in the celebrated *Brown v. Board of Education* ruling of 1954. He wrote that there was little or no evidence that the hardship of segregation prevented black schools from functioning well. Rather than focus on the "separate" part of the case, Bell, who was black, said, the high court should have more closely looked at the "equal" part.

Preston R. Wilcox, a longtime organizer in Harlem and professor of sociology and social work at Columbia University, used to argue in the 1960s that "If one can believe that a 'de facto segregated' white school could be a 'good school,' then, one must believe that a 'de facto segregated' and predominately Negro and Puerto Rican school can also be a 'good school.'"

While I couldn't articulate these ideas with that sort of insight and precision as a junior high school student, I remember feeling exactly the same way about Williston. It was black and great, those qualities not being mutually exclusive. I didn't feel that it was my sad fate to go there, but a privileged honor to attend Williston.

I didn't think it too much to expect to add my name to some of Williston's distinguished alumnae, starting with Jimmy Heath, jazz saxophonist extraordinaire, class of 1943; Althea Gibson, a one-woman Venus and Serena before there was a Venus and Serena Williams, and who was the first African-American woman to win a tennis Grand Slam, class of 1949; Meadow "Meadowlark" Lemon, dazzling basketball player and founding member of the Harlem Globetrotters, class of 1952; Joseph A. McNeil, class of 1959 and one of the Greensboro Four, students attending North Carolina Agricultural and Technical State College in Greensboro and leading historic, non-violent sit-ins in 1960 aimed at getting Woolworth's department store to drop its policy of racial segregation; Superior Court Judge Ernest Fullwood, class of 1960; Phil Terrell Flood, a singer who became the choreographer for major rhythm and blues group, The Manhattans, class of 1961; Dr. Phillip L. Clay, the first and now former African-American chancellor of the Massachusetts Institute of Technology and professor of city planning, class of 1964; and Joseph McQueen, Jr., North Carolina's former New Hanover County Sheriff, class of 1965.

At the time, I didn't know that outstanding black public schools, and their amazing adaptations to the cruelties of racial segregation, were being sacrificed in the name of doing what was best for me and mine.

I recently found an oral history compiled by the University of North Carolina at Chapel Hill. Among its entries I found a black woman from Charlotte, North Carolina, a kindred soul, wounded in much the same way I had been when Williston was abruptly closed in 1968.

INTERVIEWER:

So your first high school, they were closing it down, and that's why they had to move all of the students out?

REVEREND BRENDA TAPIA:

Umm, it wasn't so much that they needed to close it down, or they were going to close it down. That's how Charlotte-Mecklenburg decided to integrate schools. They decided to integrate at that point. As a process of their integration plan, they closed black schools. And it was really interesting because a lot of the black schools, because of racism, they were newer than the white schools, because for a long time we didn't have any schools.

So a lot of the white schools they were using were much older, and far more, in much worse physical condition. They were the more likely choices to close. But instead they closed our schools and bused us to them; because naturally they wouldn't want to come to us.

According to the oral history, Rev. Tapia was one of the first African-American students under the new busing plan to attend North Mecklenburg High School in Huntersville, North Carolina. Her experience with desegregation, the entry notes, was extremely negative.

"Moved from her black school after a successful sophomore year, she entered North Mecklenburg as an unknown, excluded from participating in clubs and marginalized in the classroom. By graduation night of her senior year, Tapia was furious. Her experience and observations led her to view desegregation as 'one of the worst things that could have been done to [African Americans].' She maintains that though it changed the law, it did not change white Americans' attitudes, and she argues that its legacy is a black community sapped by discrimination."

In the spring of 1976, the year of America's bicentennial, I sat in a drafty prison gymnasium at Odom Correctional Institution in Jackson, North Carolina. I was an inmate among hundreds more that day receiving one of the few respites from the dark drudgery of prison life. We were being treated to a recently released movie, *Cooly High*, which is now a classic.

I watched a group of black actors playing high school kids standing over the grave of their fallen friend, Richard "Cochise" Morris, whom Lawrence Hilton-Jacobs portrayed in a way that had made that character the unforgettable soul of the film. But in this closing scene, Cochise was gone, dead, cut down way before his time. As I watched, my mind harkened back to how I felt each time I walked past Williston after it had been closed. The great school had become a kind of gravesite for me, a reminder of a tragic, premature death. It was as if the whole Williston building had been turned into one huge tombstone.

In *Cooly High*, as everyone stands around Cochise's grave, the song, "It's So Hard to Say Goodbye to Yesterday," plays solemnly in the background. Damn, that reminded me—and still does—that Williston had been like a best friend to me, how we created so many dear memories in the relatively short time we had together.

It reminded me how much I was still struggling with saying goodbye to Williston.

3

SUNSET COMES TO WILLISTON

Williston's last breath came on a bright warm day in early September 1968 when its doors didn't open like welcoming arms; when they didn't open at all. It was the start of the new academic year, but the school's windows were uncharacteristically dark and absent of life. Like the doors, the windows were shut tight, and everything about the place was stone cold silent.

Death had been delivered with all the finality of an assassin's bullet.

For most of us in Wilmington's black community, still reeling from the murder of Martin Luther King, Jr., in April of that year, the undeniable demise of our only high school and cultural core was a double jolt. It was like suffering a tsunami in the wake of some life-crushing earthquake. It was overwhelmingly unbelievable. The wall of water was building all through the summer. But when that cold, gray wave finally fell over Williston there was nothing left for us but a muted shock, a kind of biting your fist to keep from crying or screaming, or both. So many of us were traumatized.

It was the day after Labor Day, the traditional beginning of the new school year. I was a tenth grader getting ready to start high school. But instead of going to Williston Senior High, forces I had little or no control over, snatched that away from me. When word came over the summer that Williston would be closed, my mother walked me to the New Hanover County Board of Education office on the north side of town, and signed me up to attend New Hanover High School. It was the white school a half dozen blocks from where Williston still stood.

I'll never forget how cruel it seemed that I would have to walk five days a week right past what should have been my high school to New Hanover, a school I never even wanted to visit. Some of my friends and I tried our best to keep up our walk-to-class routines. We sometimes stopped by Williston Junior High School's cafeteria to buy some of the best cinnamon buns ever made. A lot of days, we dropped into a neighborhood grocery store called Sellers's on Thirteenth and Ann Streets. There we would get cookies two for a penny and buy some milk or soda pop.

Sellers' was owned and run by a black man, and I could tell that he could see in our eyes what we tried to medicate away with whole milk and sugary cookies. Grocery stores like Seller's, whether they were operated by blacks or whites, were vital to our community. They treated us like family, at worse like distant cousins. As children we could take our mother's grocery lists to these corner stores and the familiar faces behind the counter would recognize the handwriting.

Need milk, bread, a pound of bologna, some fatback, cheese, a can of mackerel? They'd have it and give it to your mom on credit—if need be. That's how it was, and that's how I knew Mr. Sellers could see how hurt we were to have to go a new high school, one that he knew, as well as we did, would rather us go somewhere, any where else, but there.

Over the summer, June 26, 1968, to be exact, I read the handwriting of Williston's doom on the wall in letters that loomed larger than me. The school would not be spared a crush of good intentions churned and driven by a dark disregard for Wilmington's black community. The realization hit my gut before my head, as I sat uneasily in the crowded gymnasium of

New Hanover High School, built in the 1920s and hardly a loud shout away from Williston. This place possessed none of the grit, grace and gravitas of Williston. Yet, because it was white, it was insulated from indifference and dismissal by the powerful, also white, and fond of bending fate to favor them and theirs.

I looked around shaking my head. Even at this meeting we were segregated by race. I was among an isolated gathering of black students, black teachers, black community activists and civic leaders. A handful of flies in a big bowl of buttermilk. Everywhere else, the gymnasium, known as Brogden Hall, was swollen with hundreds, maybe a thousand, of white people, many of them red-faced with an open rage. Or was it just a baseless fear that inflamed their features?

We were not intimidated. We vented our righteous displeasure, grief and even anger at our Board of Education's decision to shutter Williston Senior High School. For many of us there, the announcement of this meeting was the first time we heard that the Board was seriously going to close Williston Senior High. It was shock that put most of us in that gym that day. At the same time, white people were there and were no less enthusiastic about expressing their displeasure, grief and even anger at the possibility of having so many blacks attending their schools.

We saw evasion. They saw invasion.

One white parent wondered aloud if her child's school's "standards would drop" if the city and county schools were fully integrated. F.L. Meier, Jr., chairman of the county's Republican party then, asked, "How many little Negro children do we have to drag kicking and screaming over to some white schools, and how many little white children do we have to drag kicking and screaming over to some Negro schools for them to be satisfied?"

Hearing all this white noise made me wonder what was being said about us in private, at white dinner tables, factory floors, tobacco fields, smoky bars and back rooms—any place we were either absent or invisible to them. As far as I knew back then, there had been no other public hearings. It was as if our views and concerns about Williston didn't matter anymore than we did. We were never honestly consulted.

Williston was being sentenced to death, and we didn't know it had actually been charged. And what was its crime, anyway? I had to come to this June meeting, even though I knew the game was rigged, that the board had made up its mind. That's the way things worked in Wilmington, especially if you were black. Only one member of the New Hanover County Board of Education was black. His name was Leland Newsome. He was a Republican, and he was appointed rather than elected to the board. His greatest qualification for the job seemed to be that he was the kind of Negro who was allergic to disappointing white wants. He voted along with the rest of the board to close Williston.

The decision was unanimous.

One of the things that really troubled me that summer was the board's insistence that its hands were tied, that Williston was being closed in the name of complying with a federal court order to integrate Wilmington's and surrounding New Hanover County's public schools. The whole thing was being framed as if the board was acting in our best interests, or being forced by outsiders to integrate. Don't get me wrong. I understood the necessity of school integration, even if the mystery of how that would exactly work terrified me at the time. But I never believed racial progress had to come at the cost of our black institutions, especially one as vital and beloved as Williston.

I was little more than a toddler living in New York City when the United States Supreme Court made its segregation-busting ruling in the *Brown v. Board of Education* case in 1954. But in the beginning, it was the most hollow of victories for millions of black students, myself included. For years, we had little choice but to attend racially segregated public schools. Before all the school integration talk started sweeping my hometown in the late 1960s, I had never sat next to a white person. For much of our lives, Old South segregation had loudly served notice that black people's place was not among white people, certainly not among their sons and daughters, learning who are destined to be on top in the world (and who are not).

My first fifteen years were defined by poverty and deprivation, mitigated only by the strength and love of my mother. The psychological stress of my childhood, an almost constant battle to keep my spirits afloat in muddy waters, was lessened by the prospect that I would someday attend Williston Senior High. I had attended Gregory Elementary School, which was to the south of a multi-block complex of school buildings on South Tenth Street between Ann and Castle Streets. North of this campus was Williston Junior High, where I also went. But in the center of the cluster was Williston Senior High, connected to its junior high school by a second-story walkway, a kind of yellow brick road into the Land of Maroon and Gold.

I desperately needed to take that road. At Williston Senior, in the Tigers Den, I knew I could find my way and make my mark. Joining that universe became a cherished goal for me, a gateway to promise. White people had not existed in that universe, not in that reoccurring dream of mine. But it had largely been white people who closed Williston. Meeting adjourned. Case closed. Go home. Suddenly, I found myself living Langston Hughes's eternal question: "What happens to a dream deferred?" I could feel it exploding in my chest.

When the meeting at New Hanover High School was breaking up, a white man whom I had never seen before, approached a knot of black people milling around in New Hanover's gymnasium. I was among them.

I stood there, a runt still waiting for my growth-spurt-to-come, my afro a defiant cloud of pride hovering over me. Hardly intimidated by us, this middle-age white man announced that he had a question.

Then, he asked it: "Why have blacks so vehemently attacked those who wished to desegregate New Hanover County Schools?"

At first, I didn't sense any malice in his words. In fact, I thought I heard a real yearning for an honest answer. It was true that a lot of black people in Wilmington weren't that anxious to integrate. It seemed that our track record of throwing in with whites hadn't been so good going all the way back to the riot of 1898. Then again, by the late 1960s, hadn't we gotten what we asked for? Hadn't our struggle been for equal rights and desegregation of the school system? Had we not struggled for years for assimilation into the so-called white man's culture? We were no longer slaves; we could vote and eat at white lunch counters. We no longer had to sit in the balconies at movie theaters. We no longer had to sit in the back of the bus or hold our bladders until we reached the next station, one not designated WHITE ONLY.

"My God, stop your whining," he said to none of us in particular, but in a tone that suggested that he was some prince addressing his lesser subjects. "Don't you know that the barriers that once existed no longer exist? There is nothing that stands in the way of your educational, political, or socio-economic progress. Why are you here? "Wasn't part of your struggle to desegregate the schools?"

Yes, asshole, but on our terms, not yours, I thought, but wasn't able to articulate it as anger. Confusion and profound disappointment squatted on my intellect. I just looked at the man, then walked away. He had no idea of *our* struggle.

The decade between *Brown v. Board of Education* and the *Civil Rights Act* of 1964 came to be known as the era of "massive resistance." It was when white school boards, especially those in the South, did all they could to slow or sneak around the decision. Wilmington and New Hanover County were no exception. But the Civil Rights Act linked federal dollars for public schools to how well those school systems desegregated, and only then did things get serious.

The Afro American newspaper reported that the New Hanover County school system stood to lose $700,000 ($4.7 million in 2013 dollars) if it had not instituted an integration plan that the federal government would accept.

A previous integration scheme, the "Freedom of Choice Plan," had lured no more than fifty black students to predominately white schools, so it was overturned by Washington. That sent the board scrambling. Earlier in 1968, a team from the federal government's Health Education and Welfare Office of Civil Rights determined that if Williston Senior High School was to continue operations under a new desegregation plan, major improvements and renovations would have to be made. The team concluded that Williston's physical plant would have to be comparable to that of the much better maintained New Hanover and practically brand new John T. Hoggard High School.

The estimated cost of bringing Williston up to par would cost more than $200,000. That was a lot of money back then.

Using a little white power sleight of hand, the cost of the desegregation plan without Williston would require the Board of Education to only purchase thirty-eight school buses to ferry Williston's 1,100 or so black students to the remaining two high schools. This move, reasoned its supporters, would also help quiet widespread white opposition to the potential for busing white students to a black school with black teachers and administrators. This part of the plan was presented as a win-win, in which most of the city's and county's white students got to stay at their home schools, while black students would be bused to vastly better white schools with superior resources.

Most of Wilmington's black community was stunned by what looked to us like a LOSE-LOSE. I was outraged.

I came to learn years later that this sort of decision was typical of white boards of education when they were faced with federal pressure to integrate public schools. Black schools were deemed by default to be inferior. If desegregation would come with costs, black schools and their faculties, administrators and staff—all of them reassigned (to white schools), retired or simply laid off— would be the first to pay.

Reginald Ennett, a 1966 Williston graduate, called Williston's closing an "act of disrespect" leveled by the city's white power structure on Wilmington's black citizens. "There was," he elaborated, "nothing fair, ethical, or compassionate about this decision. It was full of bias, corruption, and bigotry."

Linda Pearce, another Williston alumna, said after all of these years the closing "still hurts." She said losing Williston Senior High was like experiencing a death in her family. "Why? Why close our school? I was in Washington when my mother wrote and told me. I cried for days."

I felt the same way. And to simply say that Williston was closed in the name of desegregation of Wilmington and New Hanover County schools, which many—black and white—still do today, does not do justice to a richer, more complicated story of race, power and entitlement, American-style. To begin to understand Williston's closing, a decision that forever changed my life and the lives of the rest of the Wilmington Ten, we have to dig down and get into the dirt. There, we can examine the twisted roots beneath all the surface details, all the misdirection and misinformation.

Let's start with Dr. Hubert Arthur Eaton. He was a prominent Wilmington physician who was black and complicated. Like other black change agents—Harlem Renaissance's Alain Locke, Walter White and W.E.B. Du Bois come immediately to mind—

Dr. Eaton was a "race man," although he might not have embraced the term.

One thing he definitely *was not* was grassroots. While he was generally a crusader for his people's advancement, starting in the predawn of the modern civil rights movement, he was always a part of the black elite. Deep down, I always felt that he worked so hard for us to have equal rights and he did a lot of good stuff so he could go where he wanted, like golf courses barred to black golfers like him, and do what he wanted. In the end, Dr. Eaton was an aristocrat.

The story of Williston's closing cannot be told without telling at least some part of Dr. Eaton's story and his efforts to desegregate Wilmington and New Hanover County schools.

In 1951, Dr. Eaton filed a suit in the Eastern Division of the United States District Court against the New Hanover County School system, charging that the U.S. Supreme Court's 1896 landmark *Plessy v. Ferguson* decision, that made the notion of "separate but equal" law, was being violated. He conceded that black public schools in Wilmington and the county were indeed separate, but they were hardly equal to the education provided white students. He meticulously documented how dramatically inferior black schools were to white schools materially. The suit forced the county into an extensive renovation campaign that led, for one thing, to the building of a new Williston Senior High School by 1954.

When the *Brown v. Board of Education* decision was handed down that same year, Dr. Eaton became even more aggressive about school desegregation. Nine years later, Dr. Eaton, along with his daughter, Carolyn, filed a lawsuit in federal court to challenge the slow walk of progress in implementing the high court's mandate to local schools.

The Eaton's' lawsuit led to the "freedom of choice" plan for black students in Wilmington and New Hanover County in

1965. At the time, he was also instrumental in a class action suit involving fellow black doctors seeking equal opportunity for staff positions at the then James Walker Memorial Hospital. In addition, he was at the forefront of struggles to desegregate Wilmington College (now the rambling University of North Carolina at Wilmington), the New Hanover County YMCA, and the county's library.

Racial segregation really infuriated the man. But his avid activism could be traced to a single incident. In 1947, when he was thirty-one, he was called into a local court to testify in a lawsuit and realized that the county courts maintained separate Bibles to swear on; one labeled "Colored," the other labeled "White." He quivered with rage at having to acknowledge that despite his life of privilege, white folks still considered him to be a second-class citizen. This wounding realization propelled him toward being a local civil rights leader for the next thirty years.

Dr. Eaton died in Wilmington on September 4, 1991, at age seventy-four. One of the city's finer suburban elementary schools was named in his honor in 1996.

Dr. Eaton was a slight, bespectacled man with the jutting jaw of a superhero. He had a light voice, the kind that tends not to threaten white people. He realized that making important change meant flying headlong into a brick wall of Southern segregationist history. This was especially true in how Southern tradition governed the strict separation of black and white students. Still, that never seemed to stop Dr. Eaton from ramming his black privileged-class ego, right into that wall. Exhibit One: Dr. Eaton was the first African American to seek public office in Wilmington since the 1898 coup d'état in which dozens of black leaders were either murdered or run out of town. He ran unsuccessfully for a seat on the New Hanover Board of Education in 1952, 1954 and 1956.

Just four years before Dr. Eaton was born in 1916 in Fayetteville, North Carolina, Williston Senior High School was fast evolving into the institution I would come to know, love and then mourn. In 1912, the U.S. Congress passed and President William Howard Taft signed an act giving seven entire city blocks of Wilmington to the New Hanover County Board of Education. Its expressed use was reserved for the construction of an industrial school. The result was a two-story brick building called Williston Industrial School. It opened its doors in 1915 and the old school building on Seventh Street was torn down.

With the opening of Williston Industrial School, the white administrators and teachers of the earlier Williston were replaced by black educators. Among this black infusion were Mary Washington Howe and David Clarke Virgo, a new spirit of excellence. With Virgo's charismatic leadership, Williston gained its state accreditation as a Group 1, Class A high school.

Almost from the start, Principal Virgo moved to create a nurturing environment for his students. He insisted, for example, that all of his school's teachers visit the households of their students before they would receive their first paychecks. When, in 1918, North Carolina required all public schools to provide four additional years of education beyond the seventh grade, Virgo reportedly went door-to-door to convince black parents to enroll their children into the expanded instruction.

A short time later, Williston Industrial became a model for black secondary education throughout the state. In 1931, the New Hanover County Board of Education built a three-story building for Williston on South Tenth Street between Nun and Ann Streets. For the first time in Wilmington's history, black students had a school building that was just as good as what the city's white students had. This Williston had lockers, a gymnasium, auditorium and cafeteria; it even had modern science labs. It still, sadly, had to accept hand-me-downs from its white counterparts, with books and desks being chief among them.

Nonetheless, Williston Industrial thrived and soon was one of the highest rated black schools in the nation. Then in 1936 disaster struck. A fire that had apparently started in a trash bin on the building's second floor, burned Williston to the ground. Almost immediately, a new Williston was built to the same specifications using the building's original blue prints. It graduated thousands of black students until it was made into Williston Junior High School after a new, much larger Williston, now Williston Senior High School, was opened next door in 1954—thanks mostly to Dr. Eaton's lawsuit.

At the time, the school newspaper, the *Williston Echo,* proclaimed that the new high school offered "every modern convenience." It also boasted a curriculum that paralleled what white students were taking in their schools, for example, classes in literature, the sciences, social studies, foreign languages and history. The notable difference? Williston Senior High School offered a special program on black culture and heritage.

A year after Williston Industrial burned down, Dr. Eaton graduated from Johnson C. Smith University in Charlotte with a degree in zoology. Five years later, in 1942, he earned his M.D. from the prestigious University of Michigan Medical School, a rarity for blacks at the time.

Dr. Eaton was, like President Barack Obama, the product of a black father and a white mother; in her case, Scotch-Irish. Contrary to the cliché, it was Dr. Eaton's black family, not the white one, which was of a privileged class. In the late nineteenth-century, the Eaton's *had arrived,* and they were not shy about letting folks know it. The family was well-educated, well-spoken and rigidly upright. Elite.

They were the kind of black people who despite living in the nest of Jim Crow, nonetheless threw grand galas and debutante balls to introduce their daughters into society with all the best pomp their circumstance could afford. And amid all these fine trappings, Dr. Eaton, whose father was also a physician, appeared to be driven by a strong sense of responsibility to his blackness. As a young man, Dr. Eaton became an accomplished tennis player and instructor in a sport of gentlemen and ladies that happened to bar blacks from playing with whites.

Nonetheless, Dr. Eaton won a number of black-only tennis championships. In 1946, he invited a nationally ranked amateur tennis player to Wilmington. Her name? Althea Gibson. As her guardian, mentor and tennis instructor (this is when she attended Williston Senior High School) she went on to become the first black athlete, man or woman, to break that sport's national and international color line. She won the women's Wimbledon title in 1957 and 1958, and the U.S. Open in the same years.

Dr. Eaton was a self-styled black leader, a good man. Yet, in the case of Williston he totally misread the connection between Williston, our black community and its special and delicate culture in Wilmington. Dr. Eaton once wrote, "Many black citizens had a proprietary interest in Williston and a big emotional investment in it. They associated the building with fond memories. They felt they were being deprived by the closing and resented it."

But, as I hope I have made clear, Williston Senior High School was much, much more than just a piece of property filled with fond memories. Dr. Eaton was unable to understand that Williston embodied all the history, culture and values of our world in Wilmington.

It was Dr. Eaton's view on Williston that held sway with the Board of Education. For years, he seemed to be the one black person that Wilmington's white power structure tended to trust, at least trusted to speak—not too loudly now—for his people. This was especially true during the civil rights and black power struggles of the 1960s and 1970s. This was especially true as I was coming of age in the mid-1960s.

While attending Williston Junior High School in the mid-1960s, I was feeling my way toward finding my identity. I was trying to piece together the puzzle of the kind of man I wanted to be. This is confusing enough for most young men as they tread and stumble through adolescence. It was much more complex for me, a teenager burdened with the baggage of fatherlessness and poverty in a segregated society in the South.

At Williston Junior High my identity crisis was full-blown. I was becoming increasingly curious about sex. I even learned a few choice words not in Webster's to describe it, even if I didn't know what I was talking about firsthand. I did learn how to use profanity—with style and great proficiency. And I learned how to cut class and get away with it. And finally, I learned how to fight.

Armed with these newly acquired street skills, there wasn't any wonder that I began to drift further from my neighborhood. In less than a school year, I had graduated into engaging in all sorts of activities that neither my mother, nor my minster would approve of. I can hardly believe today how easy it was for me to become a gang fighter, a vandal willing to break into freight cars. Back then, I didn't take the time to think about what I was doing, or why. But looking back on it, I realize that much of my bad acting—and it was acting a role as foreign to me as Richard III—was rooted in all the anger and fractured hope I carried inside.

Frankly, I was rebelling. A lot of this had to do with the absence of my father. I knew who he was, that he was in the navy, just not where he was for most of my life. I cannot recall ever spending more than a week's time around him. For every intent and imaginable purpose, my father was nonexistent.

My mother worked hard doing menial work to provide for me and my siblings. She loved us. I never doubted that. But mothers can't really teach boys to be more than good boys, not men, and certainly not good men. I turned to hanging out with the fellas, looking for answers, for the pieces of my puzzle, in places like

Robert Strange Park, which was across the street from my junior high school.

It wasn't long before I ventured deeper into Wilmington rather than go straight home after school. I discovered the Dew Drop Inn, a greasy, black cafe that looked as if it had crawled into its painted, cinder block building, five blocks south of the park. There were always people hanging out in front of its smeary plate-glass window. There were young bloods and old street gangsters, some wearing afros, others wrapped in do rags keeping their processed hair fresh for the weekend. Most stood in soft angles of cool, drinking and smoking and talking tough. Out front, on the corner, there was always the earthy aroma of fried chicken (Dew Drop Inn was famous for its chicken sandwich) and the weedy exhalations of Acapulco Gold, Jamaican, or African Ganja.

I wanted to be a part of that world. It was just across the street from the Jervay public housing projects. It seemed free in its own don't-give-a-damn way. I had a lot to learn and there seemed no better place than this cafe also known as Dew Drop University. Anyone with eyes could see that Wilmington's most aspiring pimps, players and pushers had obtained their kick-ass diplomas there. It was where dope addicts went to get their fixes and potheads went to cop a nickel bag. I informally signed up for courses that promised a whole new level of sex, drugs, and rocking to roll with my fist.

It was in Jervay, at Dew Drop, and in the pool rooms on Castle Street where I learned that I had to step up my game with the ladies. Almost every day I had to listen to some dude bragging about he had made, the night before, some girl's pussy purr his name. It seemed that the only real arenas of manhood were in the bedroom and on the basketball court. I knew how to play ball, but sex... All I knew about that was that I desperately needed it. I couldn't be a man, not like the men I was hanging out with on Castle Street, and be a virgin.

My mother was evidently either too embarrassed to talk about the subject or she felt it was something I just didn't need to know. I'm sure my father would have had a different take on it, but, of course, he was nowhere to be found.

Ok, so I was pushing against my limits; I was beginning to act out. By this time, I hadn't done anything too wild. Williston Junior High's S.J. Howie alone would not have tolerated that. Howie was the principal and disciplinarian at Williston Junior High. We called him "Baldhead Howe," although never to his face. He tolerated no bad behavior, none, period! Parenting and mentoring surrogates like Mr. Howie, not the streets, were my most important early influences as I struggled to define myself.

At the beginning of each year at Williston Junior High, all its students were packed into the auditorium for an assembly. Howie would lead us through a series of promises that concluded with a promise from him. He told us that we would be expelled if any of us were caught smoking, drinking, fighting, kissing, or walking over the ramp to Williston Senior High. There would be no loitering in the hall between classes, nor would he allow any cutting classes. There would be no gambling on the premises. I later learned in the hardest of ways that violators would have to face the "board of education," a large, wooden paddle swung with great authority at your butt.

And there was also the likelihood of a note from the principal's office informing a parent that you had been punished and why. This note from a highly respected principal would then likely result in an additional punishment at home. Yes, I met with the " board of education" on more than one occasion, mostly for cutting class. Unbeknownst to me back then, I was in desperate need of structure and discipline. One piece of my puzzle that always stayed in place was my sense of wanting to be a good guy. And that was recognized at Williston Junior High. Mr. Howie never made me feel as if I was a criminal, or an animal like the Central Park Five were made out be before they were railroaded to prison for basically being in the wrong place at the wrong time in the wrong colored skin.

All of that would change when I started going to New Hanover High School in the fall of 1968. It was a disaster for me that whites who had no understanding of me as a student or a person, or a member of an important community, had determined that my equality depended on my sitting with them. And all of this for no reasons other than their conviction that my race made me not as good as they were.

At Williston Junior High School, I had begun to develop a social consciousness. Up until that point, I had accepted life as it had been presented to me. I didn't buck the unwritten rule in public schools that only the white version of history was to be taught in Wilmington. When we were kids, my black classmates and I had learned how the Spanish monarchy supplied Christopher Columbus with the Niña, Pinta, and Santa Maria... You know the drill. We learned that white people benevolently settled Jamestown in the New World on 1607 with John Smith and the ever helpful Indian maid, Pocahontas. And on and on.

By 1965, however, things began to change and some black teachers, emboldened by the black power movement, could be heard mimicking Malcolm saying, "We did not land on Plymouth Rock, Plymouth Rock landed on us." It was in the classrooms of Williston Junior High, that I first began to understand the kinds of injustices and indignities prevalent in the world and started feeling the weight of all of that history flattening my future.

I began to see things more clearly. I understood that while desegregation can be forced and implemented, the integration of cultures is a much more complex process. This was as true in 1968 as it is today. Racism is a moral issue that cannot be solved through just moving the deck chairs around on a sinking ship of state. What we needed then is the same thing we need today: educational environments that are conducive to learning and sensitive to our needs.

This was where my head was as an evolving, young black man when I stepped into New Hanover High School on September 3, 1968. When Williston closed I had enrolled at the nearby New Hanover High School under the banner of Dr. Eaton's "Freedom of Choice" initiative. But by the fall of 1969 a so-called "satisfactory plan desegregation" was firmly in place, and I was forced to attend school miles away in the vanilla suburbs, home of John T. Hoggard High School. Much more than a new school year was about to begin, and I knew it.

4

A REVOLUTIONARY TIME

The blaze started, like most fires, with the faintest flickers of a flame.

It was Martin Luther King, Jr.'s birthday, Friday, January 15, 1971. I'll never forget it. Weeks earlier, a delegation of black students from John T. Hoggard High School, the suburban school where hundreds of blacks like me were bused, asked its administration if there could be a school-wide program to honor the slain civil rights leader. The request was denied out of hand.

When I heard that news, I could feel myself growing hot with barely contained rage. We weren't asking for much; not a day off from school like everyone got for, say, Columbus Day, or even for George Washington's birthday. We just wanted a pause, some kind of memorial held in the school's auditorium, in the name of Dr. King and all that he had accomplished. We didn't want this just for us, but for everyone in the school.

But, no; there would be no such memorial at Hoggard. This came at a time when black folks, especially young black people, were still pissed off about Dr. King being killed in the first place; and almost before anyone could dry their tears in April 1968, more blood was spilled. Robert F. Kennedy was shot and killed in June of that year. It would be such a long, searing summer. Remember the context. We wondered, like Bob Marley later asked in his "Redemption Song," "How long shall they kill our prophets, while we stand aside and look?"

But the truth was, at the time, most of us were in no position to do anything more than simply look. We were witnesses to these hope-crushing assassinations; we witnessed the clashes of protesters and police right there in Wilmington, and the riots that swept the nation. There was death, occupation and curfews as National Guard troops stormed into American cities and patrolled black communities as if they were little more than South African townships living under the oppressive boot-to-neck of apartheid. There was Stokley Carmichael calling for black power. Black Panthers dressed in dark berets, leather jackets and gun belts, with their loaded weapons at the ready; and James Brown, who told us to "Say It Loud" that we were black and proud, was now telling us by 1971 that "It's a New Day."

Then, almost as if it happened over night, black history, even the most recent of it, took on a glistening new relevance for many of us. Wilmington's black teenagers—students ripped from their black, neighborhood school and transported against their will to cold, foreign schools teeming with hostile, white students, teachers and administrators who hardly concealed their disdain for us—began to understand something. We could see that more was in play, and at stake, than just high school. What may have once felt esoteric, now felt concrete and on point as we found ourselves in the middle of a struggle for self-expression, self-definition, and self-determination. And all the while we were insisting that we be treated fairly and regarded with dignity.

We found solace and strategies in, say, Frantz Fanon's *The Wretched of the Earth*, or in the scholarly, liberation writings of Angela Davis. We found ourselves quoting black visionaries and revolutionaries like Marcus Garvey, Malcolm X, George Jackson and Huey Newton. We began incorporating their uncompromising pro-black stance, heeding their call that we should be proud of our full lips, our hair (my own afro was bigger than ever now), the color of our skin, and our legacy of being the first men and women to walk and then settle a corner of this earth. So many of us were coming to understand that we need not be servile to any person. Contrary to the *Dred Scot v. Sandford decision* of America's nineteenth century, black people of the late twentieth century did, indeed, have rights white people were bound to respect. And those rights were written into the United States Declaration of Independence for us just as much as for all other Americans. There was no escape clause: "All men are created equal."

In short, a lot of black students who were attending Hoggard and New Hanover County high schools were becoming politicized. We were growing increasingly militant. This was a revolutionary time, a period when young black people were rising up. And we, the black refugees from Williston Senior High School, were not immune to these events crashing and banging around us. It was just a matter of time before we would start doing some crashing and banging of our own.

At first, for me, it was personal before it was political.

One school day when the fellas and I were hanging out in the hallway between classes at Hoggard, a white boy came walking through like we were invisible or worse yet, inconsequential. As he came close to me he barked, "Get out of my way, nigger." Then he pushed my skinny ass aside.

Before I had time to respond, my boys were all over him, stomping him into the hallway's freshly waxed tile floor. The next thing I knew, I jumped in and started stomping him, too. I had never been so angry. Words gurgled up and out of my throat, words I had never dared even think before.

"I'll kill you, you white muthafucka!"

But as hot as my rage was in those moments, an icy shame rose up in me when the kicks and blows stopped and the offender scampered away wounded and outraged in his own way. All I could think then was, that my mother would *kill* me if she found out what I had done. Remember, I was pretty much a good boy. She always taught me that fighting was wrong. "It's not the way civilized people solve their problems," she'd say, and I'd listen.

But there I was, in the bathroom at school, cleaning myself up, cleaning this white boy off of me, and feeling less bad every second about what I had done. After all, I had just gotten retribution. And it wasn't just for my mangled pride. Every kick and punch that I landed on this guy was a kick and punch for all the terror white folks had unleashed on black people down through the ages.

My mind picked at the tender racial scabs that I had hidden for so long. I thought about the tears that blurred my vision when, as a boy, I first saw old photographs of white men standing around, laughing and drinking beer, as three black men—all lynched— hung like gutted game from a tree behind them. I had also seen, in Wilmington's public library, pictures of once prominent black men being killed or run out of town in the city's 1898 massacre.

In a crazy way, I had wanted to go home and tell my mother how I'd gotten revenge for our shared racial wrongs and slights: for all the times Mrs. Whedbee called her "my niggra girl;" all the opportunities that had been denied her as a black woman in the South; all the days of slaving in flower farms and blueberry farms, at a sewing machine factory, and still, barely able to feed and clothe her children and pay the rent on shacks we lived in for years.

I wanted to tell my mother, too, that I had even gotten some degree of revenge for sins of Joseph Foy. He was the son of the eighteenth-century founder of the Poplar Grove Plantation, once one of the largest peanut plantations in the state. Its mansion, which was built in the mid-1800s by Joseph Foy, still stands just outside Wilmington and is on the National Register of Historic Places.

My family doesn't need a registry to always remember this place and the man who built it. It was Joseph Foy who, needing additional slave labor on his plantation, paid $1,010 for the purchase of Nancy, and her two sons, Daniel and Nathanial. Nathanial, who would carry the surname of his owner, was my great-great-grandfather, a direct ancestor to my mother, Dolores Foy Moore.

As I slipped out of the bathroom after the fight, I headed toward the gym for class. As I walked, I thought to myself, *maybe, when I know better, I'll do better. Right now, it's a powerful feeling to kick a white muthafucka's ass.*

Amazingly, I was not among those who got suspended for the beatdown. No one had ratted me out. Three of my boys had been late for class after the altercation, so their teachers sent them to the office where they were identified by the victim. I had gym that hour and as a consequence, I temporarily escaped similar scrutiny because most students were a little late after showering and changing clothes. No trip to the office. No chance of being fingered. I was scot-free.

I felt strangely good about doing something bad and not having to apologize to anyone for what I had done. No, this was not a corrective act of nonviolence. Yet, at the same time, I realized that we, black students, had to stand up for ourselves. No one else back then seemed willing to stand up for us. This was true for most black adults in Wilmington, especially those the ages of our parents and grandparents. Their will to stand up to whites, even themselves, appeared to have been snapped long before I came along. It was as if the spirit of whole generations of black Wilmington had been trampled, broken. But with us... no. We were a new generation of black Wilmington and we were finding our legs and testing our muscles. We hadn't been around a lot of white people before. Maybe we didn't know any better. Nevertheless, we were standing up. And it felt good.

I know my sense of racial justice had been inflamed that cold, January Friday in 1971. It was the forty-second anniversary of

Martin Luther King Jr.'s birth. A bunch of us on the forty-or-so-minute bus ride to Hoggard hadn't talked about having our own memorial at school that day. The idea was one of those leaderless, spontaneous things. It just made sense that we could do something, and that something started in the cafeteria.

For me, it was just human nature. We were being treated so unfairly at Hoggard. And that treatment started on day one when the big, yellow school buses packed with black students (and some poor whites who lived in or at the fringes of our black neighborhoods) pulled up to the practically brand new and previously almost lily white high school.

There, right in Hoggard's parking lot, were all these white people apparently waiting for our arrival. A lot of them looked like they were parents who likely had kids in the school. All of them were wearing these nasty expressions, yelling and holding up signs that made it clear that we were not welcomed. I heard more than my share of angry shouts that morning. Chief among them was "nigger go home."

For centuries, black people had lived in petrified fear of white people, white people who, like those screaming just a matter of feet from our school buses, knew nothing more about us than the color of our skin. It was this kind of baseless hatred that marked so many of our American decades in the pendulum swings of lynched black bodies hanging from trees. It was the kind of hatred that informed black men that they dare not gaze at a white woman, the kind of hatred seen in the heinously bloated and hauntingly disfigured face of fourteen-year-old Emmitt Till, who was fatally shot, beaten and stabbed in 1955 for allegedly whistling at a white woman in the Mississippi Delta. It was precisely this kind of blind hatred that so many white people—who even took offense if a black man looked them in the eye—had for us that first lit the flames of our own resentment of, mistrust of, fear of, and in some cases, hatred for white people.

For years, many black people did their best to hide it, if for no other reason than self-preservation in a land in which we were nearly always outnumbered and outgunned. Nonetheless, I'm sure that all black people felt it. My mother, one of the most loving and forgiving people I ever knew, would transform into a steely-eyed militant—mostly behind closed doors—when it came to how white people were treating blacks. She knew that openly speaking her mind about such matters in the early 1960s would probably accomplish little more than costing her job, and possibly landing her in jail for being, *Conscious While Black*.

My mother loved Dr. King, and saw him as a kind of messiah. But she was also very proud of the way Malcolm X stood up to white folks, calling them blue-eyed devils when they did devilish deeds. At home, my mother and I talked about the black struggle for equality, respect, self-esteem and community development. We both liked the way Elijah Muhammad's Nation of Islam taught self-reliance, and demanded that its members not wait for someone to assure them that black did not mean something inferior or dirty. The Muslims taught that we could be our own agents of change in a country that felt thoroughly committed to policing a status quo that vastly favored white people and even more vastly disadvantaged us.

I reflected a lot on what being a black American meant as I boarded the school bus for my first day at John T. Hoggard High School in the fall of 1969. Once again, our case, in this instance to keep our Williston Senior High School open, had so little weight in the scales of justice held in the pale clenched hand of whites. I searched the bewildered black faces riding the bus with me that morning that still cast night shadows where a new day's lazy light had not yet reached.

What would John T. Hoggard High School be like? I wondered. All of our lives most of us had always walked to school, in my case Williston Junior High, with every expectation of walking to Williston Senior High next door. Up until this day, the first day of school had always been a joyful occasion of reconnection with sights and sounds and faces both familiar and reassuringly comforting.

But now, on this bare-bones school bus, everything seemed quiet and subdued—somber, like we were crammed into the family's limo headed to the cemetery to bury grandma. Everyone's eyes were open that morning, but everyone seemed, like me, to be looking inwardly, trying to make sense of our collective loss. There was no one boasting about his or her summer vacation. No good-natured joking and jiving; no one was even playing the dozens, as in "Your mama's so fat that her blood type is Ragu."

No one seemed to notice all the back-to-school clothes most of us were wearing on that bus that day. Strange.

In black Wilmington, which consisted mostly of neighborhoods populated with the "have not's" and the "have less," clothes were major signifiers of status. Yes, there was status, or lack thereof, in the flare of a pair of shark-skin slacks, the cut of a jacket, the brand and designer names on a pair of sneakers, whether a coat was genuine leather or its cheap second cousin, "pleather."

Aside from the pride the community had in its institutions, like Williston Senior High, major self-esteem was long derived from the way brothers or sisters presented themselves in public. If you wanted to be somebody, if you wanted to be accepted, you had to dress for success—as it was solely translated by the tastemakers of our communities. For instance, we wanted to dress much more like Richard Roundtree's Shaft, close-knit, turtle-neck shirts and full-length leather coats rather than, let's say, Sonny Bono with his loudly striped, denim bell-bottomed pants, balloon-sleeved paisley shirts and furry vests.

This wasn't easy. For most of us, keeping up with street fashions meant working all summer long to earn enough money to buy boldly patterned, Italian-knit shirts called Blys, floppy woolen or cotton caps called Big Apples, and iridescent silk and tailored woolen pants. And on your feet? Platform shoes sporting more styles than Detroit had cars. They literally let you look down on anyone who couldn't afford them. And closer to the skin, silk socks called Thick 'n Thins.

For more casual wear? Chuck Taylor All Stars sneakers by Converse. Decades before Nike's Air Jordans, "Chucks" was the first premium basketball shoe. It was, for a time, the official shoe of the National Basketball Association, costing as much as twice the price of its nearest competitor. In 1970, that was about $10 a pair. If you wore any sneakers other than Chuck Taylors (named for Charles H. "Chuck" Taylor, a fairly minor, white professional basketball player in the 1920s) you were instantly branded crudely uncool and a nerd long before there was such a word to describe this socially challenged, outcast condition.

So much was at stake in the name of *style*, some guys went as far as to make special trips to New York to buy their rags. There, on big city streets, they could, for example, find Chuck Taylors in colors other than the standard black or white. Extra effort often payed off. One of the greatest compliments that could be bestowed on a brother back then was to say, "That nigger is the cleanest muthafucka in town."

Style was among the half dozen or so things—music, dance, speech, sports and sex among them—that black folks didn't look to whites to define the rules or set the standards of excellence and acceptance. Maybe it was a way to deflect all the none-too-subtle messages of black inferiority that were forced on us back then. A lot of that shit got through, too.

Take for instance, black entertainers who would not be seen on stage in the 1950s and 1960s unless their hair was dyed, fried, and laid to the side, emulating the so-called "good hair" natural to white people. And what about colorism? For much too long and much too often black people internalized white folk color prejudice in our own sayings like, "If you're white you're right; if you are brown stick around; if you're black, get back."

For as long as I could remember, black people had struggled with an inferiority complex that was deeply rooted in their identity. For centuries, we had been called Negroes and niggers. And even while we insisted on being called black and African American, so many of us were still ashamed of our color, our kinky hair, wide noses, full lips and round asses.

If you were black and had light skin and "good hair," you were considered by fellow blacks, as well as whites, to be better than someone with dark skin and nappy hair. One of the worst putdowns a black person could call another black person was to call him or her a "black ass nigger." Dark-skinned black people's only comeback would be, "The blacker the berry the sweeter the juice." It was at best a bitter retort.

So damn straight, dressing *clean* for us meant much more than just wearing clothes that weren't soiled in any way. It meant that you dressed with style, black style, a style that sported all the latest fashions *we* favored. That morning aboard the school bus on the first day of school at Hoggard High, Rudy Waddell, seventeen-years-old like myself, was as clean as the Board of Health. He was dressed in an expensive mohair Bly with razor-creased, gray silk and wool pants. Stacy Adams slip-ons shined on his feet and a new Big Apple sat at just the right angle and attitude on his head. All through our old school, Rudy had always been talkative, always cracking jokes, always breaking whatever ice that dared to form in his effusive, yet cool, presence.

Surely at any moment, in an icy tension that held us all frozen in our seats, Rudy would crack a joke and have the whole bus laughing. Instead, he sat in his seat, motionless, staring straight ahead all the way to green and gray suburbs, all the way to John T. Hoggard High School. It was at that moment that I began to realize the seriousness of the culture shock this hasty, ill-conceived venture into school desegregation had loosened on us. A guy who otherwise would have been one of the most animated dudes on the bus was reduced to looking—despite his pitch perfect attire (for Williston Senior High, that is)—like he was heading for the gallows.

As our bus approached Hoggard, I heard one of the fellows ask no one in particular, "Man, how we going to get along with those white people if they don't want us around."

I thought, *hell, we are not only going to be fish out of water, but black fish marked for stomping wherever white feet find us.* Then I thought about my younger brother, Harold. He was the first of my siblings to go to a majority white school. In fact, it was under the banner of Dr. Eaton's "Freedom of Choice" desegregation effort. When I knew I was going to have to go to a white school because Williston Senior was closing, I went to New Hanover High school next door to Williston. It was a white school that never held any allure to me. It wasn't that I had anything against New Hanover. It was just that I knew it wasn't for me.

But shortly before I was to start my first year of high school there in the fall of 1968, I asked Harold what I might expect to find behind its scrubbed clean, brick walls. I'll never forget what he told me. "White folks," he said. "They get scared when there are a lot of black folk around."

That first year of school desegregation in my hometown, coming years after the passage of the Civil Rights Act of 1964 and the Voting Rights Act of 1965, was like falling face first into a nest of coiled snakes. You felt a lot of people just holding their breath to see what would happen as hundreds of blacks like me were swallowed up in the desegregation plan. For the most part, that meant not much—at first. It was as each side was feeling the other out. There were some fights, almost all of them racially inspired. And, of course, if someone was sent home, suspended or disciplined in any way, you could be sure that person was black.

For me, desegregating at New Hanover *and* Hoggard was a disaster. I was at the mercy of people who had no understanding of me as a student or appreciation of me as a person and member of a community of any significance. White teachers, white school administrators and white students seemed to have determined that my equality meant that I had to attend their schools, like I couldn't derive any nutrition from food unless I ate it from their table. It was insulting, but my full understanding of this race-based insult would come to me later when I languished, still more boy than man, in prison where oppression was plainly and painfully spelled out in high relief, in black and white.

But even in the prickly months when I was forced to attend white high schools, I knew it was all wrong. I knew this with ever greater conviction as I dragged myself from class to class, learning that most whites I encountered had no use for black people other than serving as some kind of flesh and blood robots expected to work their nuts and bolts off without complaint, or shuck and jive as if living cartoons for their amusement. Either way, our humanity was not part of the program.

By 1971, in my second year of desegregation, I realized that I had no choice but to sit next to, and answer to, people who had decided they hated me for no reason other than my race being different than theirs. Not only were we unable to communicate with these strange (we were no doubt just as strange to them) people, but they were unable or unwilling to communicate with us.

I came to the conclusion that the unwillingness of white students to deal with us in any meaningful way was deeply rooted in racist Southern white supremacist traditions. Young people, black or white, can usually work out their differences. Yet, it was apparent to me that the white supremacist tradition was not dead in Wilmington, and was the guiding force in the fiasco of our school desegregation crisis. This coming together of blacks and whites actually opened old wounds that, to this day, still fester in Wilmington.

Everything I was required to read about white people in class, combined with my new experiences with them, was materializing into an omnipresent noose for me and my friends. It was like a nightmare someone else forced you to dream. Monday through Friday, all day long, I looked at frosty white faces and saw in their eyes—grey, green, blue and brown like mine—a merciless indictment against us, eyes unblinkingly ready to indict us for presuming to think of ourselves as their equals.

Nonetheless, in those early years of desegregation I tried to carry on the best that I could. I craved for something normal. A lot of black students tried hard to make it work.

But black students weren't the only ones displaced because of the closing of Williston Senior High School. Black administrators and teachers were displaced, too. All forty-seven of Williston's teachers and administrators were assigned to other schools or forced into retirement, as was the case with Principal Booker T. Washington. Assistant Principal James Harris was assigned to an elementary school. Many of Williston's teachers were sent to junior highs and elementary schools, like Roland-Grise and Sunset Park, and other historically white schools. Seventeen of Williston's finest teachers were, thank goodness for me, sent to Hoggard, including our former Wilmington City Council woman, Lethia Hankins, along with coaching legend E.A. Spike Corbin, and Williston's music instructor, Constance B. Odell.

Fourteen teachers were assigned to New Hanover High. Sixteen others, for undisclosed reasons, were never reassigned.

As a result of all of this reshuffling, everything at Hoggard was so different from what I had experienced in Williston Junior High. There, teachers really cared if I learned or didn't. They expected me to learn, and if I didn't get something, some aspect of the American revolution, for instance, I'd be asked to stay a few minutes after class so they could work with me until I got it. Black teachers were just more hands on. White teachers, on the other hand, taught like you were supposed to already know what they were teaching, that classroom topics and themes had already been warmed up around the dinner table back at home. It was like pass the peas and while you're at it, what do you think of the meat loaf and the geo-politics of Indo-China? That's not what it sounded like around my dinner table at home.

Then again, perhaps it was what teachers choose to teach at Hoggard that didn't catch our imaginations. You would likely learn, for example, that right down Highway 17 at Fort Fisher, Confederate forces fought to preserve Wilmington as the state's vital port during the Civil War. You would likely be told that the fort, which is a historic site now, was the last Confederate stronghold to fall to the Union Army (a fact that some whites still lament).

However, what you would definitely not hear in Hoggard's history classes in the early 1970s, is how Union troops captured Fort Fisher, defeating its Confederate soldiers on January 15, 1865, and how *colored troops* liberated Wilmington on January 22, 1865. Even today, I wonder how, or if the history of the Wilmington Ten is being taught in my hometown.

During my troubled days at Hoggard, I simply concluded that whites students as much as black students there were locked into a clash of cultures, and almost always it was us, the black students, who suffered the most from these clashes

I'm convinced that the racial crisis could have been mitigated if the school Board, and faculty and administrators of the surviving high schools had taken time to plan and prepare for school desegregation on such a large scale. That didn't happen. The almost daily riots and micro aggressions that flared between the races during the early years of school desegregation would not have occurred if we had been prepared for transition into this new system. If we had been treated with dignity and respect, we black students could have adjusted much more seamlessly despite the pain of being denied and removed from our school and community of equals. We were excluded from the process; and as a result many of us felt like victims and were treated like trespassers.

There was little, if any, sensitivity training. One of the consequences of that failure was that black students ended up being frequently insulted, intended or not, at almost every rung in the ladder to desegregation. It wasn't as if white teachers and administrators had never had a chance to work out school integration in Wilmington and its surrounding New Hanover County. While it was a relative trickle of black students, some, like my little brother, did attend area white schools before Williston was forcibly closed.

But black students who did integrate often did so paying a terribly high price.

Take for instance Amelia Fanning Goss. She told me a story once about being the only black student in her first-grade class. One day she said, she was surprised and confused when her teacher, a white woman, asked her to sing a song for the class.

Like many Southern blacks, Amelia had grown up around cotton. She also found, like many, anything related to cotton picking, the forced vocation of so many enslaved blacks, and later free but poor blacks, demeaning. It certainly is no accident that if you touched someone in the South who didn't want to be touched, you might be told to "Get your cotton pickin' hands off me."

But this sort of sensitivity appeared beyond little Amelia's teacher that day when she was asked to stand and sing "Cotton Needs a Pickin.' "

Cotton needs a pickin' so bad Cotton needs a pickin'
so bad Cotton needs a pickin' so bad

I'm gonna pick all over this field.

Planted this cotton in April

On the full of the moon

We've had a hot, dry summer

And that's why it opened so soon. Oh!

Cotton needs a pickin' so bad Cotton needs a pickin'
so bad Cotton needs a pickin' so bad

I'm gonna pick all over this field.

At Hoggard, white kids treated us like a disease, not wanting to get close to us. To help avoid racial polarization in the classroom, teachers had to seat students alphabetically. However, this in no way eliminated the problem that neither black students nor white students were prepared to deal with. The fact was that, at the time, few high school students were eager to associate across the color line.

I had my own reservations.

I was just an average student. While I was always interested in learning, my mind could drift all on its own out of the classroom to some ball field where base hits and line drives were immeasurably more engrossing than whatever was scrawled on the blackboard or in the day's selected reading. Maybe some of my difficulties in class helped to up the ante of my growing frustration, especially at Hoggard. I was in the eleventh grade and nothing there was getting any easier. And I wasn't alone. The school's administration did not go out of its way to explain to us why so many of our athletes that were good enough for black schools were apparently not good enough for Hoggard's teams, which were all dominated by white players. Maybe the white coaches didn't want to travel around North Carolina with blacks competing in away games, meets and matches. I found out that a lot of the school organizations were excluding black students. And why were there so few black cheerleaders? I didn't know how to handle these obvious inequalities.

I could feel a tiny flame of resentment within me begin to flicker to life.

Years later, as an unjustly convicted member of the Wilmington Ten, I would take a measure of that flame that eventually illuminated my way as, at first, an aggrieved high school student and then much more. It was the light that helped me see my way to acting righteously, forthrightly and proudly as a man in the tradition of Dr. King and a host of black leaders and activists whose names history has never fully committed to memory.

Sometimes things are just spontaneous.

A bunch of us black students at Hoggard went to the cafeteria for lunch. There was nothing unusual going on. To accommodate the full student body, some 2,000 strong, the school scheduled two lunch periods, one right after the other. On January 15, 1971, sometime during the second lunch period, some of us actually ate lunch that day.

But the group of black students that I was a part of was mostly interested in putting our lunchtime to another, higher purpose than just feeding our faces. There were a couple of dozen of us, mostly boys. We gathered around some tables and started talking loudly. A lot of us were still angry that the school was not going to have a Dr. King program of any kind. That denial really was the last straw. We grumbled about this slap in our faces as some of us sipped cartons of warm milk and chewed brown-bag sandwiches from home.

Suddenly, one of my boys jumped up on a lunch table and starting asking, rhetorically, "Yeah, yeah, how come we can't have a Dr. King celebration?"

Someone else joined in and said that we were having one right now. And then, individual voices of dissent swelled into a choir of "Yeah, yeah, let's do something about it."

Around the same time, another black student, William "Joe" Wright, Jr., got on the high school's student radio station (which was really not much more than a booth in the cafeteria) and started making the same claim. Now, thanks to the in-house radio station, our message was being heard throughout the school.

Joe Wright was confirming for all that at least some of Hoggard High's black students were staging their own celebration of Dr. King's birthday—right then and there. You could hear black students saying stuff like, "They wouldn't allow the ceremony..." We're having our own little ceremony..." "We're having a sit-in in Dr. King's name..."

We didn't go back to class that day after lunch. And I don't remember there being any particular leader at that moment. It was like one student said something, and another student said something, and then everybody said, "Yeah. Lets' do it."

I don't know that I felt any fear that day when hell took the express elevator to Hoggard's cafeteria. I just knew that something had to be, needed to be done. So, we did it. We staged an impromptu sit-in, one Dr. King, even my mother if she had been there, would have been proud of.

The following month, Joe and I and a number of student and adult activists would lead a black boycott of Wilmington and New Hanover County public schools. Benjamin Chavis, Jr., also a native son of North Carolina, would be sent by his church to help us. Almost immediately, powerful forces in and around Wilmington moved against us. These actions culminated in Joe and me, and eight other activists, including Rev. Chavis, being convicted for, essentially, firebombing Mike's Grocery, a white-owned business in Wilmington's black community. Joe and I were each sentenced to twenty-nine years in state prison. The ten of us, the *Wilmington Ten*, were sentenced to a total of 282 years behind bars.

But in Hoggard High's cafeteria on that Friday in the winter of 1971, I never felt more free. Our group of King celebrants grew to more than seventy people as we announced that none of us was going back to class. We were staging at once a celebration and a protest, and yes, in a fine example of the civil rights movement, a sit-in.

I was never in the forefront as a leader, but I was ready and available. I had become an activist because I dared, like many others that day, to take action. I know my heart raced just as much as all of the protesters. Something was happening, finally, and I was proud and excited to be a part of it.

Our impromptu sit-in quickly ended when sheriff deputies and school staff stormed the cafeteria. I was expelled after being identified as one of the persons encouraging the sit-in. I didn't realize it at the time, but that gathering in Hoggard's cafeteria, that nonviolent act of civil disobedience by a group of aggrieved, black teenagers was the Big Bang, the beginning of a movement that would, for years to come, force Wilmington into a deep re-examination of itself as a city, and a promise too long broken and unfulfilled for its black residents.

But first, I, along with seven young men, most of whom were teenagers, a white, thirty-five-year-old VISTA volunteer, and Rev. Chavis, would have to be sacrificed.

We would come to be known, likely forever, as the Wilmington Ten. I am a *soul* survivor of its tests, terrors and toil. Most of all, I survived to share its lessons and legacy.

5

THE REVOLUTION
PREPARES TO GO TO CHURCH

By 1971, there were few big city entertainments that seemed directly aimed at us. We were a restless, isolated group of black, urban Southerners coming of age on the trailing edge of the modern civil rights movement. And from our front row seats on that movement, it was crumbling under the rhetorical bombs and clenched fists of black power. These were at once exciting, exasperating and exhausting times. But you know what? We had the movies.

And I'm not talking about "Fiddler on the Roof" or the "Summer of '42" or even "Escape from the Planet of the Apes," all popular films at the time. But in '71, probably the most important year in black cinematic history, black youth like me across America were invited to a revolution on the screen that reflected and influenced the revolution that was surging in our streets, hearts and minds. For the first time, I watched black folks—black men who looked and talked and walked like me—play the hero. And win.

I was seventeen when Melvin Van Peebles' pimp slapped Hollywood by opening *Sweet Sweetback's Baad Asssss Song*, a movie he wrote, played its lead and directed. The film cost $150,000 to make and made more than $15 million, a feat that placed it eleventh among the top grossing films in the U.S. that year. And the fact that Van Peebles, a black renegade from Hollywood, created this movie as an independent production, made it that much sweeter. He was a filmmaker who had beaten the system playing a black character he invented, that had beaten the system. And all of it was set to the afro-ghetto beats of predawn Earth, Wind and Fire... I could hardly sit still in my seat when I watched the movie flicker before me bigger and bolder than life.

And then, months later, with little hype—not at all like today's flood of pre-release movie clips, star and director interviews droning from television, radio and Websites—*Shaft* exploded in movie theaters practically everywhere there were black movie audiences to see it. If you weren't around then, and especially if you weren't young and black, you cannot imagine the rush of recognition, pride and just plain coolness we felt the first time we watched Richard Roundtree stride across busy New York City streets sporting a full-length, brown leather coat, with afro picked out flawlessly smooth, jaw set and eyes expressing to anyone who had their own pair, that this is a dude you don't mess with. All business, brother.

If that wasn't enough, you had Isaac Hayes laying down the soundtrack, that iconic sizzle of high hats and guitar wah-wah from "Theme from Shaft." It all perfectly synched with the man's panther glide through a gritty urban jungle. More, he was a private detective who didn't seem to answer to anyone but himself.

They say this cat is a baadmother—

Shut your mouth.

But I'm talking about Shaft.

That was what it was like for us in Wilmington in 1971. And so it shouldn't be surprising that when I first saw Ben Chavis in Wilmington I was impressed. This twenty-three-year-old Christian activist was stepping tall, lean and brown from his blue, sun-roofed Cadillac Eldorado, a full-length fur coat draped over his square shoulders. It was February 2, 1971. And it was almost like he was unknowingly starring in his own black movie and we all were going to be part of the cast. Seriously, Ben looked like a living preview of the next big film to thrill black America with its big cars, maxi coats and all things red hot, black cool: 1972's *Super Fly*.

That film's tag line was: Never a dude like this one! He's got a plan to stick it to the Man!

But Benjamin Franklin Chavis, Jr., probably the most famous and enduring face of the Wilmington Ten, was far from some character of imagination. He was the real deal, a product of a family steeped in the church and activism for racial justice and equality. In many ways, Brother Ben was the cavalry. And we, the much maligned and mistreated black students of the New Hanover County Schools, could not be happier to see him ride into town armed with his wisdom, wit and grit—and experience of dealing with the Man.

But how had we gotten to this point where we needed a Ben Chavis? We were basically a group of black high school kids who had only wanted to be treated fairly, justly, treated like any other Wilmington high school kids. We never intended to be the center of a collision of racial hatred, racial history, violence and terror. We were just part of a rising tide of black people, especially young black folks, standing up for themselves.

In the winter of 1971, that was exactly where we were. After almost two years of enduring my middling to miserable passage from the possibility of *my* own black high school to *their* high schools, I concluded that black students were never going to be accepted—at least not in any foreseeable future—by white students, white parents, white teachers and their white school administrators. This unwillingness of them to associate or communicate with us was deeply rooted in racist Southern white supremacist traditions. This was a set of circumstances set in motion way over my head and long before I was born black, hungry and wailing.

If I needed any more proof of the racial disconnect, white parents at regularly scheduled PTA meetings came to the consensus that all the confrontations between black and white students amounted to nothing more than a disciplinary problem. That's right. We were *dangerous black brats*. And their solution? Place armed policemen in the hallways. These *adults* failed to understand the depth of the situation. We were angry as hell. We were angry because we were caught up in an untenable circumstance and no one seemed to care one bit about our pain.

When John T. Hoggard High School first opened in September of 1967, it was intended to be a state-of-the-art high school for suburban white kids. Few anticipated that a year later, its halls would be filled with black kids from Wilmington's poorest neighborhoods. Even under the best circumstances, even if racism didn't exist, at the very least, a serious cultural revolution would have been necessary to create an equitable learning environment for blacks and whites there.

The sudden integration of New Hanover County schools was a clash of cultures, and the black community's culture was the one that suffered the most and most often. There was a tremendous contrast between the kinds of things that went on at a predominantly white school as opposed to the kinds of things that were experienced at a predominantly black school like Williston. For example, at our schools, much more than the white schools we landed in, students had been expected to sing songs like *The Star Spangled Banner, God Bless America* and *This Is My Country* at assemblies. All through grade school, I sang those patriotic songs with a kind of innocent pride. They were, after all, in recognition of the fact that this was indeed the country that my ancestors had helped build. I was born in America. I was an American, so, I thought at the time, I had every right to be proud of this country.

But the years of being a darker American taught me something else. I learned that there were two Americas, one for white folk and another for black folks like me. The America that most blacks came from had little resemblance to the white one, at least from my vantage point growing up black and poor in Wilmington that treated me as if I was nothing more than raw material for demeaning white designs.

And if I, or any other young black person from Wilmington, had thought differently as a child, the rudest of awakenings awaited us in the forced integration of the county's public high schools. We saw firsthand the hatred that shaped a racist tradition deeply embedded in so many gray, green, and blue eyes that refused to meet ours. Surprisingly few reflected a glint of mercy. Their stares seemed to indict us for daring to struggle for our rights as young men and women and to presumptuously think of ourselves as their equals. It was mind blowing. What was our crime? What had we, hundreds to their thousands, done to evoke such naked hatred and resentment?

I always believed, or wanted to, that young people of any color could usually work out their differences if we could wiggle free from the yoke of entrenched Southern racism. But every day, in ways subtle and in your face, we could all feel this yoke heavy around our necks and guiding us, white and black, into a storm of deliberate chaotic school desegregation.

Throwing us all together with no plan, no understanding, no compassion, had ripped open old racial wounds that to this day still fester for black people in Wilmington—and many places beyond. In my deepest recesses, I could sense the cries of my ancestors, as if their pain comingled with mine. Everything I had read about white people, heard about them—married with my new experiences—materialized into a soul crushing, omnipresent racial reality for me and my friends.

It was like we were living in a nightmare from which none of us could awaken. It was practically open warfare between us and white students in school, at nearby bus stops and eateries after school. And then, when we were finally at home, the conflicts raged in our heads, replaying fresh slights, insults, assaults—and dreams of righteous retribution, even better, peace.

It was tiring, always bracing for attack—spiritual and physical—when you weren't receiving one, or fending one off. And remember, this was not supposed to be some battlefield, no Vietnam, no Iraq, no Afghanistan or Syria now. This was supposed to be school, classrooms conducive to learning. Black students were learning, alright, lessons no one dared to put into a textbook.

After three semesters of abuse, violence, and exclusion, I felt myself, along with scores and scores of other black students from Wilmington, becoming militant. I began to taste the flint on my tongue when the injustice we faced aroused the kinds of inflammatory words that had flown like sparks from men like Malcolm X, from Eldridge Cleaver, H. Rap Brown and Stokely Carmichael.

It was 1970, and I realized that all the major new civil rights laws of the mid-1960s were hardly ancient news. We were supposed to be living in a new era of vastly improving racial conditions. And yet, we weren't. Jim Crow might not have been kicking the asses of my people as hard as he was in the 1940s and '50s, for instance. But, I could feel old Jim Crow rabbit punching me, tripping me up, every chance he got, and he got a lot of chances each day I stepped through the doors of Hoggard high school. I never thought of myself as a leader, per se. I was just a high schooler. But I could feel responsibility weighing heavy on my chest, pressing down hard on my heart. I was ready to act. Something had to be done.

Without holding a meeting, or taking a vote, so many of us black students just arrived that spring at our own consensus: We weren't going to take this abuse anymore! We were ordinary students facing an extraordinary crisis. On one hand, we had local leaders who had fought diligently to desegregate the New Hanover County Public Schools, like Wilmington's own Dr. Eaton, who skillfully challenged the rule by using the rules. On the other hand, outside leaders, like Golden Frinks, a field secretary for the Southern Christian Leadership Conference, had been crisscrossing the state warning that the closing of black schools, like Williston, would be an act of destruction against the whole of the black community. He predicted that the shuttering of Williston Senior High School would shatter the bedrock of black Wilmington's cultural core and values. It would be devastating and a blow from which the community would not likely ever recover. Frinks was right. All these years later, we've yet to be what we were before destroying Williston. And there were other warnings, some of the loudest coming directly from us, black students caught in this race-baited trap.

On August 30, 1970, just before the start of the 1970-1971 school year, the Wilmington-New Hanover Good Neighbor Council, a group of mostly worried white citizens, held a meeting about the brewing crisis in the county's newly integrated public schools, especially in the high schools. This was high profile, in addition to the usual suspects like teachers, civic leaders, and members of the Board of Education; Superintendent Heyward Bellamy was there front and center.

I was very proud to see my friend and fellow Hoggard High student, Joe Wright, there to speak. Seemingly from the beginning, he had been an outspoken student activist for black students. And on this day at the meeting, he didn't waste any time getting to the core of the problem. He warned that the anger in the black community was real and there would be trouble in the schools if immediate action was not taken. He didn't mince words. He said everywhere he went in Wilmington over the summer he heard black students talking about waging a revolution in the schools. He said black students are no longer willing to tolerate "racist bullshit." George Clark, a school board member, appealed for calm and patience, ending with a plea: "Give us a chance." He later said, "I think every teacher in the system should be given sensitivity training."

Superintendent Bellamy swiftly called for the establishment of a faculty level bi-racial committee in all schools, "that will work to solve any problems arising out of a new school situation; an active effort to acquire upgraded and scholarly textbooks on black studies, and more black representation at the administration and counseling level." But it felt like too little much too late.

Joe Wright had already asked the board if it could institute a black studies program. The board responded by announcing that it would institute a program—but only as an elective and only one half credit would be given. Most of us resented this because if American history was compulsory, then why shouldn't black history also be compulsory? Or, as an acceptable compromise, why couldn't black history be incorporated into the American history course? Following the board's offer, Clark again called for patience. We had been patient long enough, and just as Joe had warned, fighting in and outside the "integrated" schools resumed. I believe that most of the almost daily riots that erupted during this period would have been avoided if a concerted effort to integrate black students into this white new world had been made. Had we been prepared to be transitioned into this new system, and treated with dignity and respect, it was very possible that we would have adjusted. Instead, we were made to feel like victims and trespassers in our new classrooms.

It was clear that there were deep racial and social problems at the two white high schools—involved in this forced desegregation. Like looking into Shaft's eyes, anyone with a pair of their own could see that Wilmington was drowning in racial conflict. For so long, black folk there, like old folks would say, go along to get along. And for most whites the nasty day-to-day insults of widespread discrimination, injustice and inequality that we black people in Wilmington suffered was largely invisible to them. And it had been that way for so long, that few, including the city fathers, its educators—even our parents—few seemed capable of seeing another way. Few even dreamed of a way out. But then there were Bertha Boykin Todd, a librarian at Hoggard high at the time, and Superintendent Heyward Bellamy, who both seemed to dream wide awake of a solution.

Mrs. Todd, which is what we called her out of respect and good home training, was sort of a legend for a lot of us black students at Hoggard. First of all, she was a strikingly beautiful black woman with butter pecan smooth complexion and clear, almond brown eyes. She, along with her twin sister, had been majorettes at North Carolina Central University, in Durham. It was there, a historically black college, Mrs. Todd had received her master's degree in library science in 1952. All of this lent her a kind of jaunty, sure-footed confidence in the way she spoke and moved through the world, white or black. And she was very aware of her gifts of smarts and smart looks. Almost as if to cool down her Miss Everything Good Looks, she wore her once long beautiful hair in a short and rather unflattering bob.

Mrs. Todd started her many years in education as a librarian in the fall of 1952 at Williston Industrial High School. The following year, she transferred to Williston Senior High School, then so new it still smelled of fresh paint. I guess the hairdo was her way of telling the world—nonverbally—that she was, indeed, a librarian. In the fourteen years that Mrs. Todd served as librarian at Williston, she was repeatedly recognized for her dedication to students and her respect for learning. The Williston class of 1963 honored her, writing:

> *There is no one member of rank or commission, or warrant, or enlistment on the Good Ship S.S. Williston Senior High who has guided more crew members in reading, writing, research, and a respect for learning than the beloved Captain Bertha B. Todd, to whom we, the graduating seamen, dedicate this log for 1963. To all she has been a counselor and a guide. Her charm and grace have endeared all of us to her; for to know her is to love her.*

In the wake of public school desegregation in 1969, Mrs. Todd became much more than a librarian. She was a force for positive change on the ground, not some administrative paper pusher in some distant office. She took it on herself to reach out to students, to help them cope with this huge and upsetting upheaval. It didn't seem to matter to Mrs. Todd if students were filled with rage or fear, and just plain lost—all emotions that roiled through me in the early years of my forced attendance of white schools. She just offered that warm smile of hers, and spoke in her firm but gentle voice, and everything always seemed better because of her. But Mrs. Todd wasn't just charming. She had ideas.

When relations between black and white students were getting raw in the first year of desegregation, Mrs. Todd came up with a plan. She picked sixteen male students, black and white, that she thought other students would follow. Then she gave them a job: Come up with ways in which black and white students could, like the famous plea of Rodney King, just get along.

The group came to be known as the *Viking 16*, and created ten resolutions aimed at bringing a lasting peace to Hoggard High School. Among them were:

- That we make a special effort to respect each other.
- That we try to understand why the other person has a difference of opinion.
- That we make a great effort to stop using abusive language and ask other students to do the same.
- That we try to see each person as a member of the human race instead of black and white.
- That, if two students engage in a conflict, we are to discourage the conflict rather than encourage it.
- That we make a special effort to provide a calm atmosphere for the benefit of everyone.

It was pure Mrs. Todd. But according to her autobiography, *My Restless Journey*, she began to experience resentment from many black students at Hoggard because of her growing close relationship with white students there. Some black students even went as far as calling her an "Uncle Tom." They questioned her apparent closeness with some white students, exclaiming, "Mrs. Todd, you belong to us!"

But she would respond, "No, I belong to all the students."

Still, most black students continued to show a great deal of respect for her. I know I did. It was that high regard for her that gave her the power to quell a near riot at Hoggard in the winter of 1969.

It all started when a group of black students—I was not yet attending Hoggard—marched down the school's hallways demanding that there be more black cheerleaders. Mrs. Todd quickly came on deck like a ship's captain, and took charge. She hurried off to the gym and asked Coach Jim Hebbe to pull out the bleachers there. He did. Then she ran back toward the library and approached the students, moving like one of those tornado chasers who run into trouble rather than run away from it.

"We are going to the library!" she recounts in her book. And like obedient students, they followed her to the gym. There, she told them that if they wished to voice their grievances, "now was the time to do so." And she promised to do everything she could to make sure that the administrators paid attention to their concerns. They were not sent back to class that day. Instead, the students were ordered by two assistant principals to not leave the gym for the next four hours, which was the remainder of the school day. Out of respect for her, everyone did just that.

Black students were less, let's say, compliant when it came to Superintendent Bellamy. He was a Southerner in bearing and birth, being born in Conway, SC. In fact, his paternal line goes way back, helping to settle South Carolina in the 1760s. The Bellamys even owned slaves. Heyward Bellamy's family made their way to Wilmington in 1935. He graduated from New Hanover High School in 1943, and then served in the Air Force during World War II, but never left the U.S.

After earning multiple degrees at the University of North Carolina at Chapel Hill, he left academia in 1965 after earning a PhD in science and zoology. The following year, Bellamy was named superintendent of New Hanover County Schools. We would come to learn that he wasn't such a bad guy, just one mired in a very, very bad situation.

Shortly before Thanksgiving 1970, a group of black students at Hoggard staged a protest over the unequal representation of blacks in student government and other extracurricular activities at the school. And I was there, in the middle of it, throwing in my dime's worth of two cents; provoking disturbance in Hoggard's hallways where a lot of black students were fighting and cutting up. I even had a black teacher, compromised in trying to keep her job, who called me "disturbed" for pressing for even further protests.

C.D. Gurganus, Hoggard's principal at the time, immediately dispatched his deputies to the cafeteria like storm troopers. All the students there, although peacefully sitting in, were arrested. Apparently the form of protest didn't matter to the authorities. Any form of protest, whether violent or nonviolent, resulted in arrests, suspension, or expulsion.

That day, the words of Frederick Douglass became all too clear to us: "Where there is no struggle, there is no progress! Those who propose to favor freedom, and yet depreciate agitation, are men who want crops without plowing the ground. They want rain without thunder and lightning, they want the oceans' majestic waves without the awful roar of its waters."

I had never taken the lead in anything—nothing—but at that point, I was more than willing to be a follower if it was to follow other right-thinking black people on a path to progress and respect. I soon heard that a modest group of black students at both New Hanover and Hoggard were beginning to vehemently protest the outright disrespect the board and administration of both schools were showing our grievances. I gladly joined in.

These protests ranged from a crew of students storming Principal Gurganus's office to attacks on white students for no other reason than to gain attention for our cause. Yes, I confess, I was a part of all of that. Anyone at Hoggard back then will tell you I was.

Just before Christmas—on December 18, 1970, to be precise—riots again broke out at both schools. After all was said and done, police had arrested seventeen black students for loitering, disturbing the peace and resisting arrests. On Friday, January 15, 1971, Principal Gurganus expelled fifteen students, including me, for organizing a sit-in after we were denied a request for a program honoring Dr. King. I was expelled for the remainder of the school year. I wasn't surprised or scared. I was proud. I knew my mother, who had an activist heart and iron constitution for right and wrong, would also be proud that I had taken a reasoned stance. But I would be lying if I said here that I was not concerned about my future.

Then, before anyone, including me, could catch their breath, an intolerable indignity came a short time later. Barbara Swain, a popular black student at New Hanover High School, was hit in the head with a bottle thrown by a white student during a melee involving more than fifty black and white students at a student hangout across the street from New Hanover. It was called, appropriately, the Wildcat Cafe. Fortunately, Barbara's wounds were not life-threatening. Unfortunately, after she was treated and released, Barbara and several other black students were—without the benefit of a hearing—immediately suspended by New Hanover's principal, John Scott.

It certainly didn't calm our explosive emotions regarding these suspensions that Scott was involved. Most Wilmington-area black students widely regarded the man as an outright racist. And he didn't help dissuade us of that opinion when he explained that Barbara Swain was suspended because she wasn't in class when she should have been. I guess bleeding, crying and passing out at her desk would have been fine. To make bad matters even worse, the white student who threw the bottle, who was also supposed be in his class when the incident occurred, was not suspended at the time.

Patricia Rhodes, then a recent graduate of New Hanover High School and social activist, sent word through the grapevine that any interested student from either Hoggard or New Hanover high schools should meet her at Hemenway Hall, the headquarters for the Board of Education, on Tuesday, January 26, 1971. There and then we could express our grievances directly to Superintendent Bellamy. Only about fifteen students showed up at this building downtown. But among them, though, were some of our strongest, smartest student voices. Leading the way were Benjamin "Bob" Wonce, Annie Mclean, Connie Tindall, Joe Wright, and Richard McCoy.

According to Ben Wonce, the group's meeting with Bellamy was unsatisfactory. Wonce told me that Bellamy simply tabled acting on the grievances until he could meet with the school principals and members of the Board of Education. Then the true upshot of the gathering materialized when Patricia Rhodes stood before the student group now standing around the front of the hall.

With little forewarning, words that would change Wilmington, change me, forever sprang from her lips:

> *The only way we're going to get anything done is to boycott the schools, and that's exactly what we're going to do. We are going to call for a countywide boycott of the schools. But, first we have to find a place to meet. I will work on that this evening. As soon as I find a place, I'll send word. By tomorrow morning everyone should know where to meet.*

Pat Rhodes found a small abandoned storefront on North Fourth Street, where on the following morning, January 28, she and Joe, Connie, Ben, Annie McClain, Bernard Morgan, Richard McKoy and Joseph Selby met and formed a boycott committee. The space was barely large enough to accommodate this small cadre of student leaders, so holding a mass meeting of potentially hundreds of boycotting students was out of the question there. So a search for a bigger, better place began.

Almost right away the decision to boycott the public schools was not—Surprise! Surprise!—well received by local black civic leaders and church organizations. Community organizers Rhodes and Mollie Hicks, and other well-known social activists, along with representatives from the new boycott committee, visited several black churches and community organizations looking for a home for the boycott. I was part of that search and was deeply disappointed when every black-led organization in Wilmington, every one of them, turned us down. Here we were standing up against injustice, responding to injustice in ways Dr. King himself might have acted, and when we turned to the black community for a home there was no room at the inn.

When almost at our lowest, our cause found an ally in a twenty-seven-year-old, white minister, The Reverend Eugene B. Templeton, pastor of Gregory Congregational United Church of Christ (UCC) in Wilmington.

It was Joe Wright who spoke with Rev. Templeton about our intentions and the fact that several black churches and organizations had refused to help. Without hesitation, Rev. Templeton welcomed the student boycott committee and he helped us to establish a makeshift school in an adjacent building. Pat Rhodes taught black history classes there and she covered subjects that would have been practically radioactive back at Hoggard and New Hanover high schools. We explored the events and meaning of the Wilmington Massacre of 1898, and black nationalism, for example.

The evenings were dedicated to strategy sessions held in the church's sanctuary. We would gather there among the old oak pews and beneath patterned stained-glass windows and listen to student leaders like Ben Wonce, Connie Tindall, and Joe Wright talk about the black power movement, and how brothers like Rap Brown and Stokely Carmichael had it right. The conclusion of such meetings was that the only way for black people to gain power over our own lives would be though collective, militant action to define ourselves, our needs and our own solutions as black people. In other words, black nationalism.

On some nights we would have one-hundred-fifty to two-hundred students in the church. And believe me, this didn't go unnoticed by the larger community. There were times when parents and other members of the black community joined us and spoke their hearts. Without fully realizing it at first, we, young people, high school students, had created a racism-free zone lifting the heavy burden of racism that existed in almost every other corner of Wilmington. You could see it in the faces of these black adults, our parents, our elders. You could hear it in their voices, too. It was as if they were letting their ideas and words float free into a kind racial weightlessness. It was relief.

On nights like that, we heard a lot of thoughts and emotions about the closing of Williston Senior High School, even though it had been gone for years by then. The hurt still hurt. And there were also the occasional remarks that implored us to end our boycott, the shrill call for us to "take our asses" back to school. But it was always clear, during this period, that the majority of our community wanted us to stay united and fight—peacefully—for our rights.

Back on January 29, Ben Wonce had read a list of grievances to the school board's advisory council. He warned that if the school board refused to act reasonably on them, our committee would officially call for a citywide boycott of schools. Ben was always all business and the demands he read could not have been clearer.

- Black students who have been suspended be re-instated immediately

- No more white non-students be allowed on campus at New Hanover and John T. Hoggard high schools

- Black history classes be included in the school curriculum

- January 15 be set aside to celebrate the birthday of Dr. Martin Luther King's Jr.

- There be no more harassment of black students by white male faculty

- That principal John Scott end his racist attitude toward black students

- That principal Scott order a full investigation into the Barbara Swain case

The advisory council chairman, Quintel Smith, promised us that his group would meet as soon as possible "to formulate a recommendation" on how to break the impasse and then present it to the full board. The New Hanover High School Student Advisory Committee and a group of white students all said to be working to end the racial tension in the schools were also at this meeting. We heard appeals for the creation of a policy of nonviolence and yet another committee of students and adults, blacks and whites, to monitor such a policy for violations.

It seemed that everyone that day wanted to get in on a solution, or claim a piece of the credit for it. Pam Boykin, a black student and chairman of the Student Advisory Committee, asked us to meet with her committee at City Hall. And the Good Neighbor Council, the forerunner for the Human Relations Commission, called for regular meetings among blacks and whites to establish a common understand among the races and, specifically, set up a code of conduct for the county's public school teachers and students to avert racial problems.

A number of us saw reason for some optimism when Superintendent Bellamy decided, against some stiff advice from colleagues, to accept the invitation extended by Bertha Todd, by now a black assistant principal at Hoggard, to come to Gregory Church to directly hear the grievances of the boycotting students.

On Monday, February 1, Bellamy, along with school board member George Clark, came to Gregory Church, all right. But it was to tell us that the official action of the Board of Education could not be taken at that time. While we appreciated what it must have taken for these white men to have ventured into an angry black community to deliver bad news, none in our leadership considered ending the student boycott.

The next day, we realized that Bellamy's inaction amounted to a public slap in our face. We became even more determined to be heard and to have our grievances addressed. Hundreds of students descended on Gregory Church that day, all calling for immediate retaliation for Barbara Swain's attack and injury, and, of course, her unjust suspension. Many of us were stirred up enough by insult and hurt to carry out that mission by any means necessary. But the truth was, we realized that answering violence with violence would jeopardize our chances of solving the problems. The Templetons, the young minister and his wife, Donna, could only provide a place of refuge at the church. They had no idea how to calm a storming sea of angry black students whom they knew had a legitimate cause—but no real plan of action. None of us was then experienced in the art of civil disobedience. We were just a group of young high school students desperate for relief from an intolerable situation.

Whole generations of effective black leadership had been wiped out by the Massacre of 1898. Much of what was left of established leadership in black Wilmington cringed in fear in the face of power, which almost always in this Southern port city bore a white face. We had few mentors.

The student leaders of our boycott felt that we would get more respect if we had a professional community organizer to serve as our spokesman, our point man. We made this known to Rev. Templeton, and he contacted the Reverend Leon White, director of the North Carolina and Virginia office of The Commission for Racial Justice, an arm of the United Church of Christ. From his office in Raleigh, Rev. White immediately dispatched his field director, Benjamin F. Chavis, to Wilmington.

Fortunately, Ben Chavis was in East Arcadia, NC, about forty miles from Wilmington, where he was working with high school students who were also involved in a desegregation crisis. A bomb had been discovered in the school's cafeteria in a section of the lunch room frequented by black students. It was widely believed that the bomb had been placed there by whites who were opposed to desegregation. He got the call from Rev. White, and sometime in the evening of February 1, 1971, Ben Chavis rode into town to lend a steady hand to a group of activist high school students—to lend a hand to me.

6

GREGORY CHURCH,
OUR SANCTUARY FORTRESS

Gregory Congregational United Church of Christ still stands serenely on Nun Street, between Sixth and Seventh Streets, just east of downtown Wilmington. To look at it today—with its fine, red-brick facade beneath a steeply sloping gabled roof and adjoining clock tower with a steeple that looks like, from a fair distance, a wizard's pointy hat—it is hard to imagine what it was like there in February 1971.

Gregory Congregational, named for James J. Howard Gregory, who apparently was rich enough to donate the money to build the church, was started around 1868. It wasn't the best of times in North Carolina. The Civil War had been over for three years and the Old South was still licking its wounds in defeat. It was trying to recover without the benefit of legions of slaves that had been freed in the great struggle. And Wilmington whites had their own special humiliations to weather and hope to forget. The Union navy along with ground troops, greatly assisted by the Fifth United States Colored Infantry Regiment, had not only captured Fort Fisher just outside town in January 1865, but a month later, took Wilmington. Black hands helped to hammer the last nails in the Confederacy's coffin.

The actual Gregory Church building, modest in size by most standards, was dedicated in 1881. In less than a century, its congregation had become predominately black. I think old man Gregory wouldn't have had a problem with that. After all, Williston Senior High School's history is rooted deep in the Gregory Normal Institute, which was established in the mid-1860s by abolitionists. Gregory himself had the school enlarged for area blacks while the church next door took shape.

I was raised in the church, but not in Gregory Congregational. As a child I walked past Gregory many times and tended to pay it little mind. There are so many churches in Wilmington, it sometimes feels even today that there is one on every block. Back then, I did think that Gregory Church was kind of pretty. With its tall, arched white-trimmed windows and front doors, it seemed like something out of a fairy tale, like a castle, some place strong and safe.

The church seemed a fitting backdrop when Ben Chavis stood within its light-colored, lightly adorned walls and addressed a crowd of staring faces. People had mostly gathered there, hungry to hear what this young, black out-of-towner had to say about "the trouble" in the local public schools. It was Tuesday, February 2, 1971. This would be the first time I heard Ben speak, and I felt like someone had just plugged me right into a wall socket when he began his press conference with a chant. Yeah, it was electric.

"Black Power. Power to the People. Black Power! Power to the People!"

Ok, I thought, *this brother ain't pulling any punches.* I could feel the floor boards beneath me tremble with the revolution too long suppressed. You have to understand. We all read about men like him, outspoken, well-spoken, brave, bold and black. We saw them on television news, in the movies. But here it was: black power right there close enough to shake hands with it, to throw our fists into the air with it. Now we weren't just witnesses. Ben had made us all part of it, and I could not have been more pleased.

I crossed my arms over my narrow chest and listened.

First of all, I am glad to be here in the Wilmington community. I was requested by the brothers and sisters that have been struggling with the school system here, to come here and give a helping hand, and so I am here, and I intend to stay here in Wilmington until this struggle is over. The North Carolina-Virginia Commission for Racial Justice feels that the struggle here by the brothers and sisters of this school system is a just struggle. We believe the demands are just and believe that the superintendent of schools and the school board and all other school officials have been racists, and I have listened to the racist policy against the black community in Wilmington. The Commission for Racial Justice will do whatever is necessary for the student movement here. The Commission for Racial Justice of the United Church of Christ, [is]a religious organization. As an alderman of this organization, I make an appeal at this time that all the black ministers, county-wide in New Hanover County and Wilmington too, join in this struggle, for this is not only a student struggle, this is a struggle to free the black community from the white power structure. Do not call our bluff! We mean these demands. Do not call our bluff!

Damn, was all I could say, and I said it softly to myself. Make no mistake. That wasn't because I was worried about somebody hearing me; I said it softly because that was all the air I had in my lungs to say it. Ben Chavis had snatched my breath. He was that mesmerizing. All of us, all the black students there, ones organizing and backing the school boycott, or just the curious, even the scared to act, were knocked back on our heels. His charisma was that powerful, like a wind blowing us away.

The female students were especially impressed with his image of the handsome, successful black man in the 'hood. And some of the brothers who noticed all that attention he was sweeping up, stood there with their jaws tight. But it was mostly parents and good ole' white boys and white girls from the community, ones charged with keeping the peace and Wilmington's rigid social and political order, who were the most unimpressed with Ben Chavis. They seemed to have had no patience or open mind for the black man with the Malcolm X goatee and mustache and matching rhetorical bite. I thought I noticed a few of them seething with his every word and gesticulation. I loved it! Ben not only spoke with a firm understanding of our situation, but also of the struggles of people of all races and religions for freedom and justice. We listened intently as he began to map out a strategy for our boycott.

Student leader Ben Wonce had actually opened the press conference. He, as usual, wasted no time. He stepped up to the podium and blared out a familiar list of grievances, just as he had for the school board a day earlier. This time he was emphasizing that these were not simply grievances. They were demands.

> *"We demand the immediate reinstatement of suspended and expelled black students...an end to harassment of black students by police on campus...More black studies...More black teachers...A school holiday to honor Dr. Martin Luther King... If these demands are not met by 12 o'clock, Wednesday, February 3, 1971, we as black students, will take further action."*

The church was crammed with angry, boycotting students and representatives from the local media. Ben Chavis could not have had a more primed and attentive audience anywhere. He repeated Ben Wonce's demands and he also reiterated Ben Wonce's earlier statement to Dr. Bellamy and the school board: "If all of these demands are not met by Noon, Wednesday, February 3, 1971, we will take further action."

I remember little else that Ben Chavis said that night. I was adrenaline addled, drugged by my own body. Somehow, I had been transformed by Ben's toe-to-toe facing down of local white power, leaving me feeling at once calm and enlivened. I had gone in a single day from feeling like the vanquished to feeling like the vanguard of a just and righteous global cause. I felt my ancestors, brimming with African pride and power, awakened and aroused. *We would not beg the beast for mercy anymore. We would no longer exist in a cowardly stupor like frightened slaves while heartless white men and women stripped us of our dignity, pride, and institutions. We would boldly march to the halls of justice and demand "our certain unalienable rights."*

I knew what we were up against. It was the same sensibility, far too alive and far too well, that echoed through my people's history like a midnight rebel yell. You could almost smell its breath. It reeked in Justice Taney's ruling on the Dred Scott Supreme Court decision of 1857, a stroke of the pen that rendered my ancestors less than whole human beings; and its stench hung in the air fanned by apologists of Wilmington's 1898 massacre inflicted on my people. After listening to Brother Ben, I felt redeemed and reset with a fresh sense to determine my own destiny.

No longer would any white man be allowed to define who I was. I would create my own identity: a proud black man, proud of every gift my African origins had bestowed upon me, which included my determination to struggle for true freedom and justice in America.

The following day, Wednesday, February 3, 1971, arrived. Noon came and went with no response from the school board. That evening, crowds of mostly students and some one-hundred adults met at Gregory Church, now our official headquarters. The Rev. Leon White, rose to speak first.

"The struggle will be long," he said to the roar of our cheers. "The church may have been correct in saying salvation is free, but liberation would cost everyone a lot. It is important that the protest remain peaceful." He emphasized that the white community could deal a lot more easily, and harshly, with a violent protest than with a peaceful one.

Ben Chavis listened and nodded to the implicit truth of White's statement. Then he stepped to the church's microphone:

> *What time is it? It's nation time! What time is it? It's nation time! What time is it? It's nation time? What's happening? The land is changing hands... I can't hear you! I said what's happening? The land is changing hands! Red, Black and Green, what does it mean? Red is for bloodshed. Black is for the people. Green is for the land we will reclaim after the revolution.*

I could feel myself getting revved up. We all listened closely as Ben Chavis talked about the need for solidarity if we were to succeed in our struggle against a racist Board of Education. With spirits revived and emboldened, some five-hundred students marched that day to the Board of Education and demanded that we speak with Superintendent Bellamy. He agreed to a meeting, but with only Ben Chavis and two of the students. But Ben said he wouldn't meet unless all the student leaders could accompany him. The answer was no, so there was no meeting.

The resulting realization was what Ben often talked about. In his words, the board's refusal "heightened the contradictions." It showed us that the system wasn't working for us. And with that, our student leadership officially announced to the press that a county-wide, black student boycott of public schools was on. It was a dizzying day. That night Ben held a rally at Gregory and encouraged us to continue to press for justice and equality in the schools. Then we heard them.

SHOTS.

Somebody—we didn't know exactly who at the time—was firing on the church. Students scrambled for cover like hell was knocking at the church door. No one was hurt, this time. The fact was that from the first day we began meeting at Gregory we heard shots in the night. But this time bullets were actually striking the church. It was scary stuff.

After the meeting, Ben excused himself and headed back to Oxford, NC, to take care of what he said was family business. It was decades later when I learned from Ben that the New York-based leadership of the United Church of Christ had ordered him out of Wilmington by Wednesday evening. He was told that it had reliable information that Wilmington was at the edge of explosive unrest. Ben further revealed to me this summer while I was finishing this book, that not only was he told to leave town, but he was also told to join a two-car caravan back to Oxford, with Rev. Leon White's car leading the way. That was nearly a three-hour drive, and just as Ben was crossing the Cape Fear River Bridge following White's car, he told me, he looked back to see Wilmington in flames.

That night, major fires started and they burned down several white-owned buildings in the city, mostly downtown. Among them was L. Schwartz Furniture store in the heart of the Northside, in the black community, and Lum's Restaurant on Oleander Drive, miles from Gregory Church. Almost immediately, Lum's owner blamed Ben Chavis. He said Ben had been seen in the restaurant shortly before the place caught fire. Ben flatly denied that at the time, and still does.

An FBI report would later exonerate Ben by determining that the Lum's fire was deliberately set by its owner in the midst of the city's racial turmoil. The motive appeared to be simply financial, an attempt to collect insurance money. Despite this scam, it was legitimately a terrible night. There were other mysterious fires throughout the city, including a blaze at the New Hanover

High School football fieldhouse. There were also reports that two young black men had been shot by white vigilantes riding though the city's black neighborhoods—rampaging ghosts of 1898 haunting almost a century later.

Alarmed by the extent of the violence—much of it specifically directed at blacks in Wilmington—Rev. Templeton pleaded with Wilmington Mayor Luther Cromartie to place a curfew on the city. Cromartie refused. We could feel the heightened contradictions at play.

Ben Chavis returned to Wilmington Thursday afternoon, February 4, to lead a peaceful march on City Hall to further press for a protective curfew. With hundreds of students chanting "We Want Action," Chavis demanded that the mayor and chief of police act. Again, the mayor refused to impose a curfew on the clearly racially troubled city. I had no idea until this summer that Ben Chavis returned to Wilmington because Robert W. Scott, the governor of North Carolina at the time, had phoned Ben and urged him to return to help bring a peaceful resolution to the conflict.

Ben, growing frustrated, threatened the North Carolina Highway Patrol that he would "publically charge the mayor and the city council with conspiracy in setting up the black community for annihilation," if violence revisited the city. Maybe he was playing the part of the new breed of black heroes on the big screen a little too closely. He seemed confident that he was going to ride into town—this time in a movie-pimp-perfect Eldorado Cadillac—and play the victor, standing up to the oppressors, and cruise toward sunset.

It didn't work out that way. Not even close.

Wilmington, at least the people who ran its politics, its economy, its culture, didn't care that it was a new decade—the 70s—or even that it was a new century, for that matter. As far as black people and power were concerned, Wilmington was the

Poplar Grove Plantation up the road, home to my slave roots. Local leaders were little more than overseers. The police? Slave catchers. So, it should not have surprised anyone that there was no police protection in my hometown for the likes of the Benjamin Franklin Chavis, Jr., nor for me and any of his other followers. Brother Ben was not greeted with a red carpet, nor given the key to the city. On the contrary, just as we began to shout "Black Power, Power to the People" that Thursday night in Gregory Church, a fresh shower of bullets slammed into the building from a group of white, self-appointed upholders of the racial status quo.

Ben said when he first drove into Wilmington in the predawn hours of February 1, he noticed pickup trucks bearing clean-shaven, military-styled white men with rifles circling near the church. But on this night, February 4, we weren't thinking much about the shooters, just the shots. We all hit the floor with our hearts in our mouths. Those near the church doors said they heard screeching tires. On that long, cold February night in Wilmington, an unending convoy of white men in trucks slowly drove by the church in a horror show of violence and intimidation. It was an old story updated with trucks rather than horses, modern high-caliber rifles replacing those of an earlier era. And as Ben pointed out, many of the white rioters of the Massacre of 1898 wore red shirts. The white vigilantes of 1971 drove red pickup trucks. That night, some of us decided to spend the night in the church.

Kojo Nantambu, who was there with me at the Gregory Church that Thursday night, recalled in an interview with author Larry Thomas, that he saw no less than thirty vehicles with armed whites driving through the neighborhood. Kojo, whose name back then was Roderick Lionel Kirby, said he watched some of them circle the block where the church is located and then make a second pass, this time shooting from the open windows of trucks and cars.

I'd be lying if I say I wasn't frightened. Of course, I was. Anyone would be. And to be black and demanding a piece of power in a city with such a storied history of being brutal and cruel to its black citizens, made it that much more frightening. I had visions of running for my life through rice fields along the Cape Fear River or worse floating, face down, with my fellow boycotters in its cold muddy waters. For a moment, I wondered what kind of men would attack teenage boys, but I knew the answer. I asked the same question when I first learned of the fatal shooting of Treyvon Martin in Florida on another February night, this one in 2012.

Daybreak didn't make me feel much safer at the church, or in the city in general. I feared for Rev. Templeton and his wife, Donna, a registered nurse at New Hanover County Memorial Hospital. They were such gentle and generous souls. It pained me that since they gave us refuge in the church in late January both of them had received a steady volley of death threats. Rev. Templeton was a graduate of Union Theological Seminary, famous for black liberation theologians and civil rights activists like James Forbes, James Cone and Cornell West.

It wasn't lost on us that the only initial support we could find for our cause were two white people. Right away, it was clear to me that the Templetons understood that our battle was not against white people, but instead against racism and injustice. They also understood that our grievances were more than the childish whining of ungrateful blacks. They both understood that desegregation was a much more complicated problem than simply closing the city's only black high school and busing its kids to two white schools. Rev. Templeton once said, "They tried to treat integration as just another problem without making adequate preparation and without trying to understand there are some cultural differences between blacks and whites."

Closing Williston and busing us from the predominately black inner city to the white-flight suburbs had stolen our cultural identity, dignity, and pride. That part of the issue was simple, and the Templetons clearly got it. I can't say enough good things about them. Even with bullets flying, the Templetons made us feel at home in their church and their parish home next door.

Having us there was a physically transformative act. Of course, we didn't do anything to intentionally deface the church in any way. We respected that this was a house of God. I could never forget that. The church generated a kind of sacred atmosphere with its high ceilings, electric candles along its smooth, curving walls, with its raised pulpit, a section for the church ushers and another one for the choir, and an electric organ to accompany it; and there were chandeliers hovering high over rows and rows of polished pews. This was first and foremost a church. We tried not to wear our hats inside.

But we, the students, had also turned Gregory into an underground school for boycotting students. Patricia Rhodes was basically its principal. She emphasized black studies and black nationalism, topics not even whispered in the classrooms where we had been sentenced.

We usually got to the church in the morning and stayed through the afternoon, Monday to Friday. Sundays belonged solely to the church. If we weren't attending our makeshift school there, we talked about our grievances and strategies to address them. And while we didn't like thinking about it too much, we had not only turned the church into our movement's headquarters, but—having little choice—we made it our sanctuary and fortress.

I had gotten angry earlier before the shots rang out when I looked around the church and saw a few brothers and sisters from the streets not taking our struggle seriously, playing party music on their portable eight-track players; some had apparently forgotten where they were, smoking weed and drinking wine.

Where the hell had they come from? I thought. *This boycott was serious business, not to be treated as a party. This was a bad time and place for a bunch of losers to show up.* Then later, I reconsidered my thinking. Perhaps they weren't losers, but victims of another kind of injustice. Maybe they were crying out for someone to free them from a psychological slavery, virtual manacles that chained them to self-destructive attitudes and behavior.

But when the bullets flew, lethal lead was the great equalizer, and even these hard cases from the streets were reminded that, yes, indeed, this was serious business they were employed in. The patrolling racists weren't checking to shoot only the savvy or politically conscious. They were outside doing their damnest to shoot any of us inside. Period.

I saw fear and bewilderment in the faces of the hundreds of people huddled in Gregory Church. But it took only moments for that fear to congeal into rage. George Kirby, the right hand man of longtime civil rights activist, Golden Frinks, stood up and shouted, "Those crackers aren't going to get away with this shit!"

Despite the very distinct possibility of being shot, my black brothers and sisters were not intimidated by Wilmington's past, not America's past, not even by a stone-hearted contempt for black life so often and repeatedly demonstrated. No one wanted to die in the church during those early days of February 1971. Yet there was a noble sense of higher mission there. Perhaps our leaders had empowered us to truly stand up to the white man. Perhaps generations of denial and disrespect had stirred revolution in our blood. I knew I was willing to sacrifice everything if I had to. Dr. King once said, "If you have nothing worth dying for, then you aren't fit to live." I want to believe that everyone in Gregory Church during those times of terror and tears felt that our struggle was worth dying for.

Nonetheless, Rev. Templeton again pressed the mayor and the police for a curfew to end the violence against the church. City manager E. C. Brandon, speaking on behalf of Mayor Cromartie and Chief Williamson, said that there had been no evidence of any impending racial clashes or violence against the church, that we had "nothing to worry about."

Ben even invited police to the church and showed them the drive-by bullet holes in its walls. Still, the police refused to provide us adequate police protection. Instead, they set up some wooden barricades on a couple of streets, blocks from the church. We realized that a few wooden barricades would not protect Gregory Church from these determined, demented vigilantes. Ben suggested that we erect our own barricades around the church perimeter. Led by Kojo Nantambu, we found heavy, five-foot concrete sewer pipes used by city workers to repair a broken sewer line, to block all street access to the church.

Undeterred, the vigilantes returned at night and just fired their high-powered weapons at longer range from the barricades. As the weekend approached, much of Greater Wilmington's black community started to become involved in our defense. Later that Thursday night and into the next day, armed black militants—grown men—voluntarily converged on Gregory Church from within and outside of North Carolina. They were the real deal, well trained, disciplined and no bullshit. Among them were Vietnam War veterans, marines from Camp Lejeune who called themselves the Mau Maus, and a group of Black Panthers from Greensboro and Winston-Salem.

When word had reached them that a group of high school kids were under deadly siege at a church in Wilmington, they came strong, most of them brandishing the international language of revolution, and weapons—some of them military issue—to teach and defend us.

Almost right away, we found ourselves in an armed camp governed by military tactics and procedures. For instance, we now had armed sentries posted to protect the church against further drive-by shootings. There were armed men with binoculars all around the church grounds watching warily for new vigilante attacks and activity. There were even secretive, identifying handshakes called "daps" and armed lookouts in the church's clock tower.

The code word for trouble was RABBIT.

But life inside the church was never the way Allan Hall, a kind of hanger-on and late-comer to the struggle at Gregory, described the scene in court. He was one of the state's key witnesses against the Wilmington Ten, and he, like reciting a script, told of tables of weapons in the church and orders from Ben Chavis to firebomb locations and shoot fleeing whites.

None of that happened. All of the firepower was strictly defensive.

Around 7 p.m. Friday night, February 5, Kojo's brother, who everyone called June-Bug, came running through the church door yelling, "Rabbit! Rabbit! Rabbit!" Before June-Bug could catch his breath, Marvin "Chili" Patrick stumbled through the door bleeding with a bullet wound to his chest. Things broke down suddenly. The church filled with chaos, the nastiest kind that is contagious. Young *brothers* who, just hours earlier, had vowed to protect the church with their lives, were transformed into what seemed like a gaggle of scared little boys as our sister-warriors screamed in horror.

Although Chili seriously needed medical care, we were reluctant to take him to the hospital. Someone in the church convinced us that decision would probably not be in his best interest. Outside the church walls we just didn't know who to trust. Donald Lee Salter, another victim of vigilante gunfire, had been arrested when he arrived at the hospital bleeding and disoriented. Rev. Templeton's wife rushed to set up a homemade trauma center in the church to treat Chili, which she successfully did, bringing all of her nursing experience to bear. She kept her little field hospital up and running for the sake of other potential gunshot victims that week.

In less than two hours, at about 9 p.m., we learned that a black minister had been shot outside Gregory Church. He was the Rev. David Vaughn from Central Baptist Church. He was not a supporter of our boycott. He wanted us to lay down our guns, leave Gregory and go home, telling us that our tactics were no way to get anything done. But we held our ground, saying that we were not leaving until our demands were met. The next thing, recalled Kojo, someone broke through one of the barricades around Gregory and shot the minister. Rev. Vaughn was talking with some brothers on the sidewalk by the church, Kojo said, when "a green pickup truck pulled up behind a yellow cab, which had been parked on the corner of Sixth and Nun, and the crackers blasted him with shotgun pellets." Rev. Vaughn was shot in the leg.

In an article published in *The Afro American* newspaper seven years later, Rev. Vaughn confirmed that shooting broke out in front of the church, and that he was hit when he tried to run for cover behind his car. In the same April 15, 1978, article in the Baltimore, Maryland-based weekly, an unnamed source said he participated in a meeting of forty or so angry whites who assembled in a field just outside of Wilmington. The source said the men planned an armed assault on Gregory Church, to "move in and destroy that church." The source's account was corroborated, according to the article, by a television journalist who attended the meeting with the condition that he not report it.

While no one was convicted for the minister's shooting, we believed this was the handiwork of a local group called Rights of White People, or the ROWP. It was also common knowledge that members of the Ku Klux Klan had come to town, in its words, "to help keep the peace." A few minutes later, Wilmington police officer, H. F. Genes, was shot, also in the leg, and like Rev. Vaughn, not fatally. We were told that authorities believed there had been two unsuccessful attempts that night to burn down a non-descript grocery less than a minute's walk from Gregory Church. In the meantime, Governor Scott called out the state's Riot Control Unit.

It was too late for that.

That Friday night, February 5, was definitely the turning point in the escalation of the violence that was turning Wilmington into a war zone. Sly Stone could not have said it better in his 1971 song, "There's a Riot Goin' On." There were all kinds of fires erupting, rocks being thrown and shots ranging out like a bad day in the Mekong Delta. Word of the shooting of Chili, Rev. Vaughn and others, mostly young and black, spread like a virus. The news of rampaging white vigilantes stirred fear and rage in many quarters of the black community. It even moved some to vow that 1971 was not going to be a repeat of 1898. Some blacks ran into the streets promising to destroy everything the white man owned. We students hunkered down in the church as all hell broke loose there, and seemingly everywhere else.

I was too afraid to venture into the streets. But later I decided to hell with fear. I hadn't had a bath or eaten anything except cold sandwiches since that Tuesday. Besides, I decided I needed to be in a familiar, safe place where I could think more clearly about what was happening. Shortly after midnight, when the streets looked clear, I wearily and cautiously headed home through twenty blocks of back alleys and lonely streets.

Fires flickered and blazed in the moonlit sky as I ducked behind houses and ran sneaker-soft through a neighborhood as stiff and unmoving as a corpse. This wasn't the first time I had slipped back to my home to clean up, pick up fresh clothes. Each time, I explained to my mother what was going on at Gregory Church. I could tell that she was nervous, but proud of me when I reminded her how much I wanted, needed, to be a part of it. She spoke softly to me and wore a mother's look of concern.

"That's fine," she said, "but I think you need to come home every night."

"Ok," I said, smiling at the floor, knowing that I had no intention of coming home until our grievances were resolved. I had no idea at the time that the events of the next three days would radically reorder any dreams I had ever had for my life. Nothing would ever again be like those sweet, loving mother-son moments at home.

On Saturday morning I read in the newspaper that The Chic Chic Grill, Lum's Restaurant, L. Schwartz Furniture Store, and Rooks Grocery had been among Wilmington businesses that had been destroyed in the nights of blazes and bullets. I decided that I would not return to Gregory Church, because what was gripping my hometown had gone terribly wrong and far beyond anything that we, the students, had intended with the boycott. We wanted to reform Wilmington, not see it turned into a heap of smoldering ashes.

That evening I welcomed the invitation from my sister to come to her home in nearby Hillcrest Apartments to babysit my nephews while she and her husband went out. For them, life went on despite all the turmoil that was tearing my life apart. They wanted to escape into the movies. By the time I returned to my place, the 10 p.m. news was on in my living room, flashing a bulletin that Gibbs Stevenson Corbett, who we knew as Steve Mitchell, had been killed as Mike's Grocery burned to the ground in a firebombing.

According to the TV account, Steve was fatally shot while shooting at firemen trying to put out the fire at the grocery store. A reporter said a Wilmington police officer, Jackie Shaw, approached Steve who turned his weapon on the officer and tried to fire it. But the gun misfired, the report claimed, and Shaw fired his weapon. Steve was killed almost on the spot, although some witnesses told Kojo that Steve was beaten after he was shot and then pronounced dead on arrival at New Hanover Memorial Hospital sometime after 10 p.m. Steve Mitchell was seventeen-years-old.

I couldn't believe any of it—except for the part involving a police officer gunning down another brother in the streets. I knew Steve. He was one of the organizers of the boycott, and was quiet and easy going. No one who knew him would ever suspect that he was the kind of person who would confront an armed law enforcement officer. Neither was I. Right at that moment, I realized that if I had remained at the church, the body stretched out in a cold drawer in the morgue could have been mine.

My heart actually ached when I jumped to my feet and tried to walk off the rage. No one in my home was up at the time. I felt alone. My thoughts went back to Gregory Church when I couldn't. I couldn't bring myself to sneak my way back to the church that night.

I kept trying to picture the scene. Mike's Grocery was on Sixth Street, a block from the church building. It must have gone up in flames in plain view of anyone remaining in Gregory Church. It didn't add up. Almost immediately, Wilmington authorities began painting a picture of brave police and firefighters answering the call that there was trouble at the grocery store. Officer Shaw told local reporters that emergency personnel were "fired upon and that the gunfire was so intense that the firemen were unable to control the flames."

But others, including Milton Jordan, a reporter for the Wilmington *Star-News*, said this account was "blatantly untrue." He said he stood at the scene for more than an hour. He added that he had interviewed firefighters and was told that they had gotten to the fire too late to save the convenience store. Jordan said firefighters had waited four blocks away for a police escort because the neighborhood had been cordoned off by police Friday night after they arrested a carload of armed whites headed toward the church.

Jordan also said he never heard any intense gunfire, none at all, near Mike's Grocery the night it burned down. But this was clearly not enough for Mayor Cromartie to declare a curfew, saying later that night that, "I see the shooting of Steve Mitchell as a deterrent. I think we have the situation in hand now."

I was sick to my stomach. Do these people have any shame? A kid had been killed, shot in the neck, I would later learn. I should have felt relieved that I was warm and comfortable at home when it happened. But I wasn't. I wanted to do something to avenge Steve's death. But I didn't. Instead, I went up to my room, laid down fully clothed on my bed and stared at the ceiling.

Finally, I fell asleep thinking, *what next?*

7

A CRUSHING WEIGHT

Early Sunday morning, at a time when many churches of Wilmington welcome their flocks to morning and afternoon sermons of Christian charity, faith, forgiveness and brotherly love, the scene at Gregory Congregational Church was hauntingly different.

By 9 a.m. there were no worshipers at Gregory, no choir swaying and belting out foot-stomping gospel standards, no elderly black women, wearing impossibly grand hats and fanning themselves in the front pews that were as familiar to them as their home addresses; there would be no little children, over-dressed and fidgeting inches away from their parents who sat still and dignified like religious statuary. And at the pulpit, there would be no Rev. Eugene Templeton, balding, bespectacled and square-jawed, delivering the Word like he was born to the calling. No. On this Sunday, February 7, Gregory Church was a bullet-ridden, armed camp.

And perhaps, on that day—amen—it was a good thing.

Shortly after 9 a.m., a pickup truck driven by a fifty-seven-year-old white man, made its way up to the Nun Street barricades we had erected to protect the entrance of Gregory Church. The man, Harvey Edward Cumber, a retired roofing contractor, began shooting at the church. And, like a refrain from a good, old gospel song, there was a response to his call. Gunfire from the church abruptly answered his.

At 9:38 a.m., according to news reports, Cumber sat slumped dead in his truck with a 22-caliber bullet hole in his right temple. A picture of the fatally wounded man being carried away on a stretcher was splashed across the local morning newspaper. Still at home, almost two dozen blocks from the Gregory Church, I could only shake my head in disbelief. A white man was dead and likely at black hands. Just when I thought Wilmington's slide into racial violence and destruction couldn't go any faster; it broke the sound barrier with Cumber's death.

There were reports of gunfire popping off and on from the church for much of the rest of the day. I knew that the atmosphere inside Gregory had to be frigid with fear of a coming bloodbath of anyone remaining inside. Anticipating the very real possibility of violent, white retribution for Cumber's death, Ben and the Templetons warned everyone that it was too dangerous to remain in the church. In fact, Rev. Templeton wrote much later that after the killings of Steve Mitchell and Cumber, the church's Board of Deacons and Board of Trustees hastily met and asked that all of the students leave Gregory for the sake of the safety of the students and the church.

When all of this was told to the remaining students, everyone inside evacuated the building. Ben ordered that the church not only be abandoned, but locked down.

After Gregory Church was secured, the Templetons climbed into Ben's Cadillac and headed to Raleigh with Ben. Once there, they held a press conference to talk about the events of the past week. As they crossed the Northeast River Bridge out of town, a convoy of National Guardsmen passed them as it rumbled into Wilmington. Now that a white man's life had been spilled in the street, Mayor Cromartie almost immediately ordered a curfew that evening, ordering everyone off the streets from 7:30 p.m. to 6 a.m. until further notice. What we didn't know at that moment was that the National Guard had also been ordered to storm the church with guns blazing.

Wilmington's white leadership had decided to crush us and our fledgling movement that wanted nothing more than a morsel of equality and control over our own lives.

By Monday morning, February 8, after another restless sleep, I awoke at home to the news that something big was happening at Gregory Church. The news sort of announced itself in this loud, rumbling, clanking, crunching metallic sound that few of us in black Wilmington had ever heard. It was kind of the noise similar to an earth mover, but this was deeper, angrier and much more menacing. Someone told me it was a Sherman tank, I think, that was making its way down streets too narrow for its wide, heavy-metal body. It headed straight for Gregory Church. All I could think was, *Has it come to this?*

It had already been a strange day. People were really scared and seemed so unsure of what to do, how to live their lives under what was basically military control. But then we heard the loud rumbling, and everyone who heard it wanted to see what was going to happen. What seemed to be a tank rolled forward, slow and deafening, with a battalion of armed National Guardsmen moving in behind it. A group of reporters, local and national, followed them. Then this moment came when you knew anything could happen.

The personnel carrier came to a halt in the church yard as guardsmen, pointed their weapons directly at those high-arched front double doors of Gregory. They were positioned with their rifles locked, loaded and ready to fire. According to all the reports, the guard's major general called for everyone inside the church to surrender. But I knew that there was no one left inside. Ben's much earlier call to evacuate Gregory had been completely fulfilled.

The Wilmington *Star-News* reported that Tuesday, February 9, 1971, that the National Guard's raid on Gregory turned up some discarded weapons and ammunition, six sticks of dynamite and six blasting caps, and spent shell casings. The article also reported that Donna Templeton's dining table was "laid out like an army field hospital with bandages, tape, dressings and other medical equipment" all left behind. But that was about it. I couldn't find in the newspapers a hint of the truth that I lived through in Gregory during those dangerous days of defiance.

Later, I approached Cornelius "Mutt" Bryant to help set the record straight. He had been with Steve the night he was shot and killed by police. Remember, this was 1971, long before everyday people had video cameras to capture police abuses like the one that captured the 1991 Rodney King police beating in Los Angeles. No one then had video-enabled cell phones like people did in 2009 during the fatal police shooting of an unarmed Oscar Grant in the rapid transit Fruitvale BART Station in Oakland, California. I seriously doubt that justice would have been done in these cases if there had not been the irrevocable proof of terrible abuse on video.

I brought a portable recorder, but Mutt refused to talk about Steve's killing on tape. He did, however, discuss it with me over the course of several strictly face-to-face conversations. He said he and Steve had been standing post that Saturday night behind the church when they spotted a fire at Mike's Grocery just down the block. They noticed that no firefighters were on the scene, and the fire was rapidly growing very intense. Fearing that neighboring houses were in danger, Mutt said Steve ran to the corner to pull the fire alarm. Mutt added that he ran to one of the adjoining houses and started helping the residents haul their furniture into the street to save what they could.

This was their community and Mutt and Steve cared what happened to these people. Mutt said he witnessed students and others running from the church to Mike's Grocery with buckets of water, hoping to put the fire out. Then people from neighboring houses spilled into the streets, too, either trying to figure out what was going on, or wanting to lend a hand and a strong back to help.

Eventually, Mutt said, he heard the sirens of fire trucks and police cars. *Finally,* he said, he felt a moment of relief as the emergency vehicles arrived. That sense was shattered moments later by the sound of gunfire. Then he said he went cold with shock over what he saw next. Policemen were dragging a bleeding Steve through the street. He told me that he ran to the church to report the news.

Later, Mutt, like the rest of us, heard the TV news bulletin of Steve's death. And he said he knew for sure that the reporters got it wrong when they said that Steve had a shotgun and that he had leveled it at Jackie Shaw. Mutt said he knew that Steve had left his gun behind at the church when he ran off to pull the fire alarm. In a related oral history with Larry Thomas, Kojo Nantambu, who was also at the scene the night Steve was killed, said Steve had actually handed his gun to a friend who, too, was standing guard at the church. "Steve left his gun with him," Kojo recalled to Thomas. Both he and Mutt said that there was absolutely no way Steve had a gun when he encountered Shaw. Both said that they knew Shaw had no justification to gun down Steve.

An autopsy indicated that Steve was not only shot in the throat, but at close range. Police also claimed that they had fired their weapons to protect firemen who had been fired on while trying to put out the fire at Mike's Grocery. Mutt said that was "flatly bullshit." "People were all over the streets either helping the neighbors or just out of curiosity. You couldn't be shooting at the firemen without risking hitting other people in the street. Besides, it just didn't make sense when your neighborhood was burning down around you."

No further official investigation of Steve's death was conducted.

Ben Chavis told me in an interview that he knew that, "Nobody in their right mind would have set Mike's Grocery on fire because there were black-owned homes adjacent to it. Certainly none of the organizers of the boycott had anything to do with burning down Mike's Grocery, or any plans like that. In fact, as I recall, when the store caught on fire, we risked our lives going out to help the sister get her furniture out of the house".

"So, it was just a terrible thing," he continued, "and, yes, there were defensive measures taken at the church hoping that… you would think that after that first night, the violence would stop, but it went on for a whole week and finally escalated that Friday and Saturday night. It was not until Harvey Cumber was killed on Sunday morning that Governor Bob Scott, and Mayor Luther Cromartie declared a state of emergency. It was a terrible, senseless loss of lives, and all of it could have been avoided."

Ben also told me as I was completing this book, that a very elderly woman who lived across the street from Mike's Grocery had recently told authorities that she saw the store's white owner, Mike Poulos, pouring a suspicious liquid around his store and lighting matches the night the grocery went up in flames.

I was stunned when I heard this. The very focus of our wrongful arrest, conviction and imprisonment—Mike's Grocery—had finally been revealed to be the lie that we had all along been proclaiming. Of course, we, the members of the Wilmington Ten, knew we had nothing to do with the store's burning. But we never knew who had actually committed what authorities almost immediately ruled arson. I was able to confirm in writing that Marlyn Mallette, a black, Wilmington resident, spoke with Mark Davis of the North Carolina Attorneys General Office late last year during our successful campaign for a Pardon of Innocence from Governor Perdue. I learned that Marlyn told Davis that her mother, who is ninety-five years old, told her that she witnessed

Mike Poulos setting fire to his own store. I found documentation that strongly suggests that the Attorneys General Office believed the story.

I certainly do.

In conversations with Marlyn, the story emerged that her mother first told her in 1971 that she saw what happened but did not tell authorities at the time. I suspect that she kept quiet out of fear of white appraisals. The Massacre of 1898 did a number on black Wilmington, especially on those like Marlyn's mother whose parents may have lived through its terrors. And besides, it was the Mallette backyard where Steve Mitchell was fatally shot by a white police officer. But it wasn't until late last year, according to Marlyn, that her mother, (Marlyn asked that her mother not be named in my book) began to speak of what she saw at Mike's Grocery. She said her mother, in her advanced years, began suffering from dementia, but has periods when she is lucid. During one of those periods, likely triggered by our widely covered campaign for a pardon in the local press, Marlyn's mother once again told her daughter, forty-one-years later, what she saw Mike Poulos doing to his store that day.

I was relieved and dismayed to hear this. Like Ben, it is hard for me not to think about all the many lives destroyed by the city leader's failure at that time, to act fairly and forthrightly and truthfully, starting with the truth of who really set Mike's Grocery on fire that February 6 night. Without the truth, the lies that sealed the Wilmington Ten's fate, fell like dominoes in a rigged game.

Once the "raid" on Gregory was done Monday morning, February 8, it seemed that National Guardsmen, state highway patrolmen, and local law enforcement personnel were everywhere. One thing was certain. It was not Steve's death that brought them out in force. It clearly took the death of a white man, Harvey Cumber, to provide the grounds to finally establish a curfew and bring the protection to the city and county that we had pleaded for. By the time the smoke had cleared, it was obvious that authorities had not taken seriously the threat of violence we warned would come to our community. In the aftermath, twenty-seven buildings, including Mike's Grocery, went up in flames. Several people were wounded, two people dead, and irreparable damage had been done to the hearts, minds and souls of the hundreds of black boycotting students and their supporters

Our deepest desire had been not for an armed revolution, but to engage in a nonviolent protest for equality in the school system and to redeem our lost identity. We simply wanted to raise the spirit of Williston Senior High School. How simple could that have been if the city and county's leadership would have taken our concerns seriously? Instead, our struggle for a supportive and just educational environment, a struggle of teenage students, became the signature cause for everyone who had a beef with the white man. For us, the students, the transformation was a conundrum. I still struggle to this day to understand how we got there. I may never understand the insatiable appetite of white supremacists to feel superior to other human beings. But I will never rest until I can at least make sense of the real reason why we were the target of white extremists when we wanted no more than their children wanted for themselves.

We could not have anticipated what happened. I'm sure Ben Chavis hadn't. In less than a week from his arrival in Wilmington, he found himself in the middle of a boiling crisis. Although his speeches had been fiery, he never advocated violence. Ben's message to the students at Gregory Church was always that if we kept faith in God and organized ourselves in nonviolent protests, we would ultimately be victorious. He represented the United Church of Christ, which he described as a denomination with a long tradition of social justice advocacy. He told us that, with the church as our partner, we would never be alone in our struggle.

He believed that the church, by definition, would stand with the oppressed.

However, when things began to spiral out of control, Ben had armed men all around him, both inside and outside of the church. Ben's call for nonviolence seemed to fall on ears that heard only what they wanted, not just the ears of authorities charged with maintaining the peace, but those who had been shot at by white vigilantes. The militants, who had come to protect us and the church, began to shoot back. At that point, when facing down the barrels of loaded rifles, few of us talked about turning the other cheek. Some simply reloaded.

Ben led two nonviolent marches to City Hall. Both times he publicly insisted that the city authorities provide police protection for the students and a curfew for the city. But this was a city, county and state that had its highways peppered with billboards that read such things as "Help us Fight Communism, Busing and Integration" and, yes, "Join the Ku Klux Klan!"

I believe in the end, Ben underestimated the alliance between government officials and the area's racial extremists that included the Klan and the Rights of White People. And had this been a different time before there were national television and radio news, national daily newspapers quick to print, we would have been slaughtered like our predecessors had in the Massacre of 1898. Our slaughter would eventually come, but it would be largely bloodless, and done in the light of day with a public veneer of the just and lawful.

But first we had to pick up the pieces. We had to bury our dead.

Fearing more violence, the trustees of Gregory Congregational Church refused to permit Steve Mitchell's funeral to be held at the church. But Holy Trinity Church, a Holiness church about a mile away, did welcome the funeral into its chapel on February 11, 1971. Jordan's Funeral Home, where Steve's body was taken and prepared for burial, was located next to Gregory. Luther

Jordan, whose father owned Jordan's Funeral Home, was one of the last graduates of Williston Senior High before it was closed in 1969. While he never actively participated in our protests, Luther Jordan sympathized with us and the rest of the boycotting black students. The Jordan family were long-time community leaders in Wilmington and Luther Jordan went on to become a state senator.

We decided that it would be fitting to have an African-styled funeral march from the funeral home to Holy Trinity on Fourth and Red Cross Streets. Hundreds of people, some in dashikis, others wearing the red, black and green liberation colors first made famous by Marcus Garvey, joined in the mostly silent march.

I eventually learned that Cumber, too, had a funeral procession of sorts. His casket, under a deck of flowers, was loaded into the same truck in which he died and was driven to a prison camp where his son was an inmate.

For Steve's funeral, I hadn't had a lot of time to go run out and buy myself an outfit, but I did manage to find a red, black and green tam that I wore over my afro. I felt good about that. These were the colors that Ben first told me about; they were statements like the color of our skin, like the color of the blood that Steve had shed, and it was the color of the land that we had all come from. But for the most part, I felt little else. Well, there was the mad swim of anxiety and fear in my gut. It's hard to accept that somebody you were just talking to, somebody you were running around with, one minute, is gone the next. I kept thinking, and I know I shouldn't have—but I couldn't help it—that could have been me. The thought walked with me all the way to the funeral home.

It might be hard to believe now, but I wasn't feeling any fear for myself while I walked. I guess the same people, the Klan and the Rights of White People, who had threatened us daily, could have been gunning for us along the march route. But I didn't have any personal fear that day. I just feared for our boycott, our movement, and where it all might end. For Steven it was definitely over. Everything was over.

The funeral was open-casket. I heard Steve looked peaceful. I didn't go up, I couldn't. I definitely understand how Rachel Jeantel, the Florida teenager who testified in the Trayvon Martin case, felt when she said she couldn't bring herself to see her friend—whom she had been talking to on her cellphone minutes before he was killed—lifeless in his casket.

I later found out that the FBI surveilled us as we walked to Holy Trinity and as we made our way to the burial. I have no idea why. Yet, I feel compelled to share a part of the February 18, 1971, report exactly how it was written and filed to an FBI office in Charlotte.

"At approximately 1:10 p.m., the crowd outside the Holy Trinity Church was estimated to be between between four- and five-hundred. After the ceremony in the church which was over at 2:00 p.m., the crowd gathered out in front of the church until approximately 2:45 p.m., when they began marching north on Fourth St., near the Northeast River Bridge. Just before getting to the bridge, some of the marchers got in two buses and these buses along with an estimated twenty-eight cars proceeded with the hearse to Kelly, North Carolina, where the burial was to take place."

Steve's death was not the first time I had made death's icy acquaintance. I had already felt it, seen it up close. And I'm not talking about the loss of an elderly relative, or even a family pet. This was, like Steve's, a violent, bloody end.

It happened the summer when I was sixteen, when I was laughing and having good times with a bunch of buddies at Seabreeze, the jewel of the area's segregated black beach resorts for decades. But by the time me and my friends were old enough to go there, the place had been badly battered by hurricanes, neglect and changing times. Still, even in its sorry state, we liked partying there.

One of my closest friends, Donald Salter, the teenager who would get shot in the leg outside Gregory Church during the student boycott, was with me. And everything seemed great until the news exploded in our faces like a bomb that Donald's older brother, Alexander, had been shot just outside.

We all ran out of this old nightclub and found Alexander crumpled on the ground, bleeding and gasping for breath. His car was nearby, so me and the boys gathered him up and put him in the backseat of his car while Alexander's baby brother, Jerome, sat next to Donald, who jumped into the driver's seat to rush Alexander to New Hanover Memorial Hospital. It was where incidentally, Donna Templeton, the pastor's wife at Gregory, was a nurse.

The only way we could all go to the hospital was for me and two of my friends—John Green and Freddie Parker—to cram into the car's backseat with Alexander stretched out across our laps. Donald's brother was older than all of us, twenty-one, I think. He laid there across us, semi-conscious and bleeding. He was dying, and knew he was dying. He had been shot in the chest at close range with a rifle. The best we could figure out was that Donald's younger brother, Jerome, was trying to break into somebody's car parked at Seabreeze. He got caught by the owner who then slapped Jerome in the face before chasing him away. Jerome then found his big brother and told him that he had been slapped. When Alexander confronted the man at his car, the man, probably scared, pulled a rifle out of the car and started shooting.

He left Alexander dying in the street like a stray dog.

On the race to the hospital, I could feel Alexander's last breath. He was dead on arrival. All I could think at the time was—as I did when I was attending Steve's funeral—that death is so ruthlessly final. And that it can come at any time, especially if you were young, black and male.

Even Ben Chavis, our cool head and hand of a leader, was not spared this crude cruelty. The year before he arrived to us in 1971, he had to endure the murder of his first cousin in Oxford, NC, where they grew up with dreams that hadn't included premature death and prison.

None of us had endured death dreams, either.

8

BUSTING THE BOYCOTT, NOT OUR SPIRIT

By mid-April, our student boycott was completely smashed. Its demise was at the hands of a flurry of devastating blows. The first was a steady draining of student enthusiasm for it by all the rioting, rock-throwing, gunfire, wounds, worry and bloodshed that struck Wilmington in early February 1971 like white knuckles. Then came an armed invasion by the National Guard of our boycott headquarters and alternative school at Gregory Congregational Church.

But the death blow came by way of a stroke of a pen.

Welding that pen was Judge Algernon Butler of the United States District Court for the Eastern District of North Carolina. At the request of the New Hanover County Board of Education, a two-day hearing was held. It concluded April 16, with Judge Butler delivering a body shot of an order *"enjoining Ben Chavis, James Earl Grant, Rev. Leon White, Rev. Eugene Templeton, Joe Hammonds, Tom E. Houston, North Carolina-Virginia Commission for Racial Justice, Anne Sheppard, Allen Hall, Ben Wonce, Connie Tindall, Molly Hicks, George Kirby, Pat Rhodes, Joe Wright, Rev. Al B. Sutton, Annie McClean, Julius Nixon, Anthony Ray Henry, Golden Frinks, Milton Fitch, Rev. William Land, The Southern Christian Leadership Conference, and other persons known and unknown, and all other persons in active concert*

*or participation with them from (A) instituting or maintaining
a boycott of the public schools of New Hanover County; (B)
attempting in any manner to deter or obstruct the attendance
at the public schools of children within New Hanover County
School System; (C) attempting in any manner to interfere with
the lawful administration of the schools or frustrate the school
board in complying with the order of this court."*

Further, this restraining order maintained that *"Ben Chavis, et
al, by concerted action have organized and sponsored a boycott of
the schools by black students, demanded that the school boards
re-established an all-black school, threatened to bring pressure
to close the entire school system, and contributed to extensive
violence in the New Hanover County School System, resulting
in disruption of the schools and necessitating periodic closing of
the schools."*

While there were, indeed, shreds of truth in the order, its
officious language barely concealed blatant lies. First of all, by
the time Ben Chavis arrived in Wilmington February 1971, the
boycott had already been organized by Ben Wonce, Joe Wright,
and other suspended students, including me. And re-establishing
an all-black high school was never one of our demands. We had
long realized reopening the revered and once predominately
black Williston as a high school was never going to happen. And
to be clear, our call was for black students not to attend classes
in the city and county public schools until we, as a group, were
treated fairly and equally. We never called for white students
to join our boycott, and those who did so did it for their own
reasons—definitely not ours.

It was this sort of lack of understanding and disregard for the
truth by local authorities that fueled the accelerating violence
in Wilmington, not Ben Chavis or any other so-called "outside
agitator." Believe me, we had more than enough internal
agitation from homegrown white racists, their sympathizers and

their official enablers to stir up trouble. Generations of black Wilmingtonians suffered that trouble mostly in strained silence.

In a documentary about the Wilmington Ten, the judge who later presided at our preliminary hearing, Judge Gilbert Burnett, can be heard blaming Ben Chavis for all the violence that occurred in Wilmington. Blaming Ben totally dismisses the history of race relations in Wilmington. Equally disturbing was the city's white leadership's belief that Wilmington's young African Americans actually needed someone from the outside to stir them to anger.

Ben had no more to do with stirring up violence in Wilmington than a weatherman who predicts rain makes the rain fall. To blame Ben Chavis for inciting the 1971 uprising in Wilmington is like blaming Moses for turning the people of Israel against Pharaoh; like blaming Sojourner Truth for inciting slaves to be free; like blaming B.B. King for the blues. Just as the great white shark doesn't need to be told it's feeding time when it smells blood in the water, we did not need to be told that it was time to satisfy our hunger for justice. Yet as remarkable as it was that so many of us came together for a just cause, I have wondered how the call was answered by so many people—black and white— from so many different backgrounds and histories.

For example, Ben had never experienced the deprivation and poverty so many of us had known coming of age in Wilmington. I doubt very seriously if he had, like I had, choked down fatback and grits before heading off to school because there was nothing else for breakfast. I know Ben and his family hadn't depended, like I did, on monthly allotments from the Department of Agriculture for yellow grits, cheddar cheese, powdered milk, chopped meat, rolled wheat flour and corn meal for sustenance. Nor did he ever go, I'm sure, through the winter using cardboard to cover over the holes in the soles of his shoes.

My thoughts also turned to the Rev. Eugene Templeton and his wife, Donna, and wondered almost aloud why a young, white couple would commit to such a cause as ours. They both risked not only their reputations with so many fellow whites of Wilmington, but they put their lives between us—a group of confused, frightened, and determined students—and white hatred literally pounding at their church door.

I will never forget how he rose to our defense in confronting what appeared to be common knowledge that Gregory Church was a nest of snipers firing on police and firefighters. In a letter entitled, "Five Questions About Gregory's Involvement in the New Hanover School Crisis—1971," he wrote, among many things, "I firmly believe that the sniping took place from vehicles that directed their fire toward the church. I deeply regret the fact that media has convinced the community at large that the sniping came from the church."

He went on to write that the last known incident of sniping near the church occurred on a Sunday, February 14—Valentine's Day—when a white man approached the front door of Rev. Templeton's parsonage. He left after the reverend refused to let him enter the home. As the man left, Rev. Templeton wrote, he turned and fired a gun at the house. Soon after, the pastor and his wife, fearing for their safety, left town.

He concluded his letter with an appreciation of "the actions of the students whom I feel saved our lives and our property" during the crisis at the church.

Why would people like this put so much on the line for black people?

White champions and defenders of black liberation and freedom are hardly absent from American history; they are just mostly invisible because they are hardly celebrated. We're all taught all the myths of our founding fathers—George Washington's total inability to tell a lie, for one—but little about black and white solidarity in our long struggle for racial justice. Tim Wise, the white author of *Dear White America: Letter to a New Minority* makes the point in his book that if white antiracism and multicultural solidarity were better known, transformation to an inclusive society would be far less stressful.

He suggests that everyone, white people in particular, should know the names and stories of whites who have significantly helped and not hindered black racial progress. I say add to that list the names of Eugene and Donna Templeton.

And turning to blacks who had achieved some level of success and comfort in America, and yet risked it all for a mass movement to liberate their fellow blacks, Jonathan Kirsch of the *Los Angeles Times* offered some insight. In his critique of Ellis Cose's, book, *Rage of The Privileged Class,* he noted, "Cose insists, intriguingly and provocatively, that the successful black professional who has achieved a measure of affluence is precisely the one most resentful of the lingering toxin of racism."

For me, that definitely described Ben when I met and got to know him in 1971. He was a bright, successful intellectual, yet was as revolutionary as Huey P. Newton and Malcolm X. Like Fannie Lou Hamer famously said of herself, Ben struck me as a man who was "sick and tired of being sick and tired."

So, in the end, it didn't seem to matter very much that Ben and I had come from family backgrounds that were socially and educationally diametrically opposed; our sense of purpose and sense of direction were essentially the same. And although Ben was never forced by court order to integrate into a predominately white institution as I had in Wilmington, he must have experienced similar race-roiling frustrations as I had. I'm sure he got a taste of that when he found himself one of eight black students enrolled at University of North Carolina at Charlotte, a school of thousands of students. He must have also experienced the trauma of being dropped into an environment in which you are at best tolerated, never accepted.

The plain truth is that black folks in Wilmington were angry long before Ben Chavis appeared on the scene. I know I was. If anything, Ben saved the city from total destruction. Despite a widely assumed belief that the riots that occurred throughout Wilmington were a direct result of the student boycott, racial tension had been high there ever since Dr. King's assassination in 1968, the subsequent riot over his death, and then, in the summer of that year, the closing and sacrificing of Williston Senior High School.

It didn't take much to incite a city-wide riot in 1971. The fuse had been lit long before and its hissing could be heard by anyone there who cared enough to listen. And then yet again, one of the worse miscarriages of justice in the history of North Carolina may have never occurred if Benjamin Franklin Chavis had never set foot in Wilmington. You see, it was that "outside agitator," our leader that the state of North Carolina deemed too outspoken, too intelligent, too correct and therefore too dangerous. He had to be stopped. He had to be silenced. The other organizers, including me, who were eventually rounded up with Ben to become the Wilmington Ten, amounted to little more than collateral damage. Now this is not to say that there would not have been a boycott of the school system, or the ensuing riots would not have occurred; only that ten innocent people would not have ended up in prison as a result of an attempt to destroy Ben Chavis. Do I fault Ben in anyway? No way.

I do, however, fault a wicked, racist system spawned by America's past that seeps all too easily into our present. This is what black people have had to face for hundreds of years with the *de facto* physical bondage of American slavery, and more than a century of the *de jure* economic and social bondage—first during the period of Jim Crow, and today in the form of mass incarceration .

For me, the idea of ever finishing high school seemed like a notion best forgotten for a while. By early spring of 1971, before the court order that would end the boycott was delivered, city and county school administrators had become alarmed when they learned that 30 to 40 percent of Wilmington's black students were no longer attending class. By then, a lot of us— like me—were suspended or expelled for protests and related incidents. Many others were staying away to honor the boycott. When Superintendent Bellamy learned that Carter Newsome, a supportive black teacher, was concerned about the low black turnout in school, he summoned him to his office to discuss ways to solve the problem. I just happened to walk by when Newsome arrived at Bellamy's office.

I was there to plead my case for reinstatement in school. I was upset that Bellamy had refused to reinstate me, noting robotically that he had no choice but to abide by the policy of the school board. I remember glaring at Newsome although he hadn't done anything to me. I just wasn't in the mood to talk to anyone, not even saying hello, which is sort of drastic for a Southerner. But these were drastic times. What was a black boy in North Carolina going to do without a high school education? The expulsion felt like a death penalty to me. In my mind, my destiny had been determined by someone who didn't even know me.

Life can be funny. I had no way of knowing at that very moment when I walked by, that Newsome and Bellamy were preparing to discuss developing an alternative "Night School" that would allow expelled students like me to graduate with their classmates still in school. I came to learn that Bellamy had personally dispatched Newsome to assist me, in particular, after seeing the hurt look on my face when I was told that I could not return to school.

If it had not been for Bertha Todd, Bellamy and Carter New-some, and a few others, I would have never graduated from high school. This group of educators successfully convinced the North Carolina Board of Education to approve a night-time alternative school for me and others like me.

It was more an accident of geography than anything else that brought me into the stabilizing orbit of Carter Newsome. He was from a small town in the northeastern corner of North Carolina, and had graduated from Hampton Institute in Virginia. As a kid, I lived right down the street from him and he came to know me well. I often shagged golf balls for him in a field not too far from Williston where he started his career in 1951. He was a good man and I liked him, and he took an interest in my well-being. He was the kind of educator who was dedicated to the proposition that black students needed to be doubly prepared to make it in a deeply unfair and segregated society.

Newsome went on to meet with the New Hanover County Schools vocational director, James Gerhardt. Together, they came up with the idea for a night school that allowed students to work during the day and go to school at night. With funding provided with the help of state school board members Barton Hayes and Dallas Herring, the school became a model for other alternative schools throughout the state. I, along with my mother, was thrilled at the prospect of me being able to graduate, yet the rate at which black students were being expelled was rapidly escalating into a crisis of its own.

❖ ⎯⎯ ❖

In the early 1970s, a few student leaders in Wilmington realized that black progressive change was not going to happen there without them stepping up to the challenge. This realization led them to create the Black Youth Builders of the Black Community or the BYBBC.

In the beginning, the BYBBC was organized to channel the many frustrations and tensions experienced in the majority white and hostile public schools we were forced to attend. But the BYBBC quickly became more than that. Its members wanted to be a positive force in the wider community. The group took some important cues from the community-based programs that the Black Panthers in Oakland, California, were operating, like free breakfast programs for the hungry.

The first meetings, which were in 1970, were held at the Tigers Inn, a onetime hot spot for students of the old Williston high school. We didn't wear berets and leather jackets like the Panthers, but instead began wearing red, black and green to express our identity with the black struggle and in defiance of any and all efforts to suppress our solidarity with that struggle.

The BYBBC gave us a vital framework in the wake of the crushing of our student boycott. We didn't feel defeated, but instead more determined to fight on, just on different fronts. Around this time, Ben Chavis said he felt that our struggle needed spiritual guidance, especially after the loss of Gregory Church as a headquarters and the funeral of Steven Mitchell. It said it was time to call on the Black Messiah, a vision and theology of Jesus as a black revolutionary with roots in the late 1960s.

Albert B. Cleage, Jr., was a Christian leader who was part of an outreach ministry of the United Church of Christ, the same church that employed Ben and instructed him to help us in the first place. In 1967, Rev. Cleage, an author and political organizer, started the Black Christian National Movement which called on black churches to "reinterpret Jesus" and his teachings to suit the social, economic, and political needs of black people.

In March 1967, Rev. Cleage hung a portrait of a black Madonna and black baby Jesus in his Detroit church and rechristened the church the Shrine of the Black Madonna. In 1970, Rev. Cleage changed his name to Jaramogi Abebe Agyeman, Swahili for "savior of the nation," among other things. He also changed the name of his church to the Pan African Orthodox Christian Church. The following year, his transformative movement reached us.

We created the first African Congregation of the Black Messiah and moved, with the membership of the BYBBC, into the recently vacated H. Jaffe Building on 714 Castle Street. The Jaffe family had owned and operated the Castle Street Furniture Company, a modest store, in that free standing building where they lived and worked from 1922 to 1967. I remember the old store very well. For a long time, the owner, Harry Jaffe, a Jewish man born in Leeds, England, ran the shop with his wife, Dora. When he died in 1962, Dora Jaffe, operated the store for a while. Eventually, the building, surrounded by the black community, was sold to members of the Nation of Islam.

Almost immediately, we made this rented space our own. We put up a painting of a black Jesus in the main room. The classes that had abruptly ended at Gregory were resumed at the Church of the Black Messiah along with classes in liberation theology, black history, self-development and self-defense; and the work of the BYBBC continued as well.

Roderick Lionel Kirby, or Kojo Nantambu, was the BYBBC president at the time. Gloria Brown was the vice president; Dianne Fillyaw was treasurer; Wanda Vereen, correspondent secretary; Phyllis Strothers, communications secretary; Anthony Henry, "public relations man;" George Davis, head of security; and Bernard Morgan, librarian.

Under the banner of the Black Messiah Church, of which Kojo was also its assistant pastor, we worked to continue our struggle for racial justice and equality in Wilmington.

In an attempt to intimidate us, Leroy Gibson and his Rights of White People organization set up its headquarters in a building less than a block away, at Eighth and Castle Streets. We were absolutely not intimidated, and openly discussed ways to encourage ROWP to leave the neighborhood. We learned that the building, badly damaged during the racial unrest in February, was less of a headquarters and more of an excuse for ROWP to be in the area. The owner was renting the space for three months for one dollar. There was another fire there in January 1972. We never knew the cause of that blaze. We knew we were being watched by authorities, which certainly didn't add to our own sense of security at the church. We posted guards in front of our building. One surveillance report noted that during the period of 1971-1972, a black Wilmington police officer was "among those who had seen the teenage youth in the company of Chavis prior to his arrest at the building on Castle Street which served as the location of the Black Messiah Church, referred to (by him) as the "'headquarters' of the Wilmington Ten." And Ben informed us that he saw a church member speaking with a ROWP member in a local shopping center. Eventually, Gibson, who was flirting with running for public office, moved off of Castle Street. But the city's racial tensions remained taut. And the stakes seemed to grow larger by the day.

Golden Frinks, a field coordinator for the Southern Christian Leadership Conference, came to Wilmington in March 1971 to push for economic development and the reopening of Williston Senior High School, something I, again, had given up hoping to see. But Golden, who stood around six feet tall and spoke with a booming voice, had a way of making you believe.

His years of work with Dr. King's Southern Christian Leadership Conference had placed him right next to the Great Man himself, including being at his side during the infamous Selma-to-Montgomery March in 1965. Although Golden was heavily influenced by Dr. King's approach to the struggle for civil rights, he found no contradiction in bringing black power figures like Stokely Carmichael and Howard Fuller into his circle. The way he saw it, all black people agitating for change had the same goal: ending social, economic and political inequality in America.

Dark-skinned and always in thick, black-rimmed eyeglasses, Golden was, to say the very least, a commanding figure. He wore dashikis in solidarity with the black power and black nationalist movements, yet he also brandished a large cross around his neck that bespoke his allegiance to the Southern Christian Leadership Conference. And while he looked more like a black preacher than a black militant, Golden's grasp and ease of black, inner-city dialect was a thing to behold, even if it sometimes seemed to contradict his brilliant instincts as a politician and community organizer.

Golden, along with civil rights activists Milton Fitch, George Kirby and Mollie Hicks formed the Poor Peoples Co-Operative, a grassroots organization designed to empower the black community through economic development. In the months following our boycott, George assisted Golden in staging several protests, including some zeroing in on local business owners' refusal to hire blacks, similar to the fight Adam Clayton Powell waged along Harlem's 125th Street years earlier.

Part of Golden's approach was to load forty to fifty young blacks, including me, onto the back of a U-Haul truck and drive around to several local grocery stores and businesses. At each location, we would rush into the store, overflow the carts with goods and walk out of the store, leaving the carts in the aisles and headaches for the store's management.

In a speech at the Longshoreman's Hall where the group met regularly, Golden Frinks, known for his flamboyant style of protest, promised that if certain demands were not met by the managing committee of Wilmington's annual Azalea Festival Parade he would turn the high-profile affair into a "chaotic adventure." His plan included the multiple threats of "sit-ins, stand-ups, and lie-ins and general agitation" to be climaxed by the release of 1,000 white chickens along the parade route of this Old South ritual of remembrance that conveniently left out our pain and subjugation as slaves.

What Golden wanted from the festival was that six percent of its profits be turned over to the Poor Peoples Co-Operative to open economic opportunities for local black people.

The committee's response was prompt: It sought and got a restraining order against Golden Frinks and all of his followers. No chickens literally came home to roost that year, but that didn't mean Wilmington was no less the hot bed of racial strife that broke into the open in 1898, then in 1968 following Dr. King's assassination, and in February 1971.

On the last day of August 1970, just before the start of the new school year, nineteen school buses were "mysteriously" burned. Many believed it was Leroy Gibson and the ROWP's way of protesting busing. Most of the vehicles had been designated to transport black students to New Hanover and Hoggard high schools. Later that same day, a leader of the Ku Klux Klan, Tex Gross, met with Superintendent Bellamy and presented a request that he and the Board of Education cease and desist from desegregating New Hanover County Schools.

In the months following what many called "the incident of February 1971" the Wilmington police became increasingly abusive. On October 1 a fight broke out between black and white students at a football game between New Hanover and Hoggard at Legion Stadium. No one was shocked when police bum-rushed and brutalized black students with nightsticks and mace. Six policemen beat down Kojo Nantambu, Rodney King-style. As a result, Kojo suffered a skull fracture and was arrested for assaulting a police officer and resisting arrest.

Kojo's arrest precipitated continued violence and hostilities in the schools and city. Less than a month later, police kicked, maced, and arrested nine black students after an argument on a school bus. Another state of emergency was declared on November 12, 1971, and a sinking feeling in the pit of my stomach was telling me that we were all slipping off into hell again. Almost overnight, Wilmington, once deemed an "All American City," was again a war zone.

As many as fifty vehicles were damaged by bricks as they traveled along Dawson Street, which was a main route in and out of the city for white commuters. Anyone commuting on Dawson Street had to run a gauntlet through two large, black housing projects—Hillcrest and Jervay. As cars and trucks drove between them, they were fluffy, white sitting ducks for young angry blacks who would, as in a guerilla war, aim at the vehicles and let loose a flurry of rocks and sometimes gunfire. According to local police reports, several vehicles were fired upon and hit by bullets. But no one was killed.

Unable to quell the rage and violence that was engulfing the city, authorities began to focus their attention on the night-riders of the Ku Klux Klan and the Rights of White People organization. Ever since the 1898 Massacre, white supremacist organizations had met in Wilmington's Hugh McCrae Park, an idyllic-looking spot of tall, thin trees, flower groves and pond, to spew their hatred of African Americans. Hugh McCrae, for whom the park is named, was one of the ring leaders of the 1898 Massacre.

In an effort to restore the city's longtime reputation as a peaceful port city of the New South, local authorities banned ROWP and the KKK meetings in the park. Shortly before the ban, large caches of weapons were confiscated in police raids on the park. Mayor Cromartie flatly turned down an offer from the local KKK's Exalted Cyclops, Tex Gross, to provide five-hundred Klansmen to restore local law and order. Open racism would no longer be tolerated, Cromartie indicated, adding that, "It only tended to stoke the rage and fury among the blacks."

All attempts by the KKK and the Rights of White People to strike old-fashioned fear and intimidation in the hearts of Wilmington's black community failed. We all held firm. Certainly an unintended consequence of all the ham-handed attempts by white supremacists to control us was that people like Tex Gross and Leroy Gibson had become a nuisance, even an embarrassment, to the real white power structure of the city. What became clear for the city's leadership was that a different and more subtle approach was needed.

In December 1971, authorities began a series of arrests that targeted Ben Chavis. This conveniently fed into a brewing outrage among Wilmington whites that no one had been hauled to jail for the many arsons—especially the burning of Mike's Grocery—that choked the city's skies in February. And many of them started demanding that someone would have to answer for the killing of a white man, Harvey Cumber.

At first, Ben and Jim Grant, another activist who had been working with us, were arrested on charges of conspiracy to aid individuals to escape custody and possession of explosive devices. Their arrests were in connection with an incident more than a year earlier in Charlotte, where a horse stable had burned down.

A week after being released on bond on that case in which he was eventually cleared, Ben was arrested in Wilmington five days before Christmas 1971. This time, he was charged with being an accessory after the fact to the March 13, 1971, murder of Clifton Eugene Wright. Wright was a black, seventeen-year-old street hustler who was playing poker at the Wilmington home of Mollie Hicks, an activist who had been important in the student boycott.

The story was that Wright had gotten up from a friendly game of poker at Mollie's apartment in the Taylor Homes public housing project to answer a knock at her front door. When he opened the door, a white man was standing there with a shotgun.

It was said that this man fired at point blank range, killing Wright, and then ran off into the night. When asked about the shooting during a press conference in Raleigh, Ben suggested that the murder was another casualty of Wilmington's racial unrest. Authorities believed that was nothing more than a likely story.

Charged along with Ben were Mollie Hicks; her daughter, Leatrice, nineteen; Jerome McLean, twenty-one, one of the poker players that day; and Donald Nixon, also twenty-one. Nixon was charged with the actual murder and later pled guilty to the charge and was considered to be a key witness in the case against Ben.

Although Ben had been in Raleigh at the time of the shooting, and it was later determined that Mollie was also not at home at the time of the incident, the indictment concluded that all five conspired to cover up the murder by making it appear as if had been carried out by white vigilantes.

Although Nixon faced murder charges, his bond was set at $3,000, while Ben's bond was set at $10,000. The message was clear: Ben Chavis you'll leave town immediately or face dire consequences.

But Ben refused to leave and continued to assist the Black Youth Builders of the Black Community in Wilmington.

Sometimes I didn't know where he got it, or kept it, but Ben never seemed to suffer a shortage of courage.

At this point, I had no idea that my own courage was about to be tested in ways I never dreamed. Not even in a nightmare.

9

NOOSES AROUND OUR NECKS

Almost a year after our student boycott ended, the editorial pages of the local newspapers were screaming that no arrests had been made in connection with the rioting and the death of Harvey Cumber. It was a killing never fully investigated, probably because Cumber was likely Klan-connected and had recklessly shot first and forgot to duck.

By the spring of 1972, Wilmington law enforcement agencies were beginning to buckle under tremendous pressure to answer louder and louder calls for blood, black blood. And it seemed that all levels of white Wilmington were taking up this call, from the city's Chamber of Commerce to the Rights of White People.

"We get a lot of criticism, which we accept as police officers," Chief H. E. Williamson said at the time, attempting to tamp down some of the civic noise being heard in much of Wilmington. But the criticism only mounted. Then, seemingly coming out of the thinnest of air, Ben Chavis and his bodyguards, Marvin Patrick and Tommy Atwood, were arrested on charges of conspiracy to murder in Cumber's death. All three were jailed under $75,000 bond. Also arrested were Connie Tindall, twenty-two, James McKoy, seventeen, Jerry Jacobs, nineteen, Cornell Flowers, seventeen, and Anne Katherine Sheppard, thirty-five, the white social worker who had worked with us during the student boycott.

All were charged with burning an unoccupied building with an incendiary device and assault on emergency personnel in connection with the Mike's Grocery fire.

Ben and some of the brothers were meeting on Castle Street at the Church of the Black Messiah when they were ambushed by a special forces unit during an early afternoon raid on the church. It was a S.W.A.T. attack—body armor, helmets, boots and automatic weapons. Ben and the guys never had a chance to do more than go along like kidnapped victims, like captured Africans marched off by slavers. It was a sickening sight and I, like a lot of the black community, wondered when all this craziness would stop.

Immediately following those arrests, Police Chief Williamson quipped, "I'm the happiest damn police chief in the country. I think that we have the majority of those who made trouble for us last February. I'm the happiest I've been since I was appointed police chief."

He wasn't alone. Suddenly whites in Wilmington seemed to start calming down. All the criticism directed at police subsided and was swallowed up in a hushed self-satisfaction. It was a collective "We got 'em now."

Over the next two months, more were arrested and charged with the Mike's Grocery fire and alledged assault on the emergency personnel that arrived at the scene February 6, 1971. They were Michael Peterson, Willie Earl Vereen, Joe Wright, Reginald Epps, James Bunting, George Kirby ...

* — *

It was May 1, 1972, and I was thinking—with a smile—about a girl.

I'd met Shirline some months earlier at the alternative night school I had been attending since being expelled from Hoggard high shortly before the boycott began. She was tall, leggy and shorn with bronze skin and a radiant smile. Being around her felt like being in the sun. I was immediately attracted to her.

Yet, when you're a teenager in high school, in a special high school held at night, it is very hard to see the difference between want that's fueled by raging hormones and want that's driven by the ageless romanticism of love at first sight. Whatever the case, when I spotted this pretty, young woman wearing this beautiful afro, I fell into a spell of fantasizing about what we may have in common, about how I could come to know her better. Maybe, I asked myself, she likes to go to the movies, or maybe to the park...? I had no idea who she was or how she had ended up in night school like me. In the same classroom with me. As far as I knew, she wasn't a part of the boycott.

Then suddenly, I realized that none of that mattered. I was caught up. My longing for Shirline overrode rational thought. I couldn't imagine anything that she could do or say that could change the way I felt at that moment. Then she caught me staring at her. Rather than roll her eyes at me, or suck her teeth as she utterly dismissed me, in the way only high school cuties can, she smiled. It was the most disarming smile I had ever seen. It was as if she had already read my best intentions, as if they had been splashed across the morning newspaper. I took her smile as an unspoken yes, accepting my invitation to the movies and the park.

I was struck even more by how I had not noticed her before. I learned that she had attended Williston and Hoggard before starting night school. Apparently, we ran in different circles. While she wore an afro as glorious as the one that adorned the militant head of Angela Davis, Shirline's finely painted nails and glossy lipstick seemed to suggest that she wasn't interested too much in the raging revolution.

In my case, though, I wore my high school expulsion for standing up for what I believed in as a badge of honor. I wondered what she would think about my involvement in the boycott and its aftermath. I would come to find out, and learn so much more about her.

On this spring evening, I had just walked the twenty or so blocks from Blocks Shirt Factory, at Third and Marstellar Streets, where I worked as an order clerk in the shipping department. As I was about to enter the alternative school, which was held on the campus of New Hanover High, at Thirteenth and Market Streets, two deputy sheriffs walked up to me and dutifully placed me under arrest.

I was the last of the Wilmington Ten—at that time, the Wilmington Sixteen—to be arrested. I was nineteen years old and two months shy of graduating from high school.

I was actually surprised by how courteous the sheriffs, both white middle-age men, were when they approached me, considering the seriousness of the charges being brought. They simply read me my rights and placed me under arrest. At that moment, all thoughts of Shirline suddenly disappeared.

Ordinarily, I would have been frightened out of my mind after all the stories I had heard on the streets about life in jail. My mind and body had gone into shock the minute I was placed into the backseat of the squad car. I know that I was processed, had my mug shot taken and was fingerprinted, but I don't recall any details. Reality didn't begin to set in until I was taken to the top floor of the New Hanover County courthouse and then through a series of clanging steel doors. After passing through the final door, I was hit in the nose by a smell that was like the odor that reeks inside ripe port-a-johns, probably the result of drunks and the habitual indifferent urinating and defecating all over the place.

The jailer pointed to a stack of thin rubber mattresses and told me to grab one. After picking up a set of jangling keys, he led me to the door of a cage leading to an open area containing two steel tables in a cell block. I looked into the dimly-lit cage and all down the row of cells, I could see the whites of eyes, as curious heads pressed against the steel bars to see. The jailer opened the door and ordered me inside this cage. He then pulled a lever which opened one of twelve cells. I walked like a zombie into the seventh one and the door closed violently behind me. Nothing can pierce the human soul like the sound of jailhouse doors being slammed shut behind you.

There was nothing in the cell but two steel bunks stacked on top of each other, a steel sink, and a steel toilet with no seat, no privacy. Although I didn't have a cellmate at the time, I chose the top bunk to get as far away from the stench of the toilet as I could. Imagine waking up to the sound of someone using a toilet just a few feet from your head. At the far end of the open area was an open shower stall. Just outside the bars in the open area was a set of windows facing the east—or so I was told. I was so disoriented at this point. All that I knew was that I was in jail.

It turned out that I was processed too late to get the evening meal. As I laid on my steel bunk staring at my cell's peeling ceiling, I heard jangling keys and someone calling my name. I jumped from the bunk, my spirit suddenly lighter thinking that someone had bailed me out. The door to my cell rolled open. I walked out into the cage. There, the jailer handed me a peanut butter and jelly sandwich and a half pint of warm milk. Freedom would have tasted so much better, but I took the little food and drink. I hadn't eaten since lunchtime at the shirt factory.

Crude curses swirled in my head, but I took the meal back to my bunk. No need to buck the system just yet; *it would only make things worse,* I thought.

At night, we were all locked in our cells. During the day, we were allowed in a common, open area where we could either play cards or look out of the window onto the streets. There wasn't much to do in jail to pass time. At least I could see people passing on the sidewalk seven floors away and witness the sunrise each morning. Little things. Any connection to the outside world is important when you've lost your freedom. I was in jail. I would not be able to graduate high school if I were in jail. All the hopes that my mother had of me making something out of myself seemed lost forever. That's what jail had me believing. Jail wreaked havoc on my mind. I spent a lot of time believing that the state would figure out that they had made a mistake and set me free.

As I tried to adjust to sleeping on the cold hard steel with a thin mattress I could not help but think about the times when my mother said, "You made your bed, now you have to sleep in it." But that was when I was being punished for disobeying her. But here I had done nothing wrong, yet I had been condemned to sleep on cold steel, a bed I certainly didn't make for myself.

Things may have gone a little easier for me if my codefendants had been there with me. I looked around the cage in vain for the brothers like Joe Wright, George Kirby, like Ben. I needed to talk with them about the charges, about our strategy to win our freedom. But they were not there. Overcrowding was a reason, I was told. But I realized that the real reason was that authorities wanted to keep us separated. It was a tactic, a taunt. The others were held either at Central Prison or at Odom Prison Farm, both maximum security facilities. And even there, they were not permitted access to one another.

I was the only member of the Wilmington Ten to be held at the New Hanover County jail. None of the parents of the jailed students could afford to post bond or hire attorneys. Anne Sheppard, though, was able to make bail almost immediately after she was arrested and charged with only one count of conspiracy. Her bail was by far the lowest.

On the other hand, Ben was being held without bond in the case of Harvey Cumber's killing.

It only took three days in jail for my own head to become one of the many pressed up against the bars, shadowy faces, panting inside at the sound of jangling keys. Jangling keys signaled any number of things, most of which were welcomed. Jangling keys could mean chow time, could mean someone was getting out, or someone new was coming in. Jangling keys could mean a visit from someone from the outside. Jangling keys could also mean there was going to be a shakedown. That's when a goon squad of corrections officers rush into your cell, performing full-body searches and ripping through your personal belongings in search of contraband, like shanks or drugs. You know something has gone terribly wrong in your life when mail call and chowtime are the highlights of your day. Of your existence.

Although the food was usually terrible, it did break the grinding monotony behind bars. There were other reliefs. The jailed were allowed to listen to radios—with headsets, but only those sold in the jail's canteen. Guys like me couldn't afford them. And for guys like me days and nights passed like weeks. That is exactly how it felt to me, time stretched and shredded and dragged through the jail like a dirty blanket.

I tried things I could do to break the monotony. I started an exercise routine in which I would flip playing cards to determine how many pushups or sit ups I would do. But I still looked forward to mail call, hoping to receive a letter or something, anything from the outside world that would provide a human touch to an otherwise animal-like existence. I did get lots of mail. It mostly came from people expressing solidarity. Those letters meant a lot, but not as much as letters from my mother or Shirline. I could say things to her and my mother that I would be ashamed to say to a supporter who viewed me as some kind of martyr for the cause.

I could express my doubts about the future and fears about the present situation to them, knowing that they would not see me as a coward who couldn't handle the pressure of being locked up. And I could bare my heart to Shirline.

＊ —— ＊

I still laugh a little to myself when I think about how Mr. Newsome caught me in class one night transfixed by Shirline, this too pretty girl I hardly knew (and would have a pretty hard time getting to know).

"What do you think, Mr. Moore?"

He'd caught me totally off guard. I had no idea what this educator was talking about. All of my attention had been focused on Shirline while Mr. Newsome had been going on about something I am sure he was convinced was essential to my education. Somehow, none of what he had to say held the tiniest of candles to this girl's wordless incandescent gaze. I was enchanted.

"I didn't come here tonight to waste my time," Mr. Newsome said a little too loudly. "Either you want to graduate from high school or you don't. If you do, you will have to pay attention in class."

For the rest of class that night I played my hand, bluffing Mr. Newsome into thinking that my poker face showed him I was paying attention to him. The real deal was that I had receded back into my sweet daydreaming about Shirline, rehearsing how I would approach her, what I would say, what would be my *move*.

What came to mind was lame, tired stuff like, *I would really like a chance to get to know you better.* Well, at least it sounded better than the standard street lines like, *You sho look fine girl. I want to spend some time with you...* I have to admit that I was not the best, in those days, at reading women. But she seemed to be interested in me, and that was all the music I needed to make the next step in this mating dance. *Hell,* I thought, *I had nothing to lose.*

Class was finally over. As she walked out of the building, I stepped to her all cool and nonchalant, but anxious, nonetheless. I opened my mouth.

"I really like you," I said, my voice soft and silky with sincerity.

Shirline smiled that smile and replied with a two-parter, a question and a statement.

"How can you like me? You don't even know me."

I smiled back knowingly, confidently. For me, her smile had said it all. I asked if I could carry her books. She said, no thanks, then pointed into the near distance. I turned and saw a parked car. Then she dropped the bomb.

"My ride is here."

I tried to stay cool as I peeked in the car a little, hoping to see her mother or father, even a big brother or sister behind the wheel. But I didn't. Shirline had made a fool out of me, or so I thought. For a fleeting moment, I had been hopelessly in love. In another instant, the heart that had been so infatuated and knotted with love's loopy hope, crashed into the pit of my stomach.

I turned and started the long, lonesome walk home. It was autumn and the sky, filled with stars and a crescent moon, was almost overwhelmingly beautiful. I thought in that instant that, *yes, the sun, the moon and the stars may rule the sky*, "but women," the word formed into a whisper I barely heard myself, "rule the world."

Shirline had completely hypnotized me and made a fool out of me. She was right: I hardly knew her. But I did realize that night that the world hadn't ended because she had rebuffed me. Tomorrow the sun would rise again, I reminded myself, and so would my hopes.

I made my way home satisfied in the knowledge that I would approach Shirline and try again.

The next day I arrived at school twenty minutes early. I was sitting at my desk when she gracefully strutted past me into class wearing jeans so tight they looked painted on. The slight scent of her perfume scrambled my senses. I hadn't noticed it the day before. She must have worn the jeans and perfume on purpose, knowing that it would drive me crazy. I decided that she was playing games with my head. Although every bone in my body yearned to be with her, I would resist with all my might any attempts she made to control my mind. At least that was the plan.

Just as she had done the day before, she smiled every time she caught me looking up at her. As she walked past me after class, she handed me a note, smiled, and said, "Call me." My knees began to shake and my lips trembled as I sheepishly said, Ok. I didn't bother to look up at the sky as I hurried home, hoping that no one would be on the telephone. It was almost 9:30 p.m. by the time I got home and no one, thank God, was on the phone. I threw down my books, not bothering to shower or brush my teeth, nor see if there was any food left to eat. I picked up the rotary phone and dialed the number she had handed me. My heart thumping with each ring,. She finally answered on the forth.

"Hello, Shirline speaking."

"It's Wayne."

"Oh. How are you doing, Wayne?"

I told her good, and that she had asked me to call her. Then I asked her why had she said that she liked me?

"I don't know. I just do," she replied.

"I like you, too."

We went back and forth for what turned into hours, talking about each other's likes and dislikes and then she dropped another bomb on me. "You know I have a little boy don't you?"

Suddenly I felt as if my emotions had betrayed me. Blinded by lust and beauty, I felt I was being led into the trap of a ready-made family. What would my mother say if I fell for someone who already had a child? It didn't matter. Once again, I was not about to let rational thought get in the way of my feelings. I was thunderstruck. That's all there was to it.

After that night, Shirline and I began to hang out on a regular basis. We went to the movies or walked in the park whenever she could afford a babysitter for her two-year-old. I would often spend time with her in the living room of her aunt's house. Shirline was one of two children. She and her brother lived with her aunt in a small, wood-frame house near Jervay projects. Her mother had died when she was just a little girl. Her aunt took to me right away, saying that I seemed to be a nice young man. She would often fix big meals, like fried chicken, collards and macaroni and cheese for me, whenever I came over. I never bothered to tell my mother about Shirline. Somehow I knew that not telling her was the best available option if I wanted to remain under her roof.

I was drawn to Shirline in every way imaginable. I wanted to be around her all the time. She had a great sense of humor and we laughed a lot. She went out her way to make me feel important. When I told her that I had gotten expelled for engaging in school protests, she responded by saying, "I love a man who fights for what he believes in."

Out of nowhere she once asked me if I could fall in love with a woman who had a child out of wedlock. I told her that it would be easy for me love someone who loved me. I refused to believe that having a child out of wedlock was an irreversible mistake. Then Shirline asked me in a gentle voice that complimented her warm smile, whether I loved her. For a moment, I contemplated the difficulty of determining the difference between love and longing.

● ── ●

Jail is the womb of paranoia.

I can't think of another environment where a person's sanity can be so easily compromised. You don't trust the system. You don't trust the jailer. You don't trust inmates, and you don't trust the women you left behind on the outside. Shirline had promised to stand by me no matter what. She would wait for me even if it took, as she'd said, "forever and a day." Nothing in the many love letters she sent to me gave me any reason to believe otherwise. Yet my paranoid thoughts had, on several occasions, served her an unrelenting indictment accusing her of cheating. Each time she visited me, I would gaze into her deep brown, giving eyes to see if I could find reflected there the shame of a woman who was lying to me and lying with another man.

Crazy. I had no idea what infidelity looked like in a women's eyes, nor did that matter to me as I turned a stone stare on her. It was nothing like the way I stared at her when I met her in Mr. Newsome's classroom.

Several weeks later, turning like a Pavlovian dog to the sound of jangling keys, I looked to see a frightened white man who was standing near the cage door. Jail is one of the few places in America where blacks are guaranteed to be in the majority. The man, who had probably not been this close to black men in his life, peeked inside the cage, then looked incredulously at the officer and shouted, "You got to be crazy if you think I'm going in there with all them niggers."

This man, whose face was beet red, knew full well that after a statement like that, there was no way he would ever be allowed in that cell block. He had decided that he would much rather be in isolation than be amongst the blacks. To guys like him, black people were the scum of the earth. It's an old story, but he had probably been shaped in the same mold of white supremacy that had sanctioned slavery—Jim Crow and organizations such as the KKK and the Rights of White People. To such people, it did not matter whether his crime was first-degree murder or child molestation, in his mind, his skin color made him superior to any black man, regardless of his status.

I could not help thinking that this was the same mentality that had led to the conflict in the schools. There were too many white folks like this guy who could not bear the thought of having to share space with black people. Despite my mother's insistence that I keep believing, it was becoming hard for me to believe that we could receive a fair trial in a system controlled by whites, when even white criminals thought they were better than we were.

● —— ●

One day, early in my first stay in jail, I stood, as I often did there, with my head pressed against the bars. I heard the jailer yelling. "Wayne Moore—front and center." Was I finally getting out? Couldn't be. No way my mother had $1,000 or ten percent of that amount to spring me. That's what it would have cost for a bondsman to stand my bond. I walked briskly to the door of the cage wearing soiled and wrinkled, clothes. "Yes sir," I answered. "Wayne Moore."

I was to prepare to come out in five minutes. I had a visitor. It was my mother. I hadn't combed my hair in three days. I didn't even have a comb. I looked disheveled, like a bum and probably smelled like one too. It was bad enough I was in jail, but my mother would have a fit if she saw the way I looked. Prisoners always like it when someone gets a visitor because it's almost like they get one too. They look forward to any contact they can have with the outside world. I would be asked to deliver several messages through my mother. For instance, a brother I barely knew named Shackdick said, "Tell your mother to tell my brother to come down here and get me out."

Really?

A guy I knew from the streets named Deebee Leebee came over to me and told me the obvious. "Brother, you need to comb your head before you go out there."

He handed me an afro pick. I stepped fast to the steel mirror above the steel sink in my cell and combed my hair. Before long, I saw, staring back at me, a blurry reflection wearing a neat afro. Presentable, I thought.

Before I knew it, I heard the jailer returning. I hurriedly splashed some cold water on my face and adjusted my clothing. I so wished I could have worn some uniform of success, a fine three-piece, pin-striped suit, a crisply ironed shirt, tasteful silk tie, clothing befitting an audience with a queen, because my mother, Dolores Foy Moore, was, in, indeed, a queen.

My mother was the person that I most respected, and to me, she was the smartest person in all the world. That's the only way she could have maneuvered as proudly as she did in the face of such abject poverty. She had been through a lot raising eight kids essentially by herself. She taught us to always hold our heads high. Even if we didn't have a dime in our pockets, she taught us that we had a dream in our heads and the Lord in our hearts. If that wasn't enough to lift your head in mixed company, nothing would. I loved her. I appreciated her considerable common sense and sheer force of will to shelter us from most of the cruelest realities of poverty.

My mother gave birth to me on November 5, 1952—in Harlem. My roots were ripped out of the industrial Northeast when my family moved to a rural area outside of Wilmington in 1958.

My mother, a Southern girl by birth and upbringing, hadn't been able to get her bite of the "Big Apple" in the post-war era of great prosperity for other folks. So when my father's mother, who we called Grandma Hannah back in Castle Hayne, NC, took ill, my mother thought it was an opportunity to return to her own roots and nurse her back to health.

It had been her own mother, Grandma Lease, who had sent her north in the first place, sweeping her up in the Great Migration of millions of black folk escaping the Jim Crow South.

It was in New York City where my mother met Willie Moore, Jr., who had joined the navy shortly after World War II began and was stationed at a naval air station near Atlantic City, New Jersey. When on shore leave, he would often drive into Manhattan to visit friends from back home who moved to New York from North Carolina. People moving to New York from the South were considered "country" by so-called "native" New Yorkers. Homeboys and homegirls usually found each other in the Big Apple, if for no other reason than to be around people they could identify with. It is exactly this dynamic that brought my mother and father together. But in time, urban poverty and crime were beginning to make the "capital of black America" unlivable for so many, including my mother. Dolores Moore, now married and a mother, was ready to leave.

I was very enthusiastic about moving South. Little did I envision, at five years old, the perils of poverty, deprivation, and racism that were yet to come, the whole jumping-from-the-frying-pan-into-the-fire kind of thing. I was a little kid and thought that anything would be better than living in our old apartment building on West 123rd Street.

I remember very little about that trip South except that my mother and father seemed to argue the whole trip. My father was in the navy then, and this was one of the few times that I had ever seen him. Besides the bickering, I was struck by how quickly the city began to fade away, replaced by farms and more farms and a few scattered houses. No more apartment buildings. No more overcrowding. No more hot, smelly subways with victims and victimizers all packed together like pickles in a jar. I assured myself that wherever we were, we would be leaving behind noisy neighbors disturbing my dreams, sirens crying outside my window, and roaches crawling up my nose. My mother made me realize that our lives would be better.

But I soon learned that life Down South would not necessarily be better at all, even as my mother worked so hard to make it so. My Grandma Hannah's house turned out to be even more rundown than the old apartment building in Harlem where we had lived. And in Harlem we never had to battle winter's "hawk" to run out to use the toilet, nor did I have to take baths in a portable tin tub in Harlem. Of course, there was no running water. My brothers Tom, Harold and myself used to take turns walking a half-mile to a well to pump for water.

Before long, I knew just when to feed the hogs and the chickens and take care of other chores that little boys do. I didn't mind feeding the chickens, although I never understood why the hens clucked after they had laid eggs, or why roosters crowed. These strange animals possessed a bit of grace, unlike those ugly, unscrupulous, disgraceful pigs, which would not only eat sour leftovers, and dishwater from meals past, but wouldn't hesitate to devour any form of putrefaction.

Decades later, I still shoved away any meal that included the flesh of that beastly swine.

Once we were settled in Castle Hayne, my father returned to his ship in the navy. Not long after that, my mother divorced him. I thought he would have stayed with us longer, at least long enough for me to get to know him. But he didn't, and it would be a long time before I would ever get to see him again.

Thankfully, my grandmother did get better. And as her condition improved she slowly returned to her kitchen; to her pots and pans. She was one of the best cooks the world has ever known. Her butter beans and okra, buttermilk biscuits, candied yams, and sweet potato pies were unsurpassed. And she was a shrewd little lady, a woman who ran a general store and who had a great deal of respect for traditional values, and very little understanding towards those who violated them.

She had a cure for every ailment. For instance, when a bee stung me once, she dipped some snuff into her mouth and spit the grotesque looking liquid on my wound. When I was too sick to chop wood for the stove, she would arrive at my bedside with a bottle of cod liver oil. Just the smell of the stuff would have me on my feet in minutes. When Grandma Hannah, the healer, was completely healed, she moved to Wilmington, finding a house on McRae Street, named for one of the leaders of the 1898 Massacre. At almost the same time, my mother rented a three-room shack about a mile away from my grandmother's old house in Castle Hayne.

The shack was located on the property owned by people most folks from those parts referred to as Ms. Ethel and Mr. George. The place was so small it must have been used for a tool shed before we moved into it. Again, we had no running water and there was a well pump and outhouse out back. Although we didn't have any hogs or chickens of our own, Mr. George had a large chicken coop on the property. The only animal we owned was a brown, short-haired mutt hound named Skippy. Just like the rest of us, Skippy loved chicken. Every now and then, Skippy would catch one of Mr. George's chickens outside of the coop and have chicken dinner, feathers and all.

Evidently, Mr. George didn't find much humor in Skippy's eating habits. One day, my brother Harold and I, came home from grade school and found Skippy dead in Mr. George's cornfield. Our dog had been shot in the head with buckshot from Mr. George's shotgun. My mother told me that I wasn't a boy given to cry. In fact, until the day Harold and I found Skippy dead, she said I hadn't cried since I was a baby. But, yes, that day I could not hold back the tears.

When Harold and I finally went over to Mr. George's to borrow a shovel to bury our dog, he greeted us with an expressionless look on his face. He simply said, "That crazy dog ate my chickens." To my brother and I, Skippy wasn't crazy; he was just being a dog.

In the meantime, my mother kept her job on a flower farm in Castle Hayne. There, she made a penny for every dozen daffodils or gladiolas that she picked. It was in the early 1960s, and around this time my brother, Willie, was born. There were now four boys and one girl. My sister, Stephanie, had been living with my grandmother at the time we moved away from New York. She followed my grandmother to Wilmington and lived with her there. But for us, we crowded into this one-bedroom shack my mother rented. She felt it right that we four boys sleep in the bedroom, and she slept in what could loosely be called a living room.

Like lots of other poor black people in the community, the little my mother made on the flower farm was not a living wage. Had it not been for the federal food subsidies coming from the Department of Agriculture, we probably would have starved to death

There was a man in my mother's life, and, so, in a way, in our lives too. His name was Charlie. I think he was related to our landlady, Mrs. Ethel. That probably had something to do with us living in the shack. Charlie wasn't much of the fatherly type, but he did help out around the house, and he would help Momma pay the bills.

But like my mother, he also worked on a flower farm, so he didn't make much money either. That didn't stop Charlie and my mother from conceiving my sister, Marva, who was born August 13, 1960, about a year after we moved into the shack. And my mother worked in those hot fields up until the day she gave birth to Marva, and she went right back to the fields a short time after Marva was born. The same was true during the birth of my sister, Jean, who was born a year later.

In 1964, we moved to Wilmington. Shortly after that, my brother Gerald was born. The house that we moved into was larger and nicer than the shack. And it looked like we had landed in a nice neighborhood. My mother had somehow managed to rent this comparatively comfortable home for $45 a month. This move, however, in no way eliminated our poverty stricken condition. It only provided us with a nicer shelter from the storm.

Instead of working in the flower fields, my mother began working as a $3- to $4-a-day maid in homes of white folks. Later, she got a job in a sewing factory, but she continued to work in white folks' homes on weekends and holidays. And when I would sometimes accompany her on these jobs, I would do yard work when I could. But I never got used to having whites address my mother and me as "niggras." And there was a time when I overheard one of our employers on the telephone one afternoon, during my lunch break, saying, "Yeah, that would be just fine, but I don't know whether I'll be able to get my niggras to work on the fourth of July. You know they love to sit around and eat watermelon on the fourth."

This was only a light brush of the broom of racial hatred that I knew my mother faced every day, for years, for me and my brothers and sisters. And she never complained but she did hope for brighter days for us all. And this was the woman, my mother, who appeared before me on the opposite side of the jailhouse's fiber-glass window. I looked into her eyes and saw reflected there the pain of a mother franticly wanting to rescue her child. She always had a good answer for all my questions as I was growing into the man I would be. And on this particular day I was looking for answers.

But before I could say a thing, my mother suddenly smiled, as if to reassure me that everything would be alright.

Then we spoke.

"When do you think I can get out of here?" I asked.

"Wayne," she said, her voice tender yet firm with resolve, "I don't know right now, but you should know I'm doing everything I can. In the meantime, I want you to remember what I taught you: Where there is a will, there is a way."

"Don't ever stop believing."

I listened, as her words seeped into my soul and then finally into my head. I looked into her face and knew all along that I had no reason not to believe her.

My mother had always been there for me, had been everything—mother and father, protector and provider. Momma.

10

TRIAL BY FIRING SQUAD

For me, the start of the summer of 1972 passed like the earth had stood still, stuck on the day that I had gotten arrested, struck down for doing nothing more than standing up. Being-in-jail time isn't anything like being-in-the-streets time. Days never have a way of getting away from you when they are just as locked up as you are. So, when my trial date finally arrived, it seemed strange that my tiny, gray concrete and steel world was starting to spin again. But it was.

It was June 6, and I was supposed to be tried along with my co-defendants who, with me, would eventually be whittled down to the Wilmington Ten, a description that would stick to us forever. The growl in my belly told me that it was time to eat. I looked around thinking that the jailer and his jangling keys should soon be coming to open the cage for chow time.

But instead, my gaze caught some familiar faces standing in front of my cellblock. By suppertime, the rest of my co-defendants, including Ben Chavis, had arrived at the jail. I learned that they had been bused in from various prisons around North Carolina for the trial. It was the first time I had seen any of them since I had been arrested at 4:15 p.m., May 1, and thrown in jail like I didn't deserve any better.

It's hard to describe exactly how I felt when I first saw my co-defendants. We had grown close in our struggle against the indifferent, the racist power structure, and the white vigilantes who vowed to destroy us. Until that day, jail had meant that I was separated from the only people who knew for certain that I had done nothing wrong. I needed people like Ben, and the others who were at Gregory Church, to affirm my innocence.

It wasn't like I had been locked away in solitary confinement. Although there were several other prisoners in the cellblock, I, nonetheless, had felt all alone. Human beings were never meant to be entirely alone in their thoughts. I needed acceptance. I needed camaraderie. Standing there, looking at them waiting to enter my cellblock, another part of me, the part of me reserved for my deepest feelings, was suddenly no longer numb like a foot gone to sleep, too stubborn to awaken. For some reason, I felt safer than I had just moments before. I suddenly felt emboldened as a sense of belonging made me want to smile for the first time in weeks.

I had lost touch with a lot of the brothers and Anne Sheppard. Months before my own arrest, many of them had been arrested and subjected to a series of preliminary hearings. The "well-coordinated raids," as the local press called these sweeps, were a big deal involving the combined efforts of the Wilmington Police Department, the New Hanover County Sheriff's Department, the Alcohol and Firearms Division of the Treasury Department, the State Bureau of Investigation, the Federal Bureau of Investigation and the District Solicitor's Office. Also long before this dragnet snatched me up, there were hearings concerning the charge of assault on emergency personnel brought against Ben and his bodyguard, Marvin Patrick. Police continually claimed that the two were part of a group of militant blacks that exchanged gunfire with the Wilmington police on February 6, 1971, the night that Mike's Grocery went up in flames.

During that exchange, patrolman H. F. Gene was wounded in the leg. No surprises there. But those same hearings did offer up a shock. The chief witness for the state would be none other than Allen Hall, a teenager we called " Big Al"—for good reason.

He had gotten the nickname "Big Al" for being a fiercely imposing man, weighing well over 200 unforgiving pounds. A year before, he brutally attacked a white girl who was a student at New Hanover High. I don't know why he did this. I don't think anyone knew. Hall had reportedly been in and out of mental institutions most of his life. Reason and Allen Hall never rhymed. He never scored more than eighty-two on any IQ tests. While I was jailed, I learned that Hall had confessed to authorities that he was guilty of rioting, burning Mike's Grocery down, and assaulting emergency personnel. The courts apparently got right down to business, sentencing Big Al to twelve years behind bars for all of that.

But I didn't believe any of it. Whatever you call him, Big Al or Allen Hall, *no way*, was all I could think when I heard this.

Hall, who was seventeen at the time of the trials, was like so many other young brothers back then. He found himself in a compromising position; facing jail time and legal counsel that was, at best, inadequate, and at worse, non-existent. I can't get into the man's head, but he probably figured that he had to do what he had to do. In this case, that was to serve the head of Ben Chavis on a dirty, prison paper platter. Even a guy with a borderline IQ can figure out that local law enforcement wanted Ben Chavis, and if he could deliver him, he might be able to cut a deal for leniency, maybe even earn a crisp, new get-out-of-jail card.

Ben never saw it coming.

But to this day, I have never blamed Allen Hall for what happened to the Wilmington Ten. He was manipulated. Prosecutors Allan Cobb and James Stroud, both white, and Wilmington police department detectives, W.C. Brown and Clarence Fredlaw, both black, took advantage of Hall. Big Al was clearly a mentally challenged man, but that didn't seem to matter as long as they could get their man, Ben Chavis. The rest of us were simply cover, collateral damage.

These "public servants" must have all known that everything that Hall had told them about the boycotters, Gregory Church, the burning of Mike's Grocery, and the sniper fire, was not true. Yet they allowed Hall to take the stand at a pretrial hearing and implicate sixteen people in crimes they did not commit. Worse, neither did he witness or could he even have known about events he swore he had witnessed.

Judge Gilbert Burnett accepted Hall's testimony, finding probable cause for placing eleven of the original sixteen of us on trial. The charges? Burning an unoccupied dwelling, and conspiracy to assault emergency personnel. Bound over for trial were: Ben Chavis, Marvin Patrick, Willie Vereen, Connie Tindall, Jerry Jacobs, James McKoy, Joe Wright, Reginald Epps, Anne Sheppard, George Kirby—and me.

George Kirby fled to New York after being released on bond. He didn't return to Wilmington until years later, and he was never tried. I thought about running, too, but I didn't know where to go to buy a ticket to that faraway place that Martin Luther King, Jr., talked about, that place where "justice rolls down like waters and righteousness like a mighty stream."

At the preliminary hearings, one judge, Gilbert Burnett, laughed after Allen Hall had physically attacked our attorney and Ben. Years later, in a documentary on the Wilmington Ten, Burnett suggested that Big Al's attack on Ben influenced his decision to bind us all over for trial. I'm not sure of the logic of his thinking on that.

In a previous court session on an unrelated matter, Burnett's friend and fellow judge, Johnny Walker, made a telling statement from the bench: "Maybe we should have brought in Lieutenant Calley to go in there and clean the place up," he said, clearly referring to the U.S. Army officer responsible for the 1968 My Lai massacre of hundreds of unarmed civilians in South Vietnam. I'm assuming "the place" was Gregory Church where we organized and hunkered down against attacks by the Klan and the Rights of White People and the like minded.

So, a sitting judge had wanted us dead. Having heard about this, I was convinced that it would be unlikely that we would ever receive a fair trial in my home state. But, I still hoped that we would not be convicted on the manufactured testimony of a mentally disturbed witness. That would be too obvious a miscarriage of justice, even for North Carolina.

Our lawyers requested a change of venue to Onslow County, which is about an hour north of Wilmington. That request was denied. Instead, the trial was set to be heard closer to home; the Pender County Courthouse in Burgaw, NC. At one point in history, Pender County was part of New Hanover County, but separated in 1875, making it the last of state's 100 counties to be formed. It seemed to be a good idea to W.H. James, who was a civil engineer working for the Wilmington & Weldon Railroad.

On February 6, 1876, the railroad company deeded some land for the development of Burgaw, which has the oldest railroad depot in the state. At the same time, construction was authorized on Burgaw's courthouse, built where it still stands, at the center of town on "Courthouse Square." At first glance, it looks like a green island of tranquility, with the generous shade of giant oaks and great sprays of azaleas, magnolias and drapes of Spanish moss. But for us, the courthouse was nothing less than a gateway to hell.

Each time I entered that courthouse, a place where we would later be joined by supporters that included the black liberation activist and intellectual, Angela Davis, I could not stop believing that the entire North Carolina judicial system and most of the people in it were racist. Why else would high school students be sitting before a judge and facing hundreds of years in prison? All that we had done was to speak out against the injustices in the school system. We were Americans who had acted in the best traditions of Americans. But I guess when you hyphenate Americans with "black" the rules change.

Our first trial barely made it past jury selection.

After our legal team successfully seated ten blacks and two whites, the prosecutor, Assistant New Hanover County District Attorney James T. "Jay" Stroud, Jr., told Judge Joshua James that he had developed severe stomach pains and had to be hospitalized. Judge James, who would later write a long article declaring the lack of bias in the Southern judicial system, declared a mistrial.

This was a terrible blow for our side because our legal team was satisfied that the first group of jurors was willing to hear the evidence and act fairly and impartially. One immediate good thing did come about because of the mistrial: Judge James reduced our bonds and we were all released pending a new trial. Bond was posted by the newly formed Ben Chavis Legal Defense fund. Thanks mostly to the case against us, most of us were jobless and living with our families, and couldn't afford to pay for our bond and defense.

The cases against high school students Tommy Atwood, Michael Peterson, Cornell Flowers, and James Bunting were dropped for no reason I ever learned about.

Years later, we would learn that the mistrial was a scam. Stroud had faked his illness so he could press the reset button on the trial. We were going back to court but this time with a jury impaneled more to his liking, one composed, according to his own notes, of mostly "KKK" and "Uncle Tom" type jurors.

Extensive notes scribbled by Stroud on the back of one of his legal pads, revealed a systematic approach to infusing the trial with racism, and weighing the advantages and disadvantages of having the judge declare a mistrial in the case. Decades later,

Ferguson would note that, "Most people don't list the pros and cons of getting sick."

Disappointed in Stroud's apparent inability to obtain justice Southern style, the good ole boys of Southern judiciary moved not to take any chances for a second trial. This time they called on the services of North Carolina's Attorney General, Robert Burren Morgan. Early in his political career, Morgan was considered a conservative because of his allegiance to his former Wake Forest School of Law professor and conservative politician, I. Beverly Lake, Sr. Lake had run a George Wallace-like, pro-segregation campaign for governor in 1960, and failed.

But by the time Morgan, who had been an influential state senator, became state attorney general in 1969, he was considered a moderate. Nevertheless, for the Wilmington Ten, Morgan assigned Robert Martin to hear the case. Then Morgan assigned a special prosecutor, Dale Johnson, to assist Stroud in prosecuting the case against us.

Martin set the new trial date for September 11, 1972.

◦ —— ◦

As the trial was about to begin, our attorneys—James E. Ferguson II, Charles Becton, Frank Balance, and John Harmon— were convinced of one thing; no fair and impartial jury could or would convict us based on the testimony of criminals like Allen Hall. In the meantime, we were refining our own witnesses. For example, my sister, Stephanie, and her husband, were prepared to testify that I had been at their home babysitting my two young nephews the night that Mike's Grocery burned more than a mile away.

The day before the second trial was to begin, eight of my co-defendants and I (Sheppard had her own legal counsel, Mathias Hunevol, so she did not attend) met with our defense staff for a strategy session at the Ramada Inn on Market Street.

There, we decided that none of us would take the stand or call any witnesses in our defense. The decision not to testify was made primarily because the two witnesses essential to our defense were nowhere to be found.

Rev. Eugene Templeton, the brave pastor of Gregory Congregational Church, and his wife, Donna Templeton, had fled the state. They could clearly set the record straight about the Wilmington Ten and the whereabouts of at least half of my co-defendants the night of the Mike's Grocery fire. Five of them, including Ben Chavis, were in the Templeton's parsonage house next to the church when the grocery store caught fire.

Following a visit of an unidentified white man to the Templeton's home on a Sunday in mid February 1971, the Templetons greatly feared for their lives. The man left, firing shots at the Templeton house. This sent the two of them scrambling out their backdoor as the shots rang out. They escaped by climbing their backyard fence, finding refuge with a neighbor and spending the rest of the night in the neighbor's house. The next morning, the Templetons ducked into the backseat of Ben's car and headed, with Ben at the wheel, for the Southside Bridge and out of town.

Although the Templetons were scheduled to testify at our trial, they said that they couldn't in the wake of a new wave of death threats and a new fear that they would somehow be arrested if they showed up for court. The Templetons did manage to testify at a post–conviction hearing held five years later in Burgaw. But they never again returned to Wilmington until 2011, long divorced and leading entirely separate and different lives.

Without our two key witnesses, we ended up going to court with our fate resting solely on the fairness of a court and a jury that would prove to be predisposed to rendering guilty verdicts across the board. It was like being trapped in a bad television courtroom drama and you couldn't change the station, or turn it off.

"All rise!" bellowed the bailiff as Judge Martin, silver-haired and black-robed, entered the courtroom. "Oh yes, oh yes, oh yes, order in the court, Judge Robert Martin presiding. Please be seated."

There was not enough room at the defense table inside the crowded courtroom, so all ten of us—including Anne Sheppard and her lawyer—were seated, elbow-to-elbow, on a hard, wooden bench behind the defense table. The trial, like most trials, started with a lot of procedural stuff, including instructions to the jurors, and explanations of the various charges against us, and then a grilling of each of us to determine that we were as poverty-stricken as we had claimed. The real start of the trial was when Stroud opened with his big fish of a witness: Allen Hall who appeared to be every inch Big Al.

The hardest thing about those early days of the trial was having to sit there listening to Hall describing the burning of Mike's Grocery.

Besides it all being nothing less than amateur theater, the mere mention of that grocery store flashed me back to that night when Wilmington burned like trash heaps under a moon-lit night. I sat there free associating, wondering if my hometown had burned like that when Union soldiers stormed into it, animating some of the final scenes of the Civil War. I had read that Northern forces left only a knot or two of defiant rebel soldiers singing "Dixie" as they ran off to relative safety. In the distance, voices had been heard yelling the battle cry of the Confederacy, some wishful thinking about the South rising again.

Sitting in that courtroom a century later, with memorials to the Confederate dead standing guard on the courthouse lawn, I wondered just how far we had come. Had the South with its devotion to black oppression and degradation, in fact, risen again? After all, here we were nine black men and a white woman who had the audacity to work with us—all innocent of any crime—

facing little less than a polite lynch mob that never raised its voice. I never heard a rebel yell in that courthouse; I never saw a rebel flag there, either. But I could definitely feel the cold hand of Dixie injustice tightening around my black neck—tighter and tighter with each passing day of that trial. My stomach clenched and my palms sweat with this truth.

Before the proceedings, we had all walked tall up a flight of steps into the red-brick courthouse, flanked by our group of big time black lawyers of whom Ferguson was the most prominent. Ferguson was one of the leading civil rights attorneys in the state. His booming voice belied his slender build, while accentuating his amazing gift of oratory. He had been the lead attorney or simply involved in almost every recent civil rights case in North Carolina. He had irritated the KKK so much with his courtroom genius that the Klan had targeted him for assassination.

His law partner, Julius Chambers, was almost killed in 1965 when the Klan bombed his car.

Ferguson's arrival in Wilmington to represent the Wilmington Ten had been preceded by a controversial and much publicized case in Oxford, NC, Ben Chavis' hometown. In that case, a white man, Robert Teel, and his son, Larry, had been charged with brutally murdering twenty-three-year-old Henry "Dickey" Marrow after a dispute that involved Larry's wife.

Marrow was Ben's first cousin.

There had been overwhelming evidence that the Teels had murdered Marrow in broad daylight on May 12, 1970, while he begged for his life outside their convenience store located in a rural neighborhood near Highway 158 just outside of Oxford. They called the place, "Grab-all."

Like a warm-up for our case, the same Judge Martin had presided over that trial, and our lawyer, James Ferguson, had assisted in the prosecution of that case.

The Teels were found not guilty, and black Oxford exploded into riots. Though Ben was never officially accused of participating in the burning of several tobacco warehouses, the very kind of retribution arsons common in slave rebellions, the local newspaper pointed to him as the person most responsible for inciting the riots.

A little less than a year later, Martin and Ferguson were facing each other again as gladiators in an arena where words and ideas were their sharpest weapons. But this time, Ferguson was leading a defense team consisting of other no nonsense black legal minds.

The trial went badly from the start. That became apparent from the moment Judge Martin ordered the bailiff to bring in the jury, supposedly a jury of our peers. Webster's Dictionary defines peer as "one that is of equal standing with another... One belonging to the same societal group, especially based on age, grade or status." As this jury—ten whites and two blacks— walked silently to its seats in the jury box, I felt the true tilt of imbalance that my blackness registered on the scales of justice.

During the jury selection, Ferguson asked a potential juror if he or any member of his family had ever been a member of a racist or clandestine organization, such as the KKK. Stroud immediately objected, and that objection was sustained by Martin. And there would be more outrages to fairness.

When another juror said he believed we were guilty; and that we would have to prove our innocence, Ferguson asked Judge Martin to remove this juror for cause. Martin asked the juror if he could disabuse his mind of all past and present biases. The juror answered yes. Martin then informed Ferguson that he found no reason to remove this juror. I could see the eight-hundred-pound kangaroo sitting in the middle of the courtroom. Again, I was reminded that there would be no justice here.

Once the jury had been selected, Ferguson filed a motion in Superior Court challenging the glaring racial imbalance of white to black jurors. He asked that the jury selection in Pender County be investigated in our case. He also charged that Stroud was using his prosecutor's prerogative to systematically eliminate prospective black jurors—a direct (but often tolerated practice in American courts to this day) violation of the equal protection clause of the Fourteenth Amendment of the U.S. Constitution.

Stroud had, in fact, used forty-one of his forty-two preemptory challenges to dismiss forty-one potential black jurors. And we learned that the county's black population was 43 percent (larger than New Hanover County's black population), while only 20 to 25 percent of the potential juror's pool was black.

Despite this, Judge Martin ruled against Ferguson's motion. With that, it felt to me like the entire North Carolina judicial system was out to crush us, just like the court in New Hanover County had crushed our student boycott a year earlier.

I slowly looked around at all the mothers, their faces stern and drawn with anxiety, in the courtroom during one of the early days of the Wilmington Ten trial. Then I saw the absence. Where had all our fathers gone? Most of our mothers were front and center in the courtroom. Ben's father had passed away on October 14, 1965, but for most of the eight other black men on trial that day, the question remained: Where were our fathers?

I had wondered if there was a connection, a thread of fatherly want and loss, which had tied us all to our fate? Had we, boys, been forced to act, too soon and unprepared, as men because we had no men to do the warrior's chore of protecting and defending us, our families, our community?

It was the heel of the white man's boot that had encouraged us to struggle to fight for what was rightfully ours during the boycott. We simply got tired of getting kicked around by that boot. Once I looked up again at Judge Martin sitting in his big plush chair at the bench, and then over to my lawyers. The contrast to the sheer, naked power before me, I slumped my head and said softly to myself, "We don't stand a chance in hell of walking out of this courtroom free men." I wish I could have found a reassuring nod from my father to keep me hoping for more. But, of course, I didn't.

❋ ─── ❋

Shortly after Grandma Hannah moved to Wilmington, I remember my mother making my brother Harold and I dress up in our best clothes, and then marching us a half mile down to Highway 117 in Castle Hayne to catch the Greyhound bus to Wilmington. We were going to see my father. I never looked forward to these trips because he felt like an absolute stranger to me. He never did anything to change my feelings about him. He never made me feel that I was important to him.

The worst of it was that this man who gave me little more than my last name, acted like he thought that he was better than the woman he had married, and the children he had sired with her. I never felt guilty about going through his pants and stealing his pocket change whenever he would fall asleep during those visits. As a kid, I asked myself why my father couldn't have been someone who would take me fishing and hunting, or take me to see the Yankees or the Knicks play? Why couldn't he have been someone who did more than provide the seed of my existence on this earth?

As a kid, I would let myself fantasize, like kids do, seeing my father at the wheel of a station wagon, driving me and the family cross country to Yellowstone Park, to the Grand Canyon, like those white families I saw on the television of our next-door neighbor, a lady named Mrs. Janie. She had lived across the road from my Grandma Hannah, who didn't own a TV at the time.

I don't remember when, but at one point someone told me that life wasn't fair, deal with it. Still, it has always bothered me that I never got to really know my father, that my only memories of him are those of a man who showed up every now and then in a U.S. Navy uniform, saying that he was my father. I never established a relationship with him, but my sister Stephanie and my brother Harold did. Because Stephanie had mostly lived with my father's mother, Grandma Hannah, she was able to see him more and see a better side of him than I did. My brother Harold only got to know the old man later in life, when he was in his mid-twenties, and deciding to go into the navy.

He sought out our father's advice, and that seemed to open some sort of door that I couldn't. As far as I know, none of my other siblings got any closer to my father than I did. Even so, I never hated him. Besides, if my mother didn't hate him, why should I? I kept telling myself that life isn't fair. I was about to get another severe lesson in just how unfair life could be in the Pender County Courthouse in Burgaw, NC.

I found it hard to take my eyes off of Big Al. I found it even harder to wipe the look of pure disbelief off my face as I listened to this burly, dark-skinned black man with a scraggly afro and unkempt mustache. He was given a lot of time to speak as the prosecution's chief witnesses, probably the first and last time he had been chief anything.

Allen Hall was an angry man. He had been waiting for quite some time to get back at Ben Chavis for not bailing him out after he was arrested for hitting that white girl at New Hanover High in March of 1971, following the February riots there. Hall, like a lot of us, looked on Ben as if he was some sort of hero. But Hall had badly miscalculated when he thought that Ben would look upon him as a hero once he told Ben that he and another guy, Willie Lee Jones, had firebombed Mike's Grocery.

I'd heard that Ben Chavis was livid when Hall told him that he had set fire to the grocery store. I heard that Ben called him a "stupid muthafucka" to his face and told him that he needed to leave town immediately. Supposedly, Ben had given him a one-hundred-dollar bill and sent him to New York with a man named Tom Houston. When Hall suddenly reappeared in Wilmington, he was promptly arrested and Ben would have nothing to do with him.

Hall's mother posted $200 to get him released on bail. Months later, on February 13, 1972, he gave a statement to police implicating Ben Chavis, and the rest of us, in the burning of Mike's Grocery.

My first clear memory of Allen Hall had been in the summer of 1971, months after that terrible week in February. I first saw him at one of the rallies Golden Frinks was holding in town. But I didn't actually meet him until I had joined Golden for a march to Washington, DC, later that year. We rode up to DC in the back of a U-haul truck. Hall rode almost the whole trip with this frightened look on his face. He looked tormented as a group of brothers, also going to the march with us, picked on him, calling him a "dumbass." I noticed from that point on that people always made fun of Big Al. He was an easy, slow-moving, slow-thinking target.

I tried hard to remember whether I'd ever laughed at him or made fun of him. I am sure I probably had. I guess that fact adds more weight to the saying, especially in my case, "He who laughs last, laughs best."

I was ripped from my thoughts about Big Al when I heard him blurt out from his perch on the witness stand, "Wayne Moore is the one sitting between Marvin Patrick and Connie Tindall with the red, black, and green knit sweater." I looked down at my sweater, hoping he could not possibly be referring to me. But I was the only one wearing such a sweater.

Big Al identified each of us to the court, one by one, as if we had been lifelong friends. The truth was that while at Gregory, he hadn't known most of us from Adam, and none of us crammed on that hard bench in court had ever been friends with him— except for Anne Sheppard.

Word on the street was that Big Al and Big Anne were having a sexual relationship. No one seemed to care that he was a teenager at the time and she was in her early thirties. And not much was said about him being black and she being white. But there were lots of jokes about the anatomic challenges their plus-size bodies may have posed to their physical passions. To us, Big Al had been a living punch line.

Did I laugh? Yeah, probably.

But again, the joke was on us. In the Pender County courthouse, Big Al was turning the tables and the joke was on us; he was making us pay for all the jokes made at his expense, for all the humiliation he had suffered at the hands of us and others like us. He was using the powers of a racist, black-life-devouring judicial system to get his revenge.

By the time of the trial, most of us had heard rumors on the street that Big Al, Willie Lee Jones, and another guy, known only as Brown, had gone to Mike's Grocery and tried to buy some wine. Mike refused to sell to them, saying that they were already drunk and that there had been rioting in the city the night before. Supposedly, they had cursed Mike Poulos and threatened to burn down his store. They left and returned with gasoline and had done just that, according to the talk around the neighborhood.

And despite suspicions that Mike burned down his own store that February 6 night in 1971, Hall confessed after he had gotten arrested on an unrelated charge in the fall of 1971. He told police that he had destroyed the grocery store. I sat in that courtroom listening to Big Al layer lie upon lie, like a brick layer building prison walls to entomb us. It was only recently that it occurred to me how incredible it was that a mentally challenged man who really didn't know me could identify me from over 200 people at Gregory Church; how amazing it was that he could claim that there was a gun in one of my hands, and a firebomb in the other, then describe in vivid detail how I'd used such weapons for two days and nights, and how astounding it was that he provided all of this flood of information without tremendous help and coaching and gave the same testimony against the nine other defendants. Yet, somehow he managed to remember, in precise detail, everything the ten of us had worn, done and said over the two-day period in Gregory Church. For anyone to believe him, they would have to believe that a soldier in the middle of combat, and in the black of night, could actually recall in vivid detail the exact location of each of his comrades while counting the shots coming from each of nine weapons. That would be insane.

Even a genius with a photographic memory could not have done that, especially when you consider that the events of February 5-6, 1971, had happened under the worst conditions imaginable.

For instance, Allen Hall testified in court that there were fires and bullets flying all around him in the church during those days. And yet he had coolly picked me and the others out of a stack of photographs taken by police photographer David Louis Turner at boycott rallies and at Steve Mitchell's funeral. He spoke with so much detail. And remember, Allen Hall had never come in contact with any of us at Gregory until he supposedly arrived at the church on February 5, 1971. Certainly before that, he had never participated in the boycott.

I understand how I had been a likely suspect. I had been one of the nineteen students expelled from school for participating and leading the boycott at John T. Hoggard High School. I had been bold as I roamed the school's halls wearing my liberation colors, demanding justice and inciting others to boycott. In handwritten notes, Superintendent Heywood Bellamy had identified me as a trouble-maker for fighting in the school and encouraging students to boycott.

None of that made me an arsonist or a shooter of emergency workers. But apparently the testimony of Allen Hall, and two other corroborating prosecution witnesses who, like Hall, would, years later, recant their stories, was enough to convince a jury that we were arsonists and snipers.

For example, when prosecutors asked Allen Hall if he saw Ben Chavis with a weapon in Gregory Church, this is what he said under oath during our trial.

Hall: He had a .45 automatic.

Stroud: Where was it located?

Hall: He toted it in on his side in a holster.

Stroud: Did he have it in his possession at the time he was talking over the microphone?

Hall: Yes sir.

Stroud: After the defendant Chavis made the statement that you have referred to in church, what if anything happened then, please?

Hall: Then Chavis and Marvin Patrick started handing out guns.

None of that happened. Most of his testimony was a fiction, a stage play, to place Ben Chavis at the scene of every major incident reported by police during the turmoil of February 1971. Some of the incidents did actually happen, but not when Ben and I and other members of the Wilmington Ten were there, and certainly not witnessed by Allen Hall. His physical description of Gregory Church is amazingly detailed, probably better than what Rev. Templeton, the church's pastor, could recite from memory the way Hall did on the stand.

Actually, most of Hall's testimony was about events that took place away from Gregory, and they had the officious smell of police reports, too precise for a mentally challenged, under educated teenager.

Ferguson would go on to characterize Hall's testimony, as well as the only other witnesses to directly testify against us— teenagers Jerome Mitchell and Eric Junious—as nothing less than "scripted."

"They have all been rehearsed," Ferguson said of the testimony. "They have all been rehearsed by the State. The State is director, producer, and scriptwriter. Everything had been rehearsed.

"This case," Ferguson told the courtroom, "is simply this: It is an attempt to get Chavis. That is what this case is really all about, an attempt to get Reverend Ben Chavis."

11

THE CURTAIN CLOSES
ON SHOW TRIAL, AMERICAN-STYLE

THE CHARACTERS

James Ferguson II: Black male, young lead attorney for the defense, five years out of law school

James "Jay" Stroud: White male, ambitious prosecuting attorney in his early 30s

Judge Robert M. Martin: White male presiding judge, middle-aged

Allen Ray "Big Al" Hall: Black male, mentally challenged prosecution witness, 17

Jerome Mitchell: Black male prosecution witness, convicted murderer, 17

Eric "Motor Mouse" Junious: Black male prosecution witness, troubled delinquent, 13

Wayne Moore: Black male defendant, soft-spoken student leader, 19

Benjamin F. Chavis: Black male defendant, black rights activist, advisor to student boycott, 24

Connie Tindall: Black male defendant, former high school football star, 21

Marvin Eugene "Chili" Patrick: Black male defendant, student leader, 19

Reginald Bernard Epps: Black male defendant, student leader, 18

Jerry Jacobs: Black male defendant, married and father, 19

James Matthew "Honey Bun" McKoy: Black male defendant, popular bass guitar player, 19

Willie Earl Vereen: Black male defendant, student leader and talented drummer, 18

William Dallas (Joe) Wright lll: Black male, student leader, aspiring lawyer,19

Anne Sheppard: white female defendant, federal anti-poverty program worker, 35

THE SETTING

The action takes place in 1972 in the Old South. Nine young black men, most of them teenagers, and a white woman, are on trial in the Superior Court Division in Burgaw, North Carolina, for the firebombing of a small, white-owned store, Mike's Grocery, on February 6, 1971, in neighboring Wilmington. All but Anne Sheppard are charged with shooting at emergency workers on the scene. The burning of the store, located at 602 South Sixth Street, was part of a wave of violence and arson that rocked the old port city that had been struggling for more than a year to integrate its public schools. **Benjamin Chavis,** who is a co-defendant in the case, emerged as the leader of a resurgent black power youth struggle in Wilmington. **Wayne Moore,** one of the student leaders of a county-wide black boycott of the area's public schools, also a co-defendant, provides the point of view of the story of racially inspired injustice and then eventual redemption.

ACT THREE

SCENE TWO

(The sun is shining through the high courthouse windows. It is mid-morning, and Allen Hall is on the witness stand as attorney James Stroud is leading his direct examination for the prosecution.)

Stroud: As you went back to the area between the third and fourth house on Sixth Street that you have described, what, if anything, occurred at that time, please? (The courtroom is gripped in a tense silence.)

Hall: (His words start slow, but build steam the longer he talks) After Chavis had told Reginald Epps to go on between the house and Wayne Moore, then Chavis then told us to go across the street and firebomb Mike's, and he told me to throw Willie Earl Vereen two firebombs, and then he told me to take the can of gasoline with me.

Stroud: Where was the can of gasoline at that time?

Hall: The can of gasoline was still sitting between the third and fourth house in the driveway.

Stroud: What, if anything, did you observe about Joe Wright at this time, the defendant Joe Wright?

Ferguson: Objection!

Judge Martin: Overruled!

Hall: (His eyes sparkle like he's about to cry, or laugh) Joe Wright had a pistol and a gun, and he had a field jacket with a white tape and a cross on the back of it. And he had this glue on the back of it that would shine at night. He had bullets taped on the back of the jacket also.

Stroud: Where was he at this time?

Hall: At this time he was standing between the third and fourth house.

Stroud: Did you see where, if any[where], please, he went to?

Hall: Yes, sir, he went behind the fourth house between there.

Stroud: Now after Chavis made the statement that you have described about going to Mike's?

Hall: Then we went across the street to Mike's Grocery.

Stroud: Who is "we"?

Hall: (Voice resolute) Myself, Marvin Patrick, James McKoy, Connie Tindall and Jerry Jacobs.

Stroud: Where was the defendant Chavis at this time?

Hall: Chavis was standing on Sixth Street facing Mike's.

Stroud: Which side of the street was he on?

Hall: He was standing on the east side of the street.

Stroud: Across from Mike's?

Hall: Right.

Stroud: What, if anything, did he have in his possession at this time?

Hall: He still had this .45 automatic.

Hall was so invested in this alternative universe that he was inhabiting that when grilled about his "facts" by James Ferguson II, our lead defense attorney, he whirled himself into a blathering rage during a pretrial hearing. He actually lunged from the witness stand and threw himself across the defense's table, scattering papers and people, to attack Ferguson and Ben who were seated together.

It took six officers to pull Big Al off Ferguson, and then restrain him.

I know it might sound overly dramatic, but that was exactly how the courtroom scene played, day after day, week after week, opening on September 11, 1972, and closing on October 17 of the same year. Our trial really felt like we were in some sort of stage play. It certainly played to a full house. And our chief attorney, James Ferguson, would never let us or the jury or the court in general forget that the prosecution's three main witnesses—Allen Hall, Jerome Mitchell and Eric "Motor Mouse" Junious—were giving testimony that was just as much scripted and rehearsed as anything seen and heard on the Broadway stage.

Even more damning were the bad actors who were trying to portray fair and honest eyewitnesses doing their civic duty to report on wrongdoing. Consider who they were. I was convinced that Hall was doing his best to use the trial to get back at Ben for not bailing him out of some previous and totally unrelated mess; and Big Al was getting back at some of us for bullying him. I don't think he knew, or maybe he just didn't care, that the

State of North Carolina was using him to sell their weak script to the public that the prosecution of the Wilmington Ten had something to do with law and order.

What Wilmington and North Carolina was really saying through our trial was that "outside agitators" like Ben Chavis were not going to march into town and disrupt business as usual. The real message of our trial was that nothing had really changed in and around Wilmington: black oppression would go on, as it had from the Johnny Rebel-rousing of Hugh McRae, and the Secret Nine that gave us the Massacre of 1898 to the Rights of White People that hounded and hunted us almost a century later.

As Hall lied his ass off during the trial, there were times when I looked up at him and I wanted to kill him. I looked up at Big Al wondering how he rationalized ruining the lives of people he didn't really know. Then I realized what I was seeing on the stand was not so much the man, but the shadow of a roaring racist lion, licking its chops and ready to gobble up its prey, the Wilmington Ten. I hated Hall for this, and then, a moment later, I wanted to hug and protect him.

Hall was one of us, mauled and torn like the rest of us by the bloody claws and jaws of racism. He was just too dumb to realize it. I am sure of this. No wonder he, and his collaborating witnesses Mitchell and Junious, had trouble keeping their lies straight on the stand. Their testimony was, I strongly believe, nothing more than a script that had been conceived, written and delivered to convict Ben and put him away for a very, very long time—and the rest of the Wilmington Ten for good measure.

During the trial, we were repeatedly portrayed as a bunch of thugs who had no respect for the law. I kept looking up at Hall, Mitchell and Junious. Then I would glance toward Ferguson, hoping that he would have a Matlock moment and that Hall would confess that it was him and Willie Lee Jones who fire-bombed Mike's Grocery that cold February night. None of us has ever denied defending Gregory Church. We acknowledged that there were guns at the church and that there had been several gun battles.

But none of us had anything to do with Mike's getting burned down or had shot at anyone who came to save it and the surrounding neighborhood. There were times when I wanted to jump up in the middle of that stuffy courthouse and yell, "Cut!" Of course, I never did. I was held down by invisible chains, forced to listen to the likes of James Mitchell feed us to that lion so his sorry ass might escape.

Mitchell, who was seventeen at the time of the trial, had the dubious distinction of being declared—just a month before the trial started—an "outlaw." North Carolina was the last state in America where, like in the old cowboy days, someone considered by the state to be a fugitive from justice could be singled out to be shot on sight. Jerome Mitchell became just such a person when he fled prosecution in connection with the murder of a white store owner, Billy Futch, in Wilmington in 1971.

Mitchell's status actually meant that anyone acting, for instance, like the bounty hunter Jamie Foxx portrayed in *Django Unchained,* could capture him or, if Mitchell resisted, legally put a bullet in his head.

Mitchell managed to make it to New Jersey where he was captured. Soon after he was returned to North Carolina, he agreed to turn State's witness against the Wilmington Ten. He was promptly sentenced as a youthful offender to one day to thirty years in the killing of Futch and the armed robbery of the man's store. The jury didn't seem to consider that Mitchell might be bargaining our freedom for us. Worse, none of us remember ever seeing Mitchell at Gregory Church. I could not imagine this murderer committing himself to anything more than his selfish wants and violent needs. He was nobody's revolutionary.

Even more incredible was the jury's apparent openness to the other collaborating witness, a thirteen-year-old kid who seemed to always be in trouble at school and with the law. Still, Eric "Motor-mouth" Junious testified against us, and again, talking with so much damning detail that he had to be told what to say, to mug lady justice the way he did.

The way the prosecution was making its case against us was that it had one witness, Allen Hall, to connect us to the crime, and then Mitchell and Junious to connect us to the scene of the crime. The only serious problem with that was that each of these witnesses lied under oath.

As the trial was coming to a close, James Ferguson, our attorney, captured what we had faced in Gregory Church. We should not have been defendants; we should have been heroes. And no matter what the verdict was that fall of 1972, we were heroes for millions of people in America and the world who believed in truth and justice.

Ferguson said of us in his summation:

> It's sort of like if somebody comes around to your house and starts sniping at your house. You don't have any obligation to leave home. You can stand your ground, and you can defend yourselves with whatever it takes. And I submit to you, ladies and gentlemen, that although all of us are against violence as means for accomplishing an end - I think all of us believe in right of self-defense. I think that President Nixon would say that he is against violence, but he believes the Vietnamese people had a right to stand their ground.
>
> So we are in Vietnam fighting a war. Now we have a situation here where the people are in the church and somebody wants them out. Somebody is mad with them and they got some grievances, and they feel like

they are right and what happens? Some people started shooting at the church.

Now a lot of people in the community in Wilmington, North Carolina, just like a lot of people in other places, didn't like the idea of what was going on down at the church. And they read about the shooting, and burning, and they jumped to some conclusions, they were upset, and no doubt they started to call people on the telephone and complain and so you know in the classic sense we might say that Wilmington had a problem.

But I am willing to say to you that Wilmington had a problem before February 5 and 6, 1971. Wilmington is going to have a problem after February 5 and 6, 1971, because it's going to be a long time before people learn to live together.

We have got to do it at some stage, but it's not going to happen overnight.

I am willing to submit to you that the mere fact that some students from New Hanover High School and whatever other high school is down there decided to stand on their ground, on Holy ground, you might say, that the mere fact that they made that decision was not because of any problems that Wilmington might have thought they had or may have had because I submit the problems were there before. So let's not blame people because they pointed out a problem. Let's praise them for having the courage to do so."

The trial went to the jury at 5:20 p.m. on a Tuesday evening of October 17, 1972.

At 8:20, three hours later, the jury returned, sat and delivered its verdicts.

We were all told to stand. And I had to admit that I was nervous. So much was at stake. I had been thinking through the six weeks of the trial, through the parade of photographs and charts and some ninety pieces of "evidence," and all through the testimony, forty witnesses put on the stand to condemn us with hearsay, conjecture and plain old lies, through all of that, we might very well be found not guilty. At worse, we'd be found guilty and get probation. That old saying about the truth setting you free was ringing in my head. I knew we had not burned anything. I knew we had not conspired with anyone to shoot anyone. The jury would have to know that, too.

The jury's foreman, a man named John W. Menth, handed the verdicts to the court's bailiff who then handed them to Judge Martin. A moment later everyone in courtroom knew what the jury had decided.

Judge Martin: "The jury has returned with a verdict of guilty in the case of State of North Carolina versus Willie Earl Vereen, James McKoy, Reginald Epps, Wayne Moore and..."

I heard the words, all of them, but I couldn't completely process them. It was like my mind was choking, gagging, on what it was being force fed. I was frightened and confused. The word guilty, guilty, guilty kept stabbing my ears. Ben Chavis, "guilty;" Marvin Patrick, "guilty;" James McKoy, "guilty;" Jerry Jacobs, "guilty;" Joe Wright, "guilty;" Reginald Epps, "guilty;" Willie Vereen, "guilty;" Connie Tindall, "guilty;" Anne Sheppard, "guilty;" and me, Wayne Moore, "guilty."

Unbelievable!

We had been found guilty on all the charges we had faced. State prosecutors charged me and the eight men with two crimes: Conspiracy to assault emergency personnel with dangerous weapons, and secondly, burning the building housing Mike's Grocery and all its contents with an incendiary device.

Authorities charged Anne, who suffered with high blood pressure and a nervous breakdown over the case, with being an accessory before the fact to the burning of the store.

I think I heard gasps in the courtroom when the verdicts were read. I thought I saw some young black folks in the courtroom wearing "Free Ben Chavis" buttons as I turned with my other convicted felons to be led out of the courtroom. What I am sure about is that sheriff's deputies transported us to spend the night in the New Hanover County jail to be returned to the Pender County court for sentencing at 9:30 a.m. the following morning.

It was one of a series of hard, sleepless nights to come when I couldn't even dream about freedom.

Wednesday morning arrived and the Wilmington Ten was once again standing before Judge Martin. Apparently well rested, he told each one of us to stand. He asked some of the youngest among us how old they were at the time of the grocery fire. Once they answered, he sentenced them. He sentenced each one of us, handing out time like party favors.

"Wayne Moore," Judge Martin began, "Judgment of the court in case number sixteen seventy-six the defendant be imprisoned in the North Carolina Department of Correction for a period not less than twenty, nor no more than twenty-four years; that he be assigned to work under the supervision of the State's Prison. Sixteen seventy-four, judgment of the court is the defendant be imprisoned in the State's Prison for a period not less than three, nor more than five years to be assigned to work under the supervision of the State Department of Correction."

I was facing no less than twenty-three years behind bars. In all, the Wilmington Ten was sentenced to terms of imprisonment that ranged from fifteen and thirty-four years each, totaling 282 years.

Most of us would not be eligible for parole until 1978; Ben, not until 1980.

＊ — ＊

I was still stunned when we were led out of the Pender County Courtroom and into some anteroom in that grim pile of bricks and wood. There, we were handcuffed and shackled together by Pender County sheriffs, and then marched in our street clothes outside to a waiting prison bus. It was white and looked more like a school bus, except its driver sat in a cage and wore a service revolver. There was also a guard on board who was carrying a loaded shotgun.

A crowd of our supporters sang Negro spirituals as we boarded. I saw some children and defiant faces cheering us on; others, like Ben's mother, Elisabeth Ridley Chavis, broke down in tears. I craned my neck to find my own mother's face in the crowd before I stepped into that bus. There was more of a well of sadness in Mom's eyes than tears. In fact, she wore an expression of total disgust with the system; a system that was unjustly sending her son off to prison.

Anne Sheppard was being transported separately to Women's Prison in Raleigh.

Everything seemed to be hurried, and yet I felt like I was moving—even thinking—in slow motion. We were all uncuffed and unshackled before we were allowed to take our seats in this otherwise empty bus. There were no other prisoners on that trip. I guess all of us were thinking the same thing. We sought our own space. *No need to crowd up before we were crowded into a prison cell.*

I felt the bus rock back on its tires for a moment, heard its engine clear its throat, and then we were moving forward, heading slowly to Central Prison, also in Raleigh, some two and a half hours away. A sheriff's car, our escort, trailed the bus all the way there.

The bus threaded its way over state roads that ran through the heart of North Carolina farmland. The dark richness of the soil stood out against the autumn tans, gold and coppers of the trees and surroundings fields. The thick wire mesh that covered the bus windows could not block my sight of acre upon acre of tobacco and corn, cattle and farmhouses that slid into view and then receded like I would never see them again.

Along the way, many of the small farmhouses appeared to be throwbacks of, or even modern interpretations of, old plantation houses. It was like history was mocking me as I was being carried off in a motorized Middle Passage where my freedom could not follow.

As the bus made its way through Smithfield, in Johnston County, I saw a sign that I'd first seen when I marched with Golden Frinks to Raleigh the previous summer. I was unpleasantly surprised that the billboard was still there, that something decent, like a gust of brotherhood, hadn't blown it down. But there it was, big and clear enough in the sitting sun for me to read from the road that snaked around it.

You Are In The Heart Of Klan Country! Welcome to N.C.

Join The United Klans Of America. Help Us Fight Communism & Integration

I noticed that Ben Chavis was silently scribbling in a notebook. I would later learn that he was writing the first of his "Psalms from Prison," a moving collection of poems and meditations about freedom, human rights, and racism, all reflected through the teachings of Jesus Christ.

My gaze wandered over the darkened interior of the bus. I don't know what really moved me to turn and look at my fellow travelers, friends and comrades. Maybe it was a stirring of nostalgia, drifting back to days not that long ago when I rode the school bus with my friends, talking about sports, style and girls. But this dying day, as the bus rambled toward Raleigh, I thought about the guys making the trip with me.

Until we were ripped from our Williston Senior High School and thrust into white high schools, each of us had excelled, some in academics, others in music, and sports. But this prison sentence was meant to erase all of that, and harshly redraw the hard outlines of our lives.

I sometimes hung out in black Wilmington listening to music played by James "Honey Bun" McKoy and Willie Earl Vereen. They were two of the finest musicians the city has ever known, and I used to hang out with them. No one played drums better than Willie Earl, hunched over his snare drum with his big, curly afro shaking with each beat. And no one thumped a bass guitar better than "Bun," who never seemed more at peace than when he was squeezing funky thunder out of the neck of his guitar. Those guys weren't really militants. They would have been perfectly happy just being free to make music, make people nod their heads and shake their asses on the dance floor.

Jerry Jacobs was a first-class tennis player in high school. His game was nothing less than amazing. He had been an all-state competitor and had gone up against tennis star and basketball great John Lucas. All Connie Tindall ever wanted to do was play professional football. Unlike a lot of young men growing up in the inner city, Connie not only had the size and speed, but he possessed NFL-like skills and determination to win.

Marvin "Chili" Patrick had been in the military and life had hardened him more than most of us, but he was never hardcore black power like Ben was. He was the guy that every group of men has, who can find lightness in even the heaviest of moments. Chili, who often wore a "what the hell" expression that made his eyebrows look like an open drawbridge, was smiling when we were being sentenced. Later, when I asked him why he had smiled, he told me, "I was laughing to keep from crying." Then he laughed again.

Joe Wright, intense and tightly coiled, was just plain brilliant. During our school boycott he defended students who had been arrested during protests and charged with disturbing the peace. He was so convincing in his legal bearing and command of the law that he was holding his own until a judge found out that he was just a high school student, and had him removed from the proceedings.

Joe's future should have been practicing at the bar, not serving time behind bars.

And Reggie Epps just sat alone in his seat staring, like I had been, out of the bus window that evening. Reggie was somewhat of an enigma. A handsome and affable brother, always smiling, yet he was personally discreet and distrusting of everyone and everything. I had been around him in school ever since I moved to Wilmington. We had been friends from that time on, but I never really got to know him. The only thing I knew for sure is that he was down for the cause, always talking about righting unrightable wrongs. He never wanted anything more than for the oppressed to live a good and decent life. Prison was never a part of his plans.

For most of the ride to Raleigh no one said much. There was a nervous joke here and there, but not a lot of conversation. I guess we were all still in shock. I know I was. I found myself melting back into my thoughts as the night deepened and all I could see were the occasional cars and trucks approaching and passing us.

My deepest desire for several years leading up to this night had been to feel important in the environment that had been deliberately structured to reject me, ultimately making me feel unimportant, inferior and unacceptable. As I grew into manhood,

I realized that I could no longer bear this humiliation. I willingly took my place among the revolutionaries. It has long been a defining tradition of our struggle in America. I, like so many black people before me, wholly rejected second-class citizenship in the nation of my birth.

So that was my crime? Why was I locked in a prison bus on my way to my imprisonment? As the road growled softly beneath us, I felt something calling deep within me not to forsake my ancestors. I closed my eyes and could feel them making the ride with me through the North Caroline countryside. I could feel Sojourner Truth, Harriet Tubman, Nat Turner... I could sense Rosa Parks, Martin Luther King, Emmett Till, Malcolm X, and Medgar Evers riding into the darkness with me, but at the same time bestowing me with a light the prison guards would never see. It would be a contraband of consciousness.

I could not forget the sepia pictures of black men and women being tarred and feathered just because they wanted to learn to read, or of black men lynched because they dared to look— eye-to-eye—into a white man's face. I had chosen not to forsake my identity and to struggle just as those who came before me had struggled to defeat the unscrupulous and immoral. It was the same mentality that the Wilmington Ten had faced as we fought unscrupulous and immoral leadership in our public schools, and then the leadership of the city and state as our protests disrupted their business-as-usual control and oppression of black people.

That struggle had condemned me to prison because I had dared to look into the white men's eyes and challenged them to look into their hearts so they might recognize their own humanity and treat us as equals.

As if Ben knew exactly what I was thinking, he looked up, still writing, and whispered to me.

"Keep the faith," he said, his face serene and painted in passing shadows.

"I will," I replied.

I remembered reading somewhere that "evil cannot stand up in the face of truth." Somehow, I knew that the power of truth would set us free. I just needed to, as Ben instructed, "keep the faith."

12

PRISON

Night fell hard as the bus finally pulled up to Central Prison. Its main building was nearly a century old, and its every dark brick and shingle looked it, as this Gothic castle of a place stood over us like some haunted house, where even ghosts couldn't escape.

Central Prison was a maximum security facility, which meant that it housed inmates considered the most dangerous in North Carolina, and that required the highest level of security, like keeping inmates locked in their cells twenty-three hours a day. This place, known as "The Wall," was going to be our new home.

Only the most hardcore wouldn't fear being locked in a dungeon like this. I had never been to prison, any prison, and my fear announced that fact louder than I wanted. I could see it in my face that stared coldly back at me in the window of the prison bus as we rolled slowly toward the prison's huge gates. When the gates opened, the bus drove through. I didn't look back.

The gates closed behind us with a great noise. Reality began to settle in the very foundation of me. I was a prisoner and might very well remain one until I was more than twice my age. I shuddered.

I had to remind myself that I was not a criminal, but a captured warrior forced into this place of promised injustice, dehumanization and suffering. When the bus slowed to a stop inside the prison grounds, I saw what looked like seasoned veterans of the prison system lined up against a fence. They taunted us as we came close enough for them to get a look at us.

"Fresh meat," one yelled.

They had no idea that we were members of the infamous Wilmington Ten, that we were black revolutionaries. If they did, they didn't seem to care. One inmate directed his attention toward Willie Earl.

"Look at that curly-headed bitch right there," he yelled. "She fine as hell. You need anything, baby? Come over here a minute."

That's when I heard someone else cut in and say, "You're not going to fuck with him, that's my homeboy... He is one of the Wilmington Ten."

Up until then, it had not occurred to me that I might run into some guys from Wilmington, homeboys, people I knew, behind The Wall.

Although we weren't allowed to talk, it wasn't long before several other guys from back home began yelling out to us.

"Homeboys." "Homeboys." Homeboys!"

The sound of their recognition of us was a momentary comfort at Central Prison. But it was not enough to chase away my generalized fear of going to prison and my specific fear entering this prison.

My eyes darted involuntarily. Prison guards. Prison Dogs. Razor wire. Thick walls. Bars. Bars. Bars. As we were moved closer into the prison, I could not help noticing that some of the inmates made an effort to look like women, complete with tight pants and make-up. They tied their T-shirts up in a fashion that made the shirts resemble girlish tank tops.

My relatively short jail time had not prepared me for how long timers simply accepted prison as a way of life and made the necessary adjustments. Some of these would-be females were gay when they came to prison. Others were turned to homosexuality by inmates who used sex to dominate and exploit weaker inmates.

Prison is a microcosm of the so-called free world. In much the same way the powerful often fed on the weak—be it animal or man in prison, the unsuspecting, the unaffiliated and the unwise enter prison as easy prey. Some of them would borrow money or cigarettes from the wrong inmate, and wind up getting turned out—raped, really—when they are unable pay their bills with anything other than their bodies.

Handcuffed and shackled, all nine of us were led to a room where we were ordered to remove our clothes. Everything was packed into bags to be shipped home. Naked, we were then ordered to lift our testicles, open our mouths, and bend over and cough for an anal search. I was given prison number 2-11-52-OS. The 2 signified that I was black; the 11-52 meant that I was born in November of 1952, and the OS meant that I was born out of state.

We were outfitted in prison grays, simple draw-string pants and pullover tops made of some cheap fabric, and then separated from each other. Each of us was assigned a cell that was four feet by ten feet. Everything that wasn't made out of cold concrete in there was cold, hard steel—steel beds, bolted to steel walls, a steel sink, and a steel toilet all behind steel bars and a slot in a steel door for serving us meals on steel trays. Because of our notoriety as high-profile inmates, we had been placed in protective custody.

At the time of our sentencing, our lead counsel informed the court that he was seeking to appeal the verdicts. If something happened to us in prison before our appeal could be taken up by a higher court, it might be extremely embarrassing for the state that sold our prosecution to the public under a cover of "law and order."

Our "protection" meant that none of the Wilmington Ten men were allowed to have cellmates at first. I went to bed with an empty bunk in my cell. Protective custody also meant that none of us were allowed outside of our cells except to shower. Three times a day, a guard would yell "chow time" and a trustee rolling a cart with a guard in front and in back would hand us a food tray through a slot in the cell door.

Like all new inmates, we underwent a series of psychological and physical exams to determine how we would be classified. This process was to determine whether we were to be sent to a prison camp, or remain at Central Prison in maximum security. Prison authorities wanted to determine three things: Were you violent? Were you an escape risk? Were you suitable for work detail?

I was asked questions like, "Do you ever feel blue... angry... Are you afraid of snakes?" I answered yes to all three. I didn't know what I should be afraid of, or what they expected me to feel. How was I supposed to feel? I was caged, the victim of a calculated and deliberate attempt to destroy every aspect that defined me as a human being. Did I ever feel blue... angry? Seriously?

Classification could take up to six months. One thing I came to understand in a hurry in prison is that nothing hurries in prison. There would be so much more I would come to learn being skinned alive of my freedom. Although I had experienced poverty, deprivation, and racism—and briefly jail—I had never been so utterly held in captivity until my first days in Central Prison.

There is no feeling worse than being restrained and restricted. It forced me to take a closer look at my relationship with existence, if for no other reason than to explore ways to maintain my sanity. It was a survival instinct. A way of doing time. You look around prison and you see inmates doing all kinds of things to do time. Guys would play basketball for hours or lift weights all day.

Doing Time. It was an art form. I mean that literally.

The first week or so at The Wall, I didn't leave my cell unless I had to. Somehow I thought I could sleep my time away. But a prison trustee, and I can't remember his name, told me, "Man, you got way too much time to sleep away. You need to get something on your mind."

It was a critical insight that I took to heart. As a result, I woke up and became a voracious reader, reading everything I could get my hands on. I was searching for ways to understand how a good and just God could stand by while his own creation was being treated so cruelly. Along this path to understanding, I discovered a quote from St. Augustine:

It goes like this: "I went wandering like a strayed sheep, seeking Thee with anxious reasoning without, whilst thou was within me. I went round the streets and squares of the city seeking Thee and I found thee not, because in vain I sought without for him who was in myself."

I would say that to myself and it brought me some peace. I realized that, in essence, St. Augustine was telling me from over the centuries that the key to the reasoning and wisdom of God is not in understanding the worldly wisdom of men, but in seeking the true essence of God. And that can only be found through a prayerful and spiritual journey, one that takes place within. There is no place like prison to begin that kind of lonesome journey.

I came to see the ultimate goal of this journey was to find peace of mind. I discovered along the way that the roads there were often rugged and filled with pain and sorrow. If a rough and rocky road can be an asset in the search for peace of mind, then I was definitely on the right road, in the right place. I needed peace more than I needed my freedom. And I had the time to search for it.

My cell was in H-Block, which is located on the west side of Central Prison. Its number, a kind of address, was H (the block)-5 (the tier) –9 (the cell). I cannot explain exactly why that address remains so significant to me, but it does. Maybe it is because H-5-9 is where, for the first time in my life, I experienced almost unbearable mental anguish for days on end. From there, I saw former gang member's fresh from the streets, crying for their mommies like lost toddlers. I heard grown men crying at late hours, their weeping painting the night in the kinds of blues you can't sing.

In those early weeks behind bars, I felt tension all around me and I immediately understood that if I didn't want to be swallowed by the madness I was going to have to make some sense of prison and the experience of it. Lots of people say inmates don't get religion until prison closes off all other possibilities. No doubt there is some truth to that. But in many cases, as it was with me, exploring faith was a conscious effort to tame demons. For me, it was my anger. There were times it wanted to bust out of me almost as badly as I wanted to bust out of The Wall.

I began deliberate steps to increase my faith in God as well as my level of spirituality. I began by immersing myself in the Bible, especially the teachings of Jesus. At the same time, I fell in love with the writings of Khalil Gibran, the Lebanese poet and spiritual writer who lived and worked for most of his life in America. His book, *The Prophet,* became the source of much comfort to me.

If you are willing to work hard to keep your soul alive behind bars, you can find places of peace even there. For instance, late at night, after the lights went out, an inmate called Swamp Dog would sing the cell block to sleep with gospel songs. He was blessed with an incredible voice. No one ever complained about his singing, the least me.

I was finding kernels of peace and tranquility in many other places. My prison reading, including from the Bible and *The Prophet,* was giving me a new therapeutic perspective. In addition, the words and support of strong black women helped me through the ordeal. I owe the freeing of my mind in part to Sonia Sanchez who sent me, sometime later in my incarceration, a wonderful sample of her work. The words from her 1973 book, *Love Poems,* helped to refine so many of my thoughts about life and love and revolution.

"... in order to be a true revolutionary, you must understand love. Love, sacrifice, and death," she wrote.

She kept my mind occupied for days on end.

And there was the interest of people like Angela Davis and poet Nikki Giovanni in the struggle of the Wilmington Ten. All of this made me feel less forgotten and lost. Their words and support gave me hope. I began to feel like a martyr rather than a victim. I realized that Nikki Giovanni wrote "Ego Tripping" with black women in mind, but her work had also uplifted this black man trapped in The Wall.

I will never forget how the poem opens:

I was born in the Congo

I walked to the fertile crescent and built

the sphinx

I designed a pyramid so tough that a star

that only glows every one hundred years falls

into the center giving divine perfect light

I am bad

In *Ego Tripping,* Giovanni implies that she went deep inside of her soul and sort of transformed herself spiritually. That was my journey, too.

The work of other black intellectuals also sustained me. I discovered Carter G. Woodson and other "Negro" intellectuals after reading his book, *The Mis-Education of the Negro.* But it was in the work of Martin Luther King, Jr. in particular that I found the courage to face the enemy, and to not be afraid of it. Like Dr. King, I too read Mahatma Gandhi and was completely sold on the power of non-violent struggle in the face of unrepentant evil.

It was unrepentant evil that I faced on a daily basis during my time in prison. My faith was constantly tested. The prison guards and the system that supported them were diligent in implementing institutional methods aimed at separating me from my humanity. Oh, they called it rehabilitation, but it was *their* cover story.

Needless to say, rehabilitation is nonexistent in the North Carolina prison system. It is totally illogical to think that anyone could be rehabilitated in an environment that is built to breed resentment, hatred and violence. America's penal system, in general, is similar to a mad scientist's laboratory that creates monsters that will eventually destroy their diabolical creators.

For security reasons we had all been placed in separate cell blocks at Central Prison and not allowed to see or talk to each other. One day, about a month after we had entered the prison, seven of us, Marvin "Chili" Patrick, Jerry Jacobs, Joe Wright, Reggie Epps, Willie Vereen, James McKoy, and I were transferred— without a word of warning or preparation—to the Odom Correctional Institution.

I controlled my anger as the prison bus rolled onto Odom, a two-thousand-two-hundred acre, twentieth-century plantation in Northhampton County, North Carolina, where the prisoners were the slaves. As far as the eyes could see, there were acres upon acres of cotton fields, and mostly black men, along with a sprinkling of white inmates, bent over picking cotton while armed overseers on horses stood guard. Tears rolled down my cheeks. It was all too apparent to me that though legalized slavery had been outlawed, a more acceptable form of enslavement still existed in America's prisons. It was still perfectly acceptable to use convict labor, which built and maintained many of the roads in much of the Deep South.

I wondered whether Harriet Tubman had led slaves to freedom from this very same plantation more than a century earlier. The whole thing felt like a cruel trick of a demonic time machine. I was my own great, great, maternal grandfather, Nathanial Foy, a slave purchased on January 3, 1857, to work the Poplar Grove Plantation just outside of Wilmington.

There were so many jobs at Odom, ranging from "house nigga" chores in the kitchen, laundry, and canteen to "field nigga" jobs that, under the sights of loaded guns, used gangs of inmates to pick cotton, tomatoes and other vegetables on the prison's one-hundred-acre plantation.

My time in prison had gotten me accustomed to the outrage of being physically chained, held in bondage and caged in cold hard steel. But to have this all happen on the very land soaked with sweat and blood of generations of my people, who also had no or little choice... It was too much. I felt myself slipping into the kind of shock soldiers do when they lose a limb in battle. For me, this whole scene was a head shot. My brain shook straining to understand how any of this could be happening.

There, the seven of us were placed on administrative segregation or "safekeeping," as they called it. Although we had been processed into the system, we were not allowed among the general population because our case was still on appeal. Anne Sheppard was still being held at Women's Prison in Raleigh. Ben Chavis and Connie Tindall were sent to Caledonia Correctional Center, which was just across the Roanoke River from Odom. I guess prison authorities thought Ben and Connie were the ring leaders, and so they had to be quarantined from us.

The segregation unit at Odom was located about fifty-feet from the main building. Except for the fact that it was an isolated, one-story building with no day room, it reminded me of the New Hanover County jail. The design of the cells was pretty much the same, and there was a shower stall at the end of a row of cells. One unit was reserved as "the hole," which was normally used for punitive purposes.

Odom Correctional Institution was a medium security prison, which only meant that the general population weren't all killers and strong-arm guys. Instead of cells, most inmates were locked away in secured dormitories with fifty or so prisoners to a dorm with common toilets and showers. And make no mistake, this was no country club prison. In some ways it could be more dangerous than Central Prison, because guards in places like this tended to let inmates have more control over their affairs and activities. For some that spelled nothing less than tragic trouble.

Odom was located about as far north as you can get in North Carolina without actually crossing over into Virginia. It was a four-hour drive from Wilmington. Since my mother couldn't afford a vehicle back then, I knew the relocation was going to make it difficult for her to visit me. This was prison tugging, yet again, at some of the very things that anchored my sanity.

After the relocation was complete, I found myself reflecting on something Ben told us as we were being driven that night to Central Prison. The only reason that we were convicted, he said, was that the state of North Carolina was "racist to the bone." He said that it was important that we stick together, and not let the system use us the way it had used Allen Hall to put us away. We realized that we would have to be strong, but we also realized that some of us were stronger than others in resisting what authorities might try to do to divide us.

A lot of us thought that if anybody could break, it would be Joe Wright. Up until the unrest in the schools, Joe had always been a pretty straight-arrow kind of guy. He had attended Catholic school before being bused off to Hoggard high. He had even joined the Civil Air Patrol. We all took for granted that of all of us, Joe was the most likely to succeed in mainstream America, in other words, White America.

Joe never made it a secret that he wanted to be a lawyer. He seemed to feel right at home when he attempted to represent students who had been arrested for disorderly conduct the year before our conviction. Still, Joe was a series of contradictions. On one hand, he was an outstanding, straight-laced young man who worked hard to bridge the racial gap between white and black. And white people seemed to love him. On the other hand, he worked hard to portray himself as a radical, a black militant.

On any given day, you would see Joe walking around wearing dark shades and a black tam in the tradition of the Black Panther Party. I think that's what got Joe in trouble: He pretended to be more than he actually was.

At Odom, I could tell that being locked up was really getting to Joe. It was getting to all of us, but Joe had almost shut down. He was acting like he was at the breaking point. Other than Connie, Joe had always been the most talkative of us all. He was always talking politics or some militant shit. But in prison, we could hardly get a word out of him. Something was definitely wrong.

I decided I would trick him into talking with some lawyer questions. He was held three cells down from me, so I called out.

"Hey Joe? Do you think Ferguson fucked up by not putting us on the stand?"

"Naw man," he called back. "Those racist crackers had their minds made up before we ever went to court. We didn't stand a chance."

"Well, what are we gonna do now?" I asked. He replied. "My brother Thomas talked to Rev. White the other day. He said that they are going to try to get Ben out on bond. Then he can try to raise enough money to get the rest of us out."

James McKoy yelled out from his cell further down the line: "That's a bunch of shit. Why should the rest of us have to sit in prison while Ben is in the streets? He is the reason we are in here in the first place. They wanted him; they didn't want us."

Joe perked up even more, adding, "Ben is our only hope if we are going to get out anytime soon. It's going to take $400,000 to spring us. Ben is the only one that can raise that kind of loot."

"We have all got twenty-six years apiece and those crackers ain't in no hurry to hear our appeal. We got to trust Ben to do the right thing."

That was all it took to bring Joe back to life. He was in his element, at least for a short while. I could tell that from that point on, Joe realized he was not in this thing alone, that we were inextricably bound together by a cruel twist and tight knot of fate. We would have to keep encouraging each other to keep the faith, to keep holding on. From that day on, we did just that.

Just like what Joe's brother, Thomas, had told him, the Commission for Racial Justice of the United Church of Christ, Ben's employer, posted a $50,000 bond for Ben's release. Ben Chavis was released on December 12, 1972, and on his return to the world he promised to work tirelessly to spring the rest of us from prison. And we all believed him.

And four months later, in April 1973, our situation changed yet again, but not a step closer to gaining our freedom, not even temporarily.

The Odom prison authorities decided that the seven of us were taking up too much space in administrative segregation. Although there were two bunks in each cell, we had each been placed in an individual cell. Apparently, the Warden needed the segregation unit to house unruly inmates and others who had been found guilty of prison infractions.

We were relocated to the prison infirmary that had been turned into a makeshift dormitory that could accommodate the seven of us. For me, this move was paradise in hell. It meant going from metal bunks to army barracks-type bunks—with springs. We even got a television that was placed on a steel rack above our cage door.

The first thing I noticed when I turned on that television was Senator Sam Ervin, an old democratic lion from my home state, questioning this bookish looking guy, John Dean, about his involvement in the Watergate scandal. I learned that Dean was a lawyer who worked for Nixon. And while I had no idea of the extent of where Watergate would go at the time, I still smelled poetic justice in the air.

It was Richard Nixon's so-called "War on Crime" that had given urban law enforcement and prosecutors a nationwide mandate to destroy black people, starting with treating the black power movement like a collection of outlaw outfits. It was Nixon who sicced his criminal justice dogs on people like us, and into going after civil rights leaders like Ben Chavis. At the time, none of us, except Ben, were the kind of hard core militants that Nixon's anti-radical campaign had targeted. Most of us were simply disenfranchised high school students, unhappy about the way things were going down. We were just ordinary teenagers growing up during a period of radicalization throughout America. While young white kids gravitated toward the anti-war movement, young black people found identity in the black power movement.

Some of us became directly involved by joining organizations like the Student Non-violent Coordinating Committee and the Black Panthers. Others just showed solidarity by wearing afros and dashikis or sporting black power fists on chains around their necks. None of this was illegal nor outside our rights as Americans to express political views and advocate for change.

One day, while I was on administrative segregation at Odom, I got a call to come to the visiting area; and there was Angela Davis. She was one of the most prominent figures in the black power movement in America. I just couldn't believe my eyes. I was awestruck as she stood outside of the prison fence, a nearly six-foot-tall, statuesque beauty, with a gap-toothed smile, and an enormous afro—bigger than mine ever was.

She was upset that prison officials would not allow her inside the gate despite the fact that she had been acquitted of the murder and kidnapping charges that helped to make her as famous as infamous.

That incident involved the killing of a Marin County judge in a failed 1970 attempt by Jonathan Jackson, a high school student, to free his Black Panther brother, George Jackson. Davis had been linked to one of the armed defendants that Jonathan Jackson had freed from a Northern Californian courthouse in an effort to kidnap the judge, Harold J. Haley, and others. The younger Jackson planned to barter his hostages for his brother's release from Soledad Prison.

In the end, the judge was killed, along with Jackson and two other black men who assisted him. Two jurors and a prosecutor, also abducted, were injured in the melee between the men and police.

Odom prison authorities would only give Davis five minutes to talk to us through the prison fence. She asked us about how we were being treated inside. She also promised that she would not rest until the Wilmington Ten were free. There were no airports near Jackson, NC, the closest town to the prison. To see us, she, along with two members of the National Alliance Against Racist and Political Repression, had driven 250 miles in from the courthouse to visit us.

Everyone in the Wilmington Ten felt solidarity with the national black power movement, although our struggle was local. And every time we heard or read about another black power leader or figure being hunted down, killed, or jailed as political prisoners; we bled inside. So, yes, I felt much pleasure seeing Nixon barbecued over a pit of his own lies during the Congressional hearings being televised live for the nation to see.

It appeared as though the crime czar was himself a criminal. As I watched the hearings, I found myself fruitlessly fantasizing that the next time I heard those prison keys jangling, and steel doors slamming, those same wounding sounds would be echoing in the ears of "Tricky Dick" Nixon's as he was being led off to his own Four-by-Ten.

* — *

Any inmate will tell you that there are few things more important in prison than getting a visit from someone on the outside. Visitation at Odom was on Sundays. Guys expecting a visit began preparing on Thursday. That was the day when inmates were granted the chance to go to the prison clothes house to pick up a clean set of prison grays.

Most of the time we'd just get an old wrinkled set with holes in them, and you didn't care much. But if you wanted a brand new set on Thursday, well, then you had to slip a couple of dollars to the inmate who was running the clothes house on Wednesday. It was big business because the thing was, everybody wanted to look their best when their folks came to visit.

Although visitation didn't begin until 10 a.m., you could see guys getting ready hours early, right after breakfast the way people on the outside prepare for a big wedding. As people began to arrive, guys would fight for a position at the windows, to see if they could recognize their folks' car pulling into the prison parking lot. Others just hoped to see anyone they might have known from the outside, even if they were not coming to see them. I know it might sound funny, but some inmates got a treat out of just seeing the latest styles and fashions. And then there were others, those with the least chance of getting visits of their own, who gathered to just gawk at the women, almost any woman. Eyefulls of clothed breasts, thighs and asses would be all they could take back to their cells, where with their imaginations, they would enjoy their own kinds of visitations.

We all must have looked like a bunch of wild animals in a zoo to outsiders coming inside to see us. They could catch glimpses of us as they walked up the sidewalk and into the building. To get there, visitors had to already make it through two chain-link fences, each topped with bundles of razor-sharp, concertina wire; they had to enter a fortress bordered on each corner by an armed guard watching everyone and their every move from guard towers twenty-feet high. And between the two fences, two vicious-looking German Shepherds paced ready to pounce on anyone foolish enough to scale a fence with the guts and intention to scale another.

Just the sight of those dogs was enough to dissuade me from even entertaining a notion of escape. Besides, if I did manage to make it over both fences without being shot, attacked by the dogs, and cut to pieces by the razor wire, I would still have to make it across a river and hundreds of acres of fields and forests just to get off the two plantations that made up Odom.

Of course, it's human nature to want to be free. From the moment those handcuffs were slapped on my wrist, all I could think of was how I could escape. I would stretch out on my bunk and stare at the ceiling in despair, as I contemplated how difficult it would be to escape, even if by some miracle I could make it over the fence. I would create scenarios of my success made from snatches of movies I'd seen, that featured suspects running though snake-infested swamps, being chased by bloodhounds, desperate to escape the too long arm of the law. Seldom did any of these suspects make it.

If some did, the movies made sure we saw them damned to a life of tragic uncertainty, always looking over their shoulders, never able to trust anyone.

One night, soon after we moved into the infirmary, right after evening head count, I heard an alarm screeching and saw floodlights flashing. The dogs were barking and shots were fired. The next morning, a prison guard told us that an inmate had gotten a *Dear John* letter and couldn't handle the soul ache of losing his woman.

The guy never made it over the second fence. The razor wire on the first fence clawed several deep cuts into his body. That apparently wasn't enough for Odom. A guard in a tower spotted the inmate trying to make a run for it. A shotgun blast pumped a round of birdshot into the guy right before the German Shepherds attacked, treating this inmate as if he was raw meat, which at this point he pretty much was.

All the moving parts of this unfeeling clockwork of captivity performed the way they were designed. No one ever successfully escaped Odom Correctional Institution. And with this inmate being carried back, Odom's perfect record remained intact.

Very few inmates will ever admit that they can't handle doing time. To do so would be a sign of weakness. Most just suffer in silence. It is not natural to accept being held against your will. A wild horse must first be broken before it will allow you to ride it. I vowed to myself that I would not be easily broken. In fact, I told myself that if I was ever sent to a medium security prison, I would make my move.

But at Odom, which was, of course, that kind of prison, I could not imagine how anyone could ever make it off. I already knew what happened to a fool who gave it a shot. Still, I often thought about trying. And those were the times I tried the hardest to think of happier times, even the occasional ones I had experienced inside.

Prison authorities were not entirely heartless. For instance, Christmas was permitted to stick its reindeer antlers and red nose through the bars, at least in some limited ways. We were allowed to get holiday cards, packages, fruit, nuts, cake, and some other modest gifts at Christmastime. Back home, my family had a Christmas tradition of aging fruitcakes. My sister, Stephanie, had always aged a fruitcake for me using enough Bacardi Rum to stagger an elephant.

She never got over not being called to testify in our trial. Stephanie told me that she felt very bad about that; she had wanted to tell the world how it was that I could not possibly be guilty, that I had been babysitting her young sons the night Mikes' Grocery burned down. I guess she thought she could bring me a taste of freedom by bringing me a fruitcake that contained more alcohol than fruit. I think her 151-proof fruitcake was Stephanie's way of bucking the system, of slipping me contraband booze so I could chew my way to a good buzz.

Contraband flowed freely during visits. My rum-loaded fruitcake was mild compared to what came into the prison every Sunday: money, marijuana, heroin, LSD, syringes, knives, and tattoo materials. Visitors brought in balloons loaded with contraband, which the inmate would swallow. Later, when the balloon passed through his digestive system, he'd fish it out of the toilet like it was the catch of the day.

After every visitation, the aroma of marijuana hung in the air throughout the prison, clear evidence that contraband had made it into Odom. Other than a few random shakedowns, prison guards showed little interest in putting an end to this. It was almost as if they turned a blind eye to almost anything that didn't result in violence directed at them.

Inmates who were violent towards guards were put in solitary, "the hole," and force fed a drug called Thorazine to induce a zombie-like, docile state in them.

My Christmas visit of 1972, my first behind bars, was also the first time I had received a home-cooked meal from anyone since being sentenced. My mother went to great lengths to make sure

I didn't forget what it was like to sit at her table. She filled the largest picnic basket I had ever seen with a soul food feast that made me feel like the most important person in her world. There was fried chicken, smoked ham, collard greens, butter beans with okra, candied yams, sweet potato pie, macaroni and cheese, homemade rolls, peach cobbler, and, courtesy of my sister, my special fruitcake.

Stephanie was there herself to present her cake to me with a mischievous grin.

Because I was permitted only two hours for the visit, I found myself juggling talking and catching up, and stuffing my face. My mother wanted to know how the other guys were handling being locked up. I told her that it was understandably difficult to be locked away on Christmas. It was their first Christmas in prison, too. But I was quick to add that it was a blessing that the seven of us were still together, able to support each other and talk things out.

There had been times when the seven of us talked all night, right up until we heard the jangling keys signaling that it was time for breakfast. We spent some time talking about the case and our situation, but we spent much more time taking our minds elsewhere. We all came to realize that our thoughts could soar far beyond the confines of hard concrete and cold steel, into the worlds from which we came. And although our lives in the so-called free world had been far from ideal, we were able to mine and extract enough humor and comfort from our experiences back there to ease the suffocating tension of prison.

From the windows of our makeshift dormitory, we could see general population inmates on the yard going about their routines. We pleaded with prison authorities to allow us to have similar activities. Eventually, we were given use of the yard for two hours a day, usually while the regular population was away on work detail.

Whenever we were allowed onto the prison yard we would lift weights or play basketball. Some of us would take turns in the boxing ring, which was in a corner of the yard. We'd pretend that we were Joe Frazier or Muhammad Ali. The idea was to do whatever it took to keep our minds off being imprisoned. Sometimes it worked better than others. Either way, we were glad we got time in the recreation yard.

Then one day we heard the sound of musical instruments coming from the gymnasium, which was adjacent to the rec yard. "Bun" McKoy's and Willie Earl's ears suddenly perked up. They hadn't heard real live music since we had first been locked up. Inside, the closest we had gotten to live music was whenever we could get some empty trash cans to use for drums and our voices for instruments.

But here was real music being made with real instruments. Willie and Bun looked like junkies with their morning Jones coming down as they listened with great intensity. The next thing I knew, Willie and Bun went to Lieutenant Garrison, who was a giant of a man who stood about ssix-feet-eight-inches tall and weighing too many pounds. Garrison, who was black, was a ranking guard; there were lots of sergeants and captains around, but everyone knew that Garrison ran our compound.

We never knew his first name. And if we had, we would never have used it. Odom was not a place where guards and inmates were on a first-name basis. But none of this stopped Willie Earl and Bun from begging Garrison to let them join the prison band. But he said that would be impossible. Our status of being in safekeeping prohibited us from intermingling with inmates (band mates, too) from the regular population.

Later, and without bugging Garrison any more about the matter, the big man reconsidered.

"Let me think about it," he said. "I'll get back with you guys later this week."

On a Saturday morning, a correctional officer came to our unit and ordered us to prepare to go to the gym in fifteen minutes. We immediately knew what that meant: Willie and Bun were going to get a chance to play their music. While the rest of us picked up basketballs and started shooting jumpers, Willie Earl and Bun McKoy darted for the stage where the instruments were. They inspected and adjusted what they found. Willie Earl went straight for a set of drums. Bun grabbed an electric guitar.

Music can soothe the most tormented soul. And it can mesmerize the heart and spirit of the most hardened criminal, at least for brief moments. It was music that sweetly swung low and carried captured African souls away, at times, from the most brutal realities of American slavery that held claim to their bodies. I understood this in so many ways, especially while I lived as a captive of the state. And for all of us, but particularly for Willie and Bun, music could be our escape too.

That's how I felt when I heard Willie and Bun begin to play. I stopped in mid dribble and listened with a smile as I heard them play the "Theme from Shaft." In my head, I sang along:

Who is the man that would risk his neck for his brother man?

Shaft!

Can you dig it?

Who's the cat that won't cop out when there's danger all about?

Shaft!

Right On.

13

PREY OR PRAY BEHIND BARS

I don't remember much about the Reverend Singletary, except that he was a fiery little man who could preach up a storm, as the sisters of the congregation would say. I never knew his first name. I was a little boy, and for little black boys growing up in the South, every elder's first name might as well had been Mr. or Miss or Mrs., or in Singletary's case, Reverend.

He was the pastor of Shoulders Branch Baptist Church, the only black church in Castle Hayne, NC, where my siblings and I lived with my mother. It was a country town that didn't seem much good for anything other than the flower factory where my mother practically slaved, being paid pennies for every bunch of posies she picked. So we didn't have much. But that didn't stop Rev. Singletary from coming around every once and a while to sit at our table and eat the little that we had.

I clearly remember our shack of a home filled with the heavy scent of pan-fried this and roasting that and the lush, green fragrance of freshly snapped green beans ready for the pot. My mother would stay up the night before, preparing a grand meal to serve the next day to her pastor who had promised to stop by with a mouth full of Christian optimism and inspiration like a gambler sporting new gold fronts on his teeth. I would look at these big spreads and wonder what power did this black man have to deserve all of this special treatment by my mother.

But before anyone could raise a fork to eat the last time he visited us, I began to understand. That man would start blessing and sanctifying the meal before we could get fully settled in our seats; he would go on, in fact, so long that the food and fixings would be cold by the time he finished blessing them.

I got it. This was religion. Through this man with the bottomless stomach and restless tongue for sermons, God spoke to my mother and every other restless soul who hung on Rev. Singletary's "moms," "ahhhhs" and "Hallelujahs." This minster was, even when he was chewing and gulping at her table, a vessel of reassurance that my mother need not worry, that the Lord would make a way for her and her children somehow.

But for me, I never got the Holy Ghost back then.

Still, religion definitely has its place, even in prison. Especially in prison.

By definition, prison is a place of sin where people are brought low, a kind of Biblical, fire-and-brimstone low. What else but hell can you call being locked away from everything and everyone you know and care about for years, maybe a lifetime, maybe more? I wasn't surprised to learn that the need to lift up souls is not lost on spiritual gurus, who crop up in places like Odom prison plantation, where almost any man can find himself a walking corpse.

These holy men, often ordained by nothing more than the faith of their followers, represented every religion I had ever heard of. At Odom, there were Christians, Jews, Muslims, Buddhists, Hindus, and Satanists. The Christians and Muslims, like in the outside world, were the most aggressive in seeking converts.

After I and my six other brothers of the Wilmington Ten had spent some time at Odom, most inmates there, black ones in particular, treated us like we were heroes; this was especially true of the Muslims. The Wilmington Ten had famously fought The Man, and to them, The Man was not only white, but the white devil. And although most of these Muslims could not be considered militants, we had one thing in common: we didn't trust The Man, devil or not.

The Muslim brothers were homegrown. Make no mistake about it, despite the skullcaps, or kufis they wore, or the Holy Qurans they quoted from, none of these guys were born or raised anywhere near the Middle East or North Africa, or any other beating geographic heart of historic Islam. They started out just like us, and had found their way to Islam, in many cases, as jailhouse converts. For the most part, they discovered a modern interpretation of Islam, an urban version, that spoke to them in ways other than the way Baptist or Jehovah Witness or whatever faiths they had grown up in, often didn't.

The Muslims at Odom would do little favors for us: sneaking stuff like fruit cocktail, peanut butter and jelly sandwiches, fried chicken and milk from the kitchen. But they would never bring us any pork. Even cookies, which they pointed out contained lard, a pork product, were questionable—and they reminded us of that too.

Much more clear cut, the Muslim brothers made sure that we had brand new prison grays for visitation. They supplied us with various newspapers and periodicals including, of course, *The Final Call*, their newspaper published by the Nation of Islam.

I had seen, like just about anyone who lived in any sizable black community, representatives of the Nation on the streets selling *Final Call* newspapers and sweet, palm-sized bean pies. I had never bothered to find out what they were all about. They always seemed to have a mysterious quality about them as they moved about town in their clean, dark suits and stiff bow ties. It was as if they were privy to some high-minded secret that the rest of us couldn't access. I had started on my spiritual journey when I was at Central Prison. But at Odom, I was really eager to find anyone or anything to help me take the next steps in that journey.

Many guys in prison often fake spiritual awakening in hopes of gaining favor with the parole board. Other weak-minded inmates wave around Bibles and Holy Qurans hoping for something more basic and immediate: the mighty mystique of an unknown deity that might ward off prison predators and vultures. For me, my steps toward the spiritual were genuine, fueled by all the books I was reading behind bars. My copy of *The Prophet* by Gibran was particularly influential.

The book was sent to me by my close friend and mentor, Marilyn Moore, who worked for the United Church of Christ's Commission for Racial Justice. I had written to her a week earlier wanting to know what the Commission was doing to get us out of prison. She wrote back saying that I sounded a little down and out. She included a check for $50 along with a copy of *The Prophet*, a book first published in the 1920s, and something I didn't know existed until it arrived to me in prison.

This slender volume of poetic pearls of insight made me feel complete for the first time since I had been incarcerated. I cannot fully explain why. I just know that its pages transported me to a different, better place in my mind. When I started reading it I melted into its pages, becoming a face in the crowd of people who ventured away from their homes in the city to say farewell to a wise man. His name was Al Mustafa, and he was standing at a harbor about to board a vessel to leave this place and these people, maybe forever. But before he left, Al Mustafa stopped to answer questions from the gathered crowd.

As he answered each question put to him, Al Mustafa answered almost every question I ever had about life—among them, what is love, work, freedom, even crime and punishment. And he did this in the most soothing and thoughtful way imaginable.

In *The Prophet*, I felt as if I had uncovered a precious and never ending supply of nourishment for my soul. It also helped me be open to seeking life and spiritual knowledge wherever it presented itself. Black Muslims, as they were often called back then, seemed more than willing to step into the open door of my open mind. They introduced me to the "Plain Truth." The "Plain Truth" is an expression used to describe the teachings of the Honorable Elijah Muhammad, then the leader of the Nation of Islam and, himself, considered a prophet to deliver the black man out of the "wilderness" of his twentieth century bondage and oppression.

Prison is a nation within a nation, and it is in such places where legions of Black Muslims were made. It had been that way for years. This was the where and how Malcolm X, the most famous Black Muslim in the world, learned of Islam and came to embrace it.

Part of almost any religious conversion requires indoctrination, and indoctrination requires a captive audience. There is no better captive audience than men held against their will in prison, men willing to resort to almost anything to escape the day-to-day soul killing that is prison. A lot of brothers behind bars saw a natural appeal in the Nation of Islam doctrine that emphasized self-respect and self-reliance. These were also attitudes that were discouraged by prison authorities—which gave then even greater appeal to men like us.

Just like on the streets, the Muslims in prison emphasized being clean-shaven, well-spoken, neatly dressed, and upright in posture and behavior. In general, the Muslims seemed to be Black America's path to redemption at a time when too many rudderless black men were drowning in self-hatred and self-destruction. But in prison, the Black Muslim message, and its muscle of being a powerful and feared group, was difficult to ignore.

I took all of this in.

One day, a Muslim brother named Rashid X, dressed in freshly pressed prison grays and wearing a kufi cap, came by our makeshift dormitory to introduce us to "The Lost-Found Nation of Islam," its formal name. The religious dogma that the

Muslims taught would have sounded insane to most people, but not so much to some of us who were searching for a way to explain the world that had been so unjust to us and our people. Rashid, soft-spoken and scholarly, taught us that a big-headed scientist named Yacub had created the white man through a series of biological grafts. The original stock for these grafts had been dark-skinned black people. They were selectively bred so that only the lighter skinned babies survived. This inbreeding, the teachings say, continued until eventually only white babies resulted.

I have to confess that after being accused by whites, misjudged by whites, sentenced by whites to spend more than twenty years in prison, this weird eugenics explanation had a certain charm: whites created from blacks by an evil genius using some nefarious method.

I grew up in the Christian church that promised pie in the sky when you die as a way to help its black flocks cope with a life on earth under the perpetual misery of white American racism. I thought of Rev. Singletary and Shoulders Branch Baptist Church and all the other experiences I had with the black church.

As a child, I never understood what church was all about, so I rebelled early. From the time I was a toddler, I always wanted to know all the "whys," "where's" and "why nots." No one seemed to be able to explain to me, even deacons and pastors, if Jesus could be raised from the dead, how come my murdered dog, Skippy, could not be raised from the dead, too?

No one could explain to me why our church's image of Jesus, the most prominent portrait in the chapel, was of a blond, blue-eyed Christ. I guess that's just the way it was back then. Everyone just accepted the notion that since white people ruled the world, then Jesus, the only son of the all-powerful Father, certainly had to be white, too.

Rashid X called Christianity the white man's religion. I got that right away. The Muslims taught that slavers used it to make them feel good about our oppression at the same time Christianity was used to make black people silently suffer their inhumane treatment. It was all God's will.

Christian missionaries taught black people that they were enslaved because they were the embodiment of the Biblical curse of Ham. Blacks were told that God's word in the Bible said they were forever destined to be slaves when a naked, drunken Noah cursed his son Ham. And because of that, one of his three sons, "shall be a servant of servants unto his brethren." White people, even some well-meaning, had used that verse in Book of Genesis for centuries to justify the enslavement of black people.

At the same time, I realized that the Black church had long served as a place of refuge for the weary souls of an oppressed people. My mother found a resting place in the Bible and in the pews of the black church. I got that, too. The civil rights movement was sustained by church pastors playing the role of Moses in the story of Exodus, leading his people to the promised land.

Congressman John Lewis, the legendary civil rights activist, once decoded the link: "Slavery was our Egypt, segregation was our Egypt, discrimination was our Egypt, and so during the height of the civil rights movement it was not unusual for people to be singing, "Go down Moses way on down in Egypt land, and tell Pharaoh to let my people go."

But I have no memories of Rev. Singletary being anything like Moses, unless Moses liked fried chicken after church on Sunday.

Rashid X had no time for Moses and had run out of patience on a Christian God to rescue his black brothers and sisters. He was quick to point out to me the contradictions of Christianity, at least how it was practiced in America.

He said the Christians who supported the civil rights movement had done so solely out of guilt. On the other hand,

Christian conservatives, he noted, were the most hateful and merciless people in America. "Contrary to the teachings of Jesus, they showed little or no empathy for the plight of the poor and downtrodden," he told me.

"You need to know your history, brother," Rashid said one day in the cellblock. "If you knew your history, there is no way that you would accept the white man's religion."

Then, he went for our jugulars: "The Wilmington Ten will never receive justice in America because white America will never respect you as equals."

I could identify with what Rashid X was saying, although his rundown of how the white man was the product of a fat-headed scientist seemed ridiculous. Before I was arrested, I was studying a book called *The Stolen Legacy* by George G. M. James. I found it at our Church of Black Messiah in Wilmington. In this book, published in 1954, I learned that Ethiopia was the cradle of civilization. Based on that alone, you could make an intelligent argument that the black man was the original man, like the Black Muslims preached.

It would be decades later that scientists would confirm through fossilized remains that human's earliest known direct ancestors lived in Ethiopia more than 4 million years ago. It is now common knowledge that the first early humans were Africans, and that all people on earth are descended from them. But the idea of a Big Headed Scientist still makes me laugh.

I wish I could laugh about something else Rashid taught us. He was right when he said that black Americans had been lied to from our first steps on this land. As a child, while watching cowboys and Indians on TV or in the movies, I would pull for the people on the wagon train. I thought, back then, that the Indians circling the settlers were nothing more than bands of "crazed savages."

I was, as the black historian Carter Woodson might have said, a mis-educated Negro. In history books and television shows and movies, white people were always the heroes. And the Indians with their painted faces, feathered head gear, screams and shouts were made out to be blood-thirsty, sub-humans. Why else would they want only to kill the good, innocent white people and hack off their scalps as trophies?

I had no idea at the time, and was willfully made ignorant, that the Indians were desperately fighting cruel invaders. They were trying to hold on to the land and way of life that was rightfully theirs. Just as my school books portrayed the so-called founding fathers as heroes for standing against the British, Geronimo, Crazy Horse, Sitting Bull, Cochise, and Chief Joseph, and so many others, Indians should be honored for their courageous fight to protect their territories and their tribes.

I had been fed the same lie about Africa, once again finding myself as a boy cheering for Tarzan as he beat down and killed "the natives" in their own land, using African animals that strangely obeyed only him.

Almost everything that Rashid X had been saying to us in prison made sense. Eventually, several of us unofficially took on Muslim names and began spending a lot of time studying the "Plain Truth."

There was another document, called the "Actual Facts," that we were told to commit to memory. This list of twenty worldly measurements were concocted by Master W. Fard Muhammad, the founder of the Nation of Islam, and the original teacher of Elijah Muhammad, who himself has spent some time in prison.

The "Actual facts" are:

- The total area of the land and water of the planet Earth is 196,940,000 square miles.

- The circumference of the planet Earth is 24,896 miles.
- The diameter of the Earth is 7,926 miles.
- The area of the Land is 57,255,000 square miles.
- The area of the Water is 139,685,000 square miles.
- The Pacific Ocean covers 68,634,000 square miles,
- The Atlantic Ocean covers 41,321,000 square miles.
- The Indian Ocean covers 29,430,000 square miles.
- The Lakes and Rivers cover 1,000,000 square miles.
- The Hills and Mountains cover 14,000,000 square miles.
- The Islands are 1,910,000 square miles.
- The Deserts are 4,861,000 square miles.
- Mount Everest is 29,141 feet high.
- The Producing Land is 29,000,000 square miles.
- The Earth weighs six sextillion tons—(a unit followed by 21 ciphers).
- The Earth is 93,000,000 miles from the Sun.
- The Earth travels at the rate of 1,037 1/3 miles per hour.
- Light travels at the rate of 186,000 miles per second.
- Sound travels at the rate of 1,120 feet per second.
- The diameter of the Sun is 853,000 miles.

Rashid told us that when a Muslim rapidly recites these facts, the effect is to make listeners think Muslims are highly intelligent. Not appearing smart could be grounds for expulsion from the Nation of Islam. If nothing more, learning about the "Nation" gave us a kind of mental furlough from having to think too much about the outside world. But some of the Nation's ideas and approaches, like its explanation of the origin of white people, for one, didn't sit right with me. I didn't take a Muslim name like some of the Wilmington Ten that were with me in Odom did. Instead, I started calling myself *Timbuktu*, after the once great African city of wealth and culture.

Staying connected to something greater than me helped me through the hardest days at Odom. It helped me when I looked out over the vast fields of the prison plantation to see armed white men on horseback overseeing the inmates, as they bent to do the field work. As the prisoners would be dripping with sweat in the sweltering sun, I could hear in my spirit the voices of those who had come before me, and had come from as far away as Timbuktu.

"Keep the faith," they silently whispered to me. "Keep the faith."

The next day, I found a newspaper article with a headline that read "In the Case of the Wilmington Ten, Justice has been done." *Justice?* I thought, *compared to what?* I thought of Dostoyevsky's *Crime and Punishment*, which I had read in prison. The novel's main character, Rodion Romanovich Raskolnikov, felt that justice meant that it should be permissible to murder your enemies in pursuit of a higher purpose.

Rashid X had convinced me that the white man was the devil, and for a fleeting moment, I contemplated what it would feel like to pursue that higher purpose. Then, I recalled how the book ended for Raskolnikov—years of hard labor in a Siberian prison. Not a pretty picture.

Once again, I decided that I would just keep the faith.

I had faith that Ben Chavis was doing all he could to spring us. We had received a letter from the United Church of Christ's Commission for Racial Justice saying that Ben would be attending a General Synod gathering in St. Louis, Missouri on June 25, 1973.

When that date arrived, Ben did ask a national audience of the UCC to assist in our release. By unanimous consent, the General

Synod voted to appropriate $400,000 for our release. Ben had come through.

After some nine months in captivity, on July 20, 1973—the fourth anniversary of the first man on the moon—we set foot outside of prison control. The remaining eight men of the Wilmington Ten were ceremoniously set free at the Pender County Courthouse into a cheering crowd. By this time, Anne Sheppard, who had gotten a much lighter sentence than we did, had been paroled from prison months earlier.

The men of the Wilmington Ten knew that our freedom was a temporary state of affairs. The appeals clock was ticking. If the U.S. Supreme Court refused to take up our case, we all knew we would be ordered back to prison to serve out the reminder of our sentences—without the benefit of being under protective custody.

But on that bright summer day of our release, I wasn't thinking about that. I was thinking about getting on with my life. I was twenty years old and itching to throw on some jeans and sneakers, hit the park and play some basketball, drink a beer, see some girls, and sit at my mother's kitchen table, and give thanks that we could once again talk like mother and son, not as visitor and inmate.

It was wonderful.

But this breath of freedom would not last long enough. Not at all long enough.

14

THE SERPENT BENDS BACK TO SWALLOW ITS TAIL

I was totally unprepared for February 2, 1976.

It is a date that I will never forget like the days that mark beginnings and endings, like the birth of a child, the death of a parent. Almost three years had passed since I had been released from Odom Correctional Institution before that February day arrived, like any, with the rising sun. But before that same winter sun had set, my naive hopes for resuming a good and decent life after prison had been smashed right in front of me.

Shortly after the United Church of Christ's Commission for Racial Justice had put up nearly a half million dollars, which it had borrowed, to get me and the rest of the Wilmington Ten men out of prison on bond in the summer of 1973, I felt that justice had been given a second chance right along with me. We all were out while our legal team was appealing our October 1972 conviction. None of us knew how long that would take, but I felt that I finally had time to just be a regular guy again.

I easily managed to fold back into the neat, familiar crease of family that my mother had maintained while I was locked away. My homecoming was sweet with lots of hugs and smiles and laughter. There was great food and *"Thank you, Lords"* all around. My sisters, Marva and Jean, who still lived at home, fawned over me. The same was true with my brothers, Harold,

Willie and Gerald. They seemed like they never wanted me out of their sight again. I played basketball at the park, I watched TV, and I read and marveled at how the world looked without steel mesh and steel bars obscuring my sight of it.

No more jingling, jangling keys. No more prison food, prison grays, cellblocks and secured dormitories. My mother had kept my room just like it had been before I was swept up, chained, tried and imprisoned in a storm of hatred.

Old friends found me back at home and playfully persuaded me to join them at all the old spots where they caught me up on hot news, while we sipped cold beer. Some things had changed, like the war in Vietnam looked like it was winding down. And others had hardly changed at all, like black people still struggling to find their way in Wilmington. Still, I felt so good to be home again. And my mother... I'll never find the words, as if I had a hundred years to look for them to describe how deeply good it was to just be her son, Wayne, again. No prison number. Wayne Moore, again. But, at the same time, I was, after my release, more than simply the teenager who went to prison.

Dolores Foy Moore never had to say it directly. I knew. She was proud of me, so proud of my principles, my perseverance and my demonstration of just how strong a man she had raised me to be. I had endured and sat at her kitchen table. I was a young man with plans. She smiled and nodded her approval when I told her what I hoped to do next with my life. I wanted to get a job.

Back in 1972, when I was out on bond awaiting trial, my old teacher, Carter Newsome, had once again come to my rescue. As coordinator of the night school that I had attended before my arrest that year, he arranged for me to complete the requirements for high school graduation. He saw to it that Joe Wright and I got our homework even while being held in the New Hanover County Jail, before we got out on bond.

I received my diploma from John T. Hoggard High School just more than a year after being expelled from the school for my activism there.

Now free and with my diploma in hand a year later, I set out to look for that job I had promised my mother that I would get. I was oblivious to the still simmering resentment and general ill will that still stirred in the hearts and minds of many Wilmington whites. This was especially true of potential employers. Anyone even remotely involved in the boycott and riots of 1971 might have well been toxic waste.

No one would hire me.

This was pretty much true for all of the Wilmington Ten men—except Ben Chavis. By this point, Ben was working as a field director at the UCC's Commission for Racial Justice headquarters in New York with the likes of the Rev. Charles Earl Cobb, first executive director of the Commission and the man who spearheaded our release. Eventually, Ben would replace Rev. Cobb as the commission's executive director.

It wasn't long before I found myself hanging out in front of the Dew Drop Inn on the corner of Eighth and Dawson Street. Stubborn habits are the hardest to break. One evening, in September 1973, my old friend, Kojo Nantambu, walked up to me and took me aside.

He asked with worry and concern playing in his eyes. "What are you doing hanging out on a street corner? You need to be in college."

Kojo, no stranger to how the streets can wreck the aimless, asked me if given the chance would I go to college. I said sure, and he said, "Go home and pack your bags. We are going to Raleigh tonight."

I did exactly what Kojo told me to do. I went home, packed a duffel bag full of clothes, and rode off to Raleigh in Kojo's '67 Dodge Rambler.

Shaw University, predominately black and home of the Marching Bears, was like open arms to me. Here was a place where black pride, black identity, black American history and culture were cherished and fostered. It was very unlikely that there would be educators here who would, intentionally or not, make me feel inferior and inadequate because of the color of my skin, the width of my nose and thickness of my lips.

My ordeal with injustice had helped to convince me that I wanted to be a lawyer, someone who could defend the poor and oppressed. I entered Shaw as a freshman in the fall of 1973, joining its 2,500 students striving to be much more than this country generally had intended for us. It was literally liberating.

In stark contrast to prison, Shaw University would be the place where I felt the most comfortable in my identity as a black man in America. At Shaw, I found the black pride and nurturing spirit that had been the promise denied me at Williston Senior High School. There was something culturally comforting in stepping onto a college campus, and seeing so many people who looked like me, walked like me and talked like me. They were all searching for something higher, something special. There were quite a few students at Shaw who were the first in their families to attend college.

There was such a confident expression of blackness there. There was, as young people say today, a sweet *swag* in how almost everyone carried themselves on campus. You saw and felt it everywhere. When I saw the Marching Bears perform at halftime of a football game, when I saw the sororities and fraternities "stepping" during block shows, and the Shaw Players on stage, my spirit screamed out "home at last, home at last, thank God Almighty, I'm home at last!" If attending John T. Hoggard High School, predominately white and hostile, had been a traumatic experience for me, then Shaw University was much needed therapy. Here, everybody treated me like family. It was an amazing experience, and it had to be the greatest time of my life so far. I had never been to a black college before. I saw bright, black individuals from all over the world.

Founded in 1865, Shaw University was the first historically black university in the South. In its time, Shaw had nurtured and educated ex-slaves and generations of black Americans who went on to become prominent leaders, educators, scientists, doctors, lawyers, entrepreneurs and businessmen.

I was ready for this. And I had more than a notion of what college required. My brother Thomas attended Saint Paul's College, a private, historically black college in Lawrenceville, Virginia. And my sister, Stephanie, attended Shaw, also a private school, for a year.

For my first year I lived in a dorm. Yes, there were college rules and some regimentation to life in the dorms, but nothing like prison. I laughed to myself when I overheard some of the students talking about how they yearned to be free. I had never been more free. I didn't have a roommate, and that didn't hurt as I would sometimes romance and sneak a coed into my room. I had fun.

Nonetheless, I was a serious student. My major was political science and my minor, international studies. This was a black campus in the black power 1970s, so to say it was politically minded would be an understatement. As a result, a lot of students, especially the campus activists, knew who I was and knew a great deal about the Wilmington Ten. There were even crossed bloodlines with The Ten and Shaw. For example, John Mendez, the president of Shaw's student government just before I arrived on campus, was part of the Wilmington Ten support group. Besides, how *incogNegro* could you be when the likes of Angela Davis was holding a rally in your support that was covered in the national press?

When I was at Shaw, I really didn't talk about my struggles in Wilmington, or my time in prison. I'd say the same was true for my Wilmington Ten brother, Reginald Epps, who was also attending Shaw. We were looking forward, not backward.

Yet, we were happy to talk about our experiences when asked. In fact, the Commission for Racial Justice of the United Church of Christ sent Reggie Epps, Joe Wright, and me on an extensive speaking tour in the early 1970s. We traveled the U.S., speaking in cities like New York, Philadelphia, San Francisco and San Jose, California. I had never traveled like that. The commission paid for everything, just the way it was paying for Reggie and me to attend college. I was eating it up.

While the Wilmington Ten was out on appeal there appeared to be no restrictions on our movements. I truly felt free and confident that I would remain so. Who—after seeing what I was doing with my life, in undergraduate school and planning a path to law school—would want me locked behind bars with robbers, rapists and murders? Who could be that cruel and unjust? I was living a whole new life in a whole new world.

Then after completing four and a half semesters at Shaw University, I got word that the U.S. Supreme Court was not going to hear our case. I knew immediately that this was the end of the line. Already, the North Carolina Court of Appeals affirmed our convictions in December 1974. In May 1975, the North Carolina Supreme Court refused to hear our case.

With the U.S. Supreme Court washing its hands of us, our 1972 convictions on arson and conspiracy assault on police and firefighters would stand. Our appeal had collapsed like a rotting staircase. I could feel something straining to break inside of me, too, but I wouldn't let it.

We were promptly ordered back to prison to serve out the lengthy remainders of our sentences.

That day arrived on February 2, 1976, the bicentennial year of the birth of the United States. I wasn't feeling very patriotic that day.

We surrendered in Burgaw, North Carolina, the town where we had originally been convicted and sentenced. We had a meal with friends and family on the lawn of that damned courthouse, breaking bread and sharing wine, as one local newspaper described the scene. Then very quickly, sooner than I could get myself ready, we started walking to an awaiting prison bus. For me and much of the rest of the Wilmington Ten men, that meant returning to The Wall, Central Prison, and maximum security.

There were many tears, wailing and screams of disbelief. All around us heads were lowered in sadness and resignation. I'll never forget the pained loss and confusion on the faces of Ben's daughters, Paula, six years old, and Michele, eight. Their daddy was slapped with the heaviest sentence of all of us: twenty-nine to thirty-four years.

And as before, the bus trembled into gear, and we were gone in a haze of engine exhaust and so much emotional exhaustion.

◉ ——— ◉

With our appeals crushed, we were returned to prison with none of the little protections we had been provided before. No more protective custody. This meant that this time around, we all faced the very real possibility in the general population of being exposed to prison life—unfiltered. This also meant that all of us would eventually have cellmates.

The importance of a "good" cellmate cannot be exaggerated. It can literally make the difference in your ability to cope. In any instance, it is abnormal for two grown, adult males to co- exist in a four-foot by ten-foot space. When you mix into that the generalized frustrations inherent in prison life; it becomes almost unimaginable.

In the restricted environment of prison, no movement goes unnoticed, no word goes unheard, and every breath of air is foul. It helps to try to understand the problems of your fellow prisoners and relate to them as human beings. This is not necessarily out of any compassion you might have, but out of necessity to preserve your own life. A simple failure to communicate can easily result in serious injury or death. I witnessed several inmates get shanked for ordinary and trivial actions. For instance, Mike Brown, a short-timer—anyone with less than a five-year sentence—from Fayetteville, NC, got stabbed. His crime? He was shanked because he forgot to pass the newspaper down to the next cell on the tier after he finished reading it. Although he survived the knife attack, he learned the hard way the importance of maintaining proper prison etiquette.

During my first months at Central Prison, I was placed in H-block, primarily a transitional cellblock used for receiving and processing new or returning inmates. I had been alone in my cell for almost two weeks when someone decided that would change. Maybe a diagnostic test had shown that I could get along with other people. All I knew was that I had no choice in having to share my space with someone who could very well turn up the heat of my previously private hell.

But when I saw who my cellmate was going to be, I felt a sense of relief. He was George "Pokie" Davis.

I knew this guy from the streets. In fact, we were practically neighbors back in Wilmington. And we worked together for the cause. He had been the minister of defense for our community action organization, the Black Youth Builders of the Black Community. And Pokie had been in prison before and knew the ropes. We were glad to see each other again.

Pokie was waiting to be shipped off to a prison road camp, which was nothing less than an old-fashioned chain gang without the chains. I still have dark memories of my own experience working prison road camps. I had no idea at the time that Pokie and I would end up at the same road camp working our asses off in the heat of summer and the cold of winter. There were lots of road camps.

I was facing real time. But like almost everybody from Wilmington, Pokie knew that. He looked me over and apparently didn't like what he saw or smelled. I had not showered in two weeks. I just took bird baths every day.

I hadn't been afraid to shower in the New Hanover County jail because I had gotten to know most of the guys that were in jail with me. None of them were hardened prisoners; only one of them had ever been to prison. But behind The Wall, it was a different story. There were predators everywhere.

Maybe I was too subtle, but I tried to give Pokie a hint of my apprehension to use the common showers.

"I'm going down to take a shower," I told him as I stared out from the cell down to the ground floor where the open shower stalls were located. There were about twenty inmates already there showering. Pokie looked over at me and saw the frightened look in my youthful eyes. With a grin on his face, he told me that when I took a shower to be sure not to bend over to pick up the soap.

I guess that was a joke. He did crack a knowing smile. Of course, I knew immediately what he was talking about. A man's sexual vulnerability in prison showers was well known, as well as the terror it stirred in straight men like me. I had, like everyone else, heard the stories about rape in prison. Pokie smiled again and said, "Man, you guys don't have anything to worry about. You brothers are famous. The brothers here will look out for you. They won't let anything happen to you."

I felt some relief, but it was not complete. For the next three weeks or so, Pokie continued to school me on all the things I needed to know about prison, perhaps trying to reassure me that

I would be alright. The only problem was, the more he told me, the more doubt he stirred into the confidence that he was giving me. For instance, Pokie told me that I would probably be treated differently because I was a member of the Wilmington Ten, a black militant. Then he would add, "But you still have to be careful because there are vultures in here who don't give a shit that you are."

"They will still try to fuck you."

Those words would echo in my head for days. He told me stories about unsuspecting young guys in for the first time ending up being somebody's bitch. To help me avoid that fate he lectured me to steer clear of asking for any kind of help from anyone I didn't know, and know well.

He told me, "if you need to borrow money, make sure it is from one of your homies. Don't take any shit off nobody. It's better to fight and lose than not to fight at all."

The only thing I was interested in fighting for was my freedom. But somehow I knew that if I was to survive prison, it was important that I not take Pokie's advice lightly. As scared as I had been in the beginning, I knew that I would fight to the death anybody who tried to rape me. It must have been the militant in me. How could I be willing to fight to the death against white people who were violating my civil rights, and not put it all on the line to fight an inmate trying to violate my body? With that in mind, my greatest fear disappeared.

I was not afraid to die for what I believed in. I grabbed my towel and finally headed to the shower.

Pokie Davis also taught me how to play chess with an eye on its larger lessons about life. Before going to prison, I had always thought that chess was some kind of intellectual, elitist game, one of those things puffed up, self-important white people do to impress one another. But in prison, I quickly realized that there was a thin line between high intellect and just plain, old street smarts. I saw lots of inmates playing chess and with most of them it was seldom simply a board game; it was a means of maintaining their sanity.

Obeying a natural instinct to adapt to prison life, guys like Pokie had transformed chess into a game of how life is played on the city streets. You either play or be played. Almost twenty years later, I read a similar account about how inmates often taught and played chess as an analogy of life in Nathan McCall's 1994 memoir, *Makes Me Wanna Holler*. It must be a universal, black prison experience.

At Central Prison in North Carolina, chess pieces became pimps, bitches, and hustlers. In chess, just like on the streets, I was taught that the pimp/king stays at home, while the bitch/queen uses her power to go out into the streets to capture tricks/other pieces. If you can play the game of chess, you can play the game of life, and you can hustle for the highest of stakes.

"If you can think three moves ahead in chess, you stand a chance of winning," Pokie instructed me. "If you think three moves ahead in life, you can probably avoid irreversible mistakes."

Although Pokie had never been to college, he was one of the smartest dudes I had ever met. When people think of prisoners, they usually don't visualize a person who is not only a chess master, but a man who can also articulately analyze any kind of literature from Machiavelli's *The Prince* to Donald Goines' *Whoreson*. Pokie could do that, and then some.

Some of the brightest people I've come across were rotting away in prison. I met scores of men, mostly black, who had gotten caught up in a system that provided only the most limited means of escape, both literally and figuratively. Sadly, as smart as Pokie was, he couldn't make it in the outside world. He had been in and out of jail since he was thirteen-years-old; he got caught up in the drug game that beat him in ways I never could beat him at chess.

The Wall warehoused murderers and rapists, but the majority of its residents were in there for drug-related crimes. It was, and remains, a national shame. What a waste.

While the Thirteenth Amendment to the U.S. Constitution had declared that no American had the right to enslave another person, it left a backdoor wide open for anyone "duly convicted" for a crime. And the U.S. Constitution never said a thing about the enslavement of the black man's mind. Just like the way the king had pimped the queen in the game of chess, Pokie had gotten pimped by a drug called heroin in the game of life. He ended up in prison because he had decided that he had nothing worth living for outside its walls and bars.

"How can a guy who is as smart as you not have anything worth living for?" I asked him once.

"For all intents and purposes, my life ended when I went to jail at thirteen," he told me. "Once I got caught up in the system almost everyone seemed to give up on me."

He said the only place he had found acceptance was the streets, and street life led straight to prison life. It had been mostly a one-way street that left him a junkie and an ex-con.

"It's too late for me," he told me one day, his voice damp with regret. "Being on heroin is like being pussy whipped by a bitch who is taking all your money while screwing other guys. You know the bitch ain't no good, but you can't leave her alone because the pussy is so good."

Guys like Pokie often believed that coming to prison saved their life. I get that. You see them on some street corner, nodding after getting their fix, and you wonder if they will be dead the next morning. Then in prison, you see them full of advice on how to make it, but advice they can't follow themselves. It is a vicious cycle that usually ends only in their premature death anyway.

One of those boomeranging inmates was William "Bay Bay" Rogers. I ran into him at Central Prison when he was back for the third time, that time on a parole violation. I found him to be exceptionally intelligent, and extremely rebellious toward the system. He liked to play chess, too.

Somehow I thought I had developed a good game even though I had only been playing chess for little more than a month when I met him. After all, I had been taught by Pokie Davis, one of the best chess players in the state prison system. But man, Bay Bay was good. We played almost all day sometimes. We played chess and talked trash... trash about prison life, trash about white people, trash about black people, and trash about each other. He brought a whole new dimension to prison chess.

Then, one day when Bay Bay ended up choosing the white pieces at the beginning of the game, the first thing he said was "Slave, say hello to your master." Although I knew he was only trash talking, his words hammered home an unintended reality that wormed deep into my brain. In chess, just like in society, the white pieces always move first, giving them an immediate advantage over black pieces.

＊ —— ＊

One Saturday, back at Central Prison, I attended an Islamic service in the prison's Westside Chapel. Brother Muhammad Nubi delivered an outstanding lecture about life and its various struggles, which was just what I needed in my sad condition at the time.

In essence, he said, we are what we think. He explained that if we are going to be good human beings, then we must sow good thoughts into our minds. This, I thought, was comforting to have someone reassure me that despite my present condition, once again an inmate, I still had some control over my destiny. I felt relaxed afterward, the way I used to feel after listening to some good jazz, almost anything blown like hot glass by Miles or Coltrane. Relaxation and pleasant dreams are things that are seldom experienced when you are living like a caged animal.

The service ended at about 4 p.m., which was chow time at The Wall. I figured that since the chow hall was adjacent to the chapel, I might as well go feed my body after I fed my soul. Besides, the path back to my cell was a difficult one, a maze with several locked gates. I had a choice: report back to my cellblock or go and eat. I chose chow.

Big mistake.

On my way back to the cellblock after I ate, a guard named Mr. Barnes apprehended me. At first, I had no idea why he snatched me up. He led me to the Westside control office to see Duty Sergeant Watson and told me to explain why I had disobeyed a direct order to report back to my cellblock immediately following the Islamic service. I stated that I did not remember hearing such an order. The Sergeant informed me that it was standing prison policy, and that I should have known better.

I can still hear his words rattling around in my memory: "Ignorance is no excuse."

At the time, I had been living in K-dorm, an open-space housing arrangement of about a hundred inmates. There was an open toilet and shower facilities and televisions. Watson decided that instead of going through the trouble of writing me up for my violation, and sending me before the disciplinary committee, he would just send me back to H-block. There were no television privileges there.

I rarely watched TV anyway, so I knew that I would simply readjust to my new environment. Adjusting and adapting in prison almost always requires rationalizing, talking yourself into tolerating what at first might seem intolerable. I adapted to this new ordeal by convincing myself that where I was held captive didn't matter; it was all prison. What difference did it make whether I was housed in a dormitory or in a cellblock? It didn't matter that mattresses on springs are more comfortable than mattresses on unforgiving steel.

To learn to cope is to learn to survive. Survival in prison has a totally different meaning than survival on the streets. On the streets, survival revolves around making it from day to day, putting food on the table, keeping the rent paid and the lights on. In prison, survival is maintaining your sanity and staying alive. It's that basic.

Sergeant Watson was the duty sergeant on cellblock C. He didn't strike me as just a regular guard. He seemed to have ended up in his vocation of guarding men by default. In a place where men were hard boiled beef, Watson was veal, medium rare. He was out of place, more town idiot than keeper of dangerous men. And although Watson was black, it became clear to me that he wanted, more than anything else, to be white. Better yet, he struck me as a man who would have loved to not only be white, but some hard-assed, narrow-minded white racist. He clearly was not comfortable in his black skin and seriously uncomfortable surrounded by so many black men behind bars.

But you know, people can be complicated. He went through great pains to at least look the part of a jailer. Even though he was short and pudgy, Watson took great care to wear his prison guard uniform neatly. And where he could personalize his look, he did. For example, he apparently spent some time choosing his glasses. Their color and design were anything but standard issue. He was also smart enough to keep his mouth shut around his fellow guards and superiors so he didn't betray his ignorance. He used to strike a pose that, if you didn't look too closely, might pass for intelligence.

But intelligence can seldom be faked, not for long, and for Watson this was especially true.

On numerous occasions he would stare directly at me and say, "The only good convict is a dead convict."

What? I'd ask myself. Was he trying to intimidate me? Was this a clumsily orchestrated attempt to disturb what was left of my peace of mind? I always ended up with the same conclusion: Watson was no more than the idiot I perceived him to be. He was totally incapable of engaging in some high conspiracy to wreak havoc on my ability to deal with, and survive, my prison experience.

Yet, there were several times he forced me to reconsider my judgment.

Watson seemed to enjoy reminding me that I was one of the notorious Wilmington Ten. Most of the guards considered us to be radical and militant, but generally kept their feelings about us to themselves. But Watson really made me focus on our notoriety, and the consequences of the unwanted attention he brought down on me.

For example, while my cellmate and I went to the dining hall for lunch, someone left the water running in our cell. When we returned the water had not only flooded our cell, but had flowed out onto the tier and was dripping onto tiers below. I immediately went in search of a mop and bucket. However, I was stopped by a prison guard named Mr. Smith. He ordered me back to my cell. I tried to explain the situation, but to no avail.

"Get back to your cell, Wayne Moore," he ordered.

I thought, *how did he know my name? I had never seen him before.* But I said nothing back to him. Like an obedient child, I returned to my cell like he told me to.

Shortly after that, I noticed Watson coming down the tier as if he was in a hurry.

"What happened?" he asked me. I explained to him that my cellmate, or I had left the water on.

"I don't know whether it was my cell partner, or I who left the water on," I repeated. "At any rate it wasn't done on purpose."

My response didn't satisfy Watson. He continued to pound me with question after question, all of which I simply ignored. He then said, "I'll tell you what, get that water up right now!"

I resented how he spoke to me, giving me an order to do something that I plainly planned to do before all the harassment began. I grabbed the mop and started getting the water up as both Watson and Smith stood over me, harassing me and watching my every move I made.

When I finished, I looked up and said, "It looks a lot better doesn't it?"

No one said a thing.

I knew I had to find a solution to my Watson problem. He was like an infection that starts small, but can grow rapidly. In the meantime, I was sure that I wasn't going to allow him or anyone one else to break my spirit. So, my cellmate and I decided to file grievances against him to get him off my back. Ten days after filing the grievance, I was called out to the Westside control office where I was interviewed by a prison psychologist. He said that he had received a report that I had been "acting strangely."

After a little cajoling, he admitted that it had been Watson who had filed the report. The discussion with the shrink went well, or at least he told me what I wanted to hear: that my head was screwed on straight. I also learned that Watson had been assigned to watch me after he had reported that he deemed me to be an escape risk. But thankfully, the psychologist's report to prison indicated that I was "probably not" an escape risk.

I went back to my business of staying alive and sane. Besides playing chess, there were other diversions. I once had a cellmate named Robert Wilson. He was reasonably quiet and seemed to really enjoy reading. But it was difficult to get a read on his personality, and he certainly wasn't in Central Prison for singing too loud in church. He seemed to be pretty laid back.

During Christmas, I got some raisins from a guy in the next cell over, and using bread from the chow hall for yeast, Robert and I made some "buck," which is homemade wine for anyone who hasn't had a belt of the stuff. Making buck was easy, but risky. Easy, because all that was required to make it was to allow the bread and raisins to ferment for about three weeks. Risky, because getting caught making it could land you on segregation for six months.

We didn't get caught, and three weeks later, for more than two hours, we were the best a cappella singers in the world. At least the buck had us thinking we were. Strong stuff.

And there was Artis Mitchell, an ex-G.I. who had gotten in trouble in Fayetteville, NC, where he had been stationed at Fort Bragg. He caught twenty-five years for second-degree murder. He hardly ever talked, and I never managed to get him to talk about the circumstances surrounding the murder. But for some reason, I felt sympathetic toward him. He seemed like the kind of guy who "just didn't mean to do it."

I remember when he got a *Dear John* letter from his woman who said she couldn't wait the twenty-five years before he might get out. The very next day he asked to talk with someone from administration. He was taken to the front office. He never returned to the cellblock. Officers later came and removed his personal belongings. I had no doubt that the letter had sent him over the edge. I had seen what these kinds of letters could do to inmates.

Few things in prison are more important to men than having a woman on the outside that they can cling to. Strangely, they are often the same woman that guys treated like a piece of shit when they were on the streets. Once living on opposite sides of the bars, the women whom they had referred to as bitches on the streets are suddenly transformed into African Queens. And no matter how she looked before her man went to prison, to him inside she is now the most beautiful woman in the world. The prison system does its best to make inmates feel like complete failures, but that woman on the outside who cares about her man in prison reminds him that at least one person in this world sees some good in him.

My last cellmate at Central Prison was Rupert P. Decosto Weeks III, the effervescent one. Weeks had caught ten years for assault with a deadly weapon with intent resulting in serious bodily injury. It was his first offence. Never at a loss for words, Weeks engaged me in some very therapeutic conversations about life in general. We would talk about how we ended up in prison and what we would do if we ever made it back to the streets. We would do all the right things to avoid prison walls again. We would go to work every day and go to church every Sunday. Yet we both knew in the back of our minds that though we were sitting in prison for very different reasons, it would take much more than that for the average black man in America to avoid prison.

There were so many traps out there for us.

I was imprisoned at The Wall for six months, and then like my first stay, I was, without much notice and no explanation, shipped off to Moore County Correctional Institution in Carthage, NC, to work eight hours a day, five days a week upkeeping and beautifying the state's roads. It was hard, hard work in freezing weather. I was outfitted with a pair of work boots, a pair of work gloves, a pair of long-johns and a winter work jacket, and was told I should be happy to be earning forty-cents a day. That camp also had a sewing factory that used inmate labor to manufacture the prison grays we wore. At least that was inside.

The first thing to know is that inmates face a Don Corleone ultimatum. To work in prison is an offer you cannot refuse. If inmates work, they could earn "gained time." This is added to "good time," which the state provides inmates for good behavior, ultimately shortening their sentences. But if an inmate refuses to work, not only is there no "gained time," but there is now time to be spent in solitary confinement, "the hole."

The hole isn't really a hole in the ground, but it might as well be. An inmate is locked away in a tiny cell, alone and far away from all the other prisoners. The inmate, who is locked in twenty-four hours a day, also loses all privileges, including canteen. Any good time an inmate might have acquired up to that point would also be in jeopardy.

I know all of this because I was once thrown into a prison work camp hole. It was a single cell that resembled a brick outhouse with a shingled roof. This was a dark, dank and moldy place whose temperature depended mainly on ambient air.

Here, I was deprived of all personal belongings except paper, pencil and the Bible. Because the hole was located more than fifty yards away from the main building, I felt like I was in the middle of nowhere, isolated on a barren island. I not only felt confined, but claustrophobic with nothing to look at but four walls, a cold floor and a dark, peeling ceiling.

I remembered how I wanted to sleep away my time when I went to prison the first time. But I was looking at fifteen days in there, and who could sleep for fifteen days? Worse, the hole grinds away at your ability to sleep at all. Insomnia ruled the day and night. There was nothing to do, nothing to see and nowhere to go. More disorienting, there was no one to talk to. So you begin to talk to God in ways you never thought you would. Pleading for mercy, or at some kind of understanding.

You hear yourself pleading, asking, "Why me oh Lord?" You wait for answers that never come. You do push-ups and sit-ups until your arms and abs hurt. Then you realize how little time has passed, and you get angry at yourself for ever bucking the system in the first place.

Yes, that's how I ended up in this basement in hell.

I was stirred from my sleep at 5:00 a.m. with bright lights beaming down on my face. There was this booming voice of a prison guard shouting, "Chow-time! Work-call!"

Like a reflex, I jumped and walked hastily from my bunk to bars in the front of the dormitory. I knew what was expected of me, but for some reason that morning, I just wasn't having it. I yelled back at the guard.

"I refuse! I refuse to be a slave!"

Just the day before, a song came to me. It was a protest song I had sung with a group of activists led by Golden Frinks, the civil rights leader. We were marching from Wilmington to Raleigh. The lyrics were: "Before I'll be a slave, I'll be buried in my grave and go home to my Lord and be free." The mind is a funny thing. I don't know why that song popped into my head the day before. But it haunted me and influenced me more than I could have known at the time.

So, here I was defying a direct order to join the prison work crew.

The guard barely reacted. In a mild voice he just said, "Go pack your personal belongings and meet me up front."

At that moment, it was apparent to me that what I deemed to be a major statement of rebellion was no more than routine procedure for him. I packed my personal belongings and went straight to the hole. I had been on segregation before at Odom, but I had never experienced anything like this.

It made me begin to question my sanity as my emotions began to play tricks on me. One minute I was sad, the next I was defiant, until I realized once again what it must have been like in the bowels of those slave ships.

After I was released from the hole I decided that I would try to play along with the system. But the pain of that experience, and others associated with the work details, never fully left me.

Nonetheless, I worked hard and was eventually promoted to a minimum custody facility at Triangle Correctional Institution in Raleigh. There, I was able to get study release status and return to Shaw University.

Other amazing good things were beginning happen as the long, moral arc of justice—as Dr. King used to say—was bending toward justice for the Wilmington Ten. In August 1976, Allen "Big Al" Hall admitted that during our trial he falsely implicated us in the arson of Mike's Grocery and its related charges.

By January 1977, a second witness for the prosecution, Eric Junious, also said he lied during our trial. Junious, thirteen at the time of the trial, said he had traded his false testimony for the promise of a mini-bike and job from the prosecutor, neither of which he received. The following month, the third and the only other witness for our prosecution, Jerome Mitchell, also said his testimony was false and misleading.

When Big Al announced to the world that he had lied under oath at our trial, I jumped for joy in my cage at Odom prison when I heard this. Inmates all over Odom cheered, too.

"Man, you brothers are gonna walk," they told us. Big Al had gone into detail about how he had been coached into lying by James "Jay" Stroud, the prosecutor, and detectives Charles Fredlaw, W.C. Brown and others. He also admitted that it was special agent Bill Walden, not Ben Chavis, who had taught him everything he knew about Molotov cocktails. He concluded by saying that his entire testimony had been a lie, that his conscience had bothered him so much since we had been sent away that he had been "unable to live with himself as a black man."

He would, on May 10, 2001, die in a car accident.

Within weeks of Hall's recantation, I started getting correspondence at Odom prison from as far away as China and South Africa. I got visits in prison too, including Congressmen Don Edwards, Fortney "Pete" Stark and George Miller, all

Democrats from California and Walter Fauntroy, then the Congressional delegate from Washington, DC. We also received a tremendous amount of support from California Congressman Ron Dellums and Congressman John Conyers from Michigan, both Democrats.

At the same time, our case kept gaining wider national and international attention. Angela Davis, now a globally recognized black power figure, and Congressman Edwards, stood on the steps of the Pender County Courthouse during our post-conviction hearing in May 1977 to voice their support for the Wilmington Ten. Their voices joined New York Congressman Charles Rangel, a powerful Democrat, who had placed his support for us into the Congressional Record years earlier.

With the collapse of the prosecution's key witnesses used to convict us, our attorney, James Ferguson, wasted no time in amending a writ of habeas corpus, which we had filed earlier in the U.S. District Court in Raleigh. But Logan Howell, the U.S. magistrate, refused to act on the matter. In another blatant demonstration of justice Southern style, he kicked the matter back to the state court.

Around the same time, William Kuntsler, a widely known activist trial lawyer, said our case was part of a federal conspiracy set in motion by the Nixon administration.

Then in June of the same year, President Jimmy Carter was lecturing Russia that the Communist superpower had a poor record of respecting the human rights of its citizens and subjects. The Soviet response was swift and aimed right at the heart of Carter's argument. An article carried worldwide by the Soviet's *Tass News Agency* said, "The Wilmington Ten was another example of repression by racist U.S. officials."

Pressure to free us kept building. You could hear it hissing throughout the world. America, especially while Carter was injecting human rights as a major element of his foreign policy, was being exposed as a hypocrite. President Carter was directly pressed about our case during a press conference in early 1978.

> Reporter: *In Wilmington, N.C., The Rev. Ben Chavis and nine others have been convicted and sentenced to prison terms totaling 282 years for what they contend were human rights activities. The Rev. Mr. Chavis and his supporters, including now the NAACP and several prominent business and political leaders in North Carolina, have implored you for your intervention and comments on their behalf. What comments do you have regarding the Rev. Ben Chavis and the Wilmington Ten and their charges of political imprisonment?*

> President Carter: *Well, the only comment I am free to make under our system of government is that I hope that justice will prevail, that the ones who are accused of a crime will be given a fair trial; if they are found guilty, that they'll be punished in accordance with normal procedures for an equivalent crime committed. There is a very strict prohibition, as you know, against the encroachment of the executive branch of government on the judicial branch. The Attorney General is concerned about this particular case in that he wants the same thing I want and that is that justice be done. This has been a matter of longstanding controversy both on the domestic scene and internationally as well. And I trust the system in its entirety if there is ever a mistake made at a lower level in our judicial system there's always a right to appeal. And I believe the history of our judicial system is that ultimately they make the right decision. But I'm not trying to evade the question; I think it would be improper for me to impose what I think should be a judgment in a case*

that I've not heard tried and I don't have any direct familiarity to with the evidence. I believe that justice will prevail.

When I read this, still an inmate, all I could say to myself was one word: "Damn."

15

VINDICATION, REDEMPTION, AND FINALLY, FREEDOM

I can still hear the iconic "tic, tic, tic, tic..." of that stopwatch. Its old-fashioned clock face was, and still is, as familiar in American living rooms Sunday evenings as the faces of the television journalists who made *60 Minutes* the pioneering CBS news magazine that everyone seemed to talk about on Monday mornings.

And what America was talking about—twice, March 7, 1977, and again on March 20, 1978—was how *60 Minutes* the nights before had raised disturbing questions about the case made against the Wilmington Ten in 1972, and how the American justice system appeared to be anything but just in how it blocked our every attempt to legally win our freedom and vindication.

Morley Safer, himself an icon of the broadcasts, put it this way:

The Wilmington Ten. Every time the President—any American— gets up in a world forum to speak of human rights in South Africa or the Soviet Union, the Russians and others point the finger right back, and say, "What about the Wilmington 10? Have those people received justice in the United States?" It's a story that just won't go away.

A year ago we did a report about the Wilmington 10—nine black men and a white woman who were sentenced to a total of 280 years in prison after arson and racial violence in Wilmington,

North Carolina, seven years ago. Supporters of the Wilmington 10 continue to claim they're innocent; that they are, in fact, political prisoners. And just yesterday the protests culminated in a march on the nation's capital, yet another reminder to President Carter that human rights may be a two-edged sword.

I was still in prison when these programs first aired. In fact, I never got to see the first one, which dedicated its full hour to our story—something *60 Minutes* seldom did. I wouldn't see the second broadcast, an update, until I was released. But I heard about these broadcasts when I was inside. And it didn't take much imagination to realize the impact of America seeing Allen "Big Al" Hall looking straight into the camera and saying that it was *his* idea to set fire to Mike's Grocery that winter night in 1971; that "Ben wasn't in on it, and neither was any of the other defendants."

If that wasn't enough to put the case against us in serious doubt, Safer delivered the kill shot to prosecutor James "Jay" Shroud's fraudulent case against us:

In addition to Hall, there were two other key witnesses who supported his original testimony. One was a young man who at the time of the trial was in custody for armed robbery in which there was a murder. He too says he committed perjury. And the other was a thirteen-year-old boy who now says he was bribed with the promise of a gift and a job if he would testify against Chavis and the others.

The broadcasts also included the Rev. Eugene Templeton's comments that Ben Chavis along with Marvin Patrick, Connie Tindall and James McKoy were standing with him in the kitchen of his parsonage home the night when Mike's Grocery loudly erupted into flames a block away. It was a story that the jury never got to hear in 1972.

Rev. Templeton and his wife, Donna, did, however, get a chance to provide these defendants with this compelling alibi during a post-conviction hearing in May 1977, to an attempt to get a new trial. But Superior Court Judge George Fountain narrowly ruled against us after that hearing, saying that our guilt or innocence was not the issue. He said he was principally concerned whether our 1972 trial had been grossly unfair, that the constitutional rights of the Wilmington Ten had been denied. After nine days of testimony, Judge Fountain took only one day to render his decision that they hadn't been. His ruling stopped us cold from getting a new trial.

This was despite the three key prosecution witnesses recanting their testimony, and the new defense testimony, and also despite that our defense found there were more than two-thousand legal irregularities in the original trial.

So, no new trial. No release on bail.

Some legal observers expressed shock that Fountain could act so quickly. We later learned that a proposed draft of his ruling had been written by Assistant Attorney General Richard League and presented to Fountain prior to the hearing. This essentially meant that our hearing was little more judicial theater, a fraud.

U.S. District Court Judge Franklin T. Dupree Jr. upheld Judge Fountain's ruling, adding that "the Constitution only requires a fair trial, not a perfect one, and this court is convinced that the petitioners' trial comported substantially with all required constitutional principles."

Really?

This ruling came on the heels of an eighty-nine-page brief that the U.S. Justice Department filed in Dupree's court on behalf of the Wilmington Ten. It asked him to overturn the case in view of unsettling issues. Among them were: "Questions about whether the prosecution's chief witness, Allan Hall, told the truth when he testified that each of the defendants took part in the firebombing. The brief contends Hall was unreliable, and that Hall used notes during his testimony which were withheld from the defense."

And, "the Justice Department contends that the defense should have been allowed to question prosecution witnesses on special treatment they may have received in return for their testimony." The U. S Justice Department's petition stated, "One would conclude that the trial was imbued with a fundamental unfairness and was in violation of the due process clause of the Fifth Amendment to the Constitution."

Regardless of any of these questions, the nine of us continued to languish in prison. But one of the most devastating blows soon followed by way of North Carolina's Governor James B. Hunt. Because our verdict had been delivered by the state, and not federal, courts, even the president of the United States, if he was so inclined, could not pardon us and have us released. The only political figure in the country that had the authority to do that was Governor Hunt.

Our defense team refocused its attention to persuade Hunt to grant us a pardon. In late January 1977, Hunt had already gone on statewide-television and announced that he studied our case and had concluded that we had been given a fair trial. Worse, he said its verdict to send us away for 282 years was the right decision. It felt like he was hammering the last rusty nails into our coffins of conviction; he added that the appellate courts had acted properly and ruled correctly.

I was disgusted. But at the same time, I didn't feel alone. Even before Hall, Mitchell and Junious took back their damning testimony, we had a great deal of support from people and organizations already deeply immersed in the struggle for human rights. Among them were the NAACP, the Southern Christian Leadership Conference, the United Church of Christ and National Alliance against Racist and Political Repression. There were also black Congressmen John Conyers and Charles Rangel, both, who almost from the beginning recognized in our struggle an outrageous violation of human rights.

All the attention and support that the Wilmington Ten was getting, especially after the state's case against us was crumbling before the public's eyes—if not for its public officials—made me feel that so many people had our backs. We were getting even more letters from around the world, people telling and showing us that they believed in us and that they were fighting for us. That makes a lot of difference in your attitude and perspective. Millions of people now knew about the travesty of justice that was manifested in the trial, conviction and sentencing of the Wilmington Ten. It had finally been exposed in all its nakedness.

Our early attempts to get judicial redress in our case became a real education for me in justice North Carolina style. Appealing in the state's judicial system at that time was synonymous to the Wilmington Ten attending a KKK rally expecting anything else but attending our own lynching party. I know that may seem harsh. But consider this for starters: Robert Martin, our judge in our 1972 trial, had been appointed to preside over our case by Chief Justice Susie Sharp. She was the first female justice to head the North Carolina Supreme Court. Following our convictions, Martin was swiftly appointed to the state's Court of Appeals, a promotion. So, by the time we are appealing Judge Martin's conduct of our trial, he turned out to be one of the justices appointed to hear our appeal.

Conflict of interest? No one important enough to make a difference seemed troubled by this apparent conflict.

Needless to say, in December 1974 the North Carolina Court of Appeals affirmed each of our convictions. The court, of which Martin was a member, upheld the ruling that Judge Robert Martin did not abuse his discretion in conducting our trial, and that errors made, individually and collectively, were constitutionally harmless ones.

Next stop: Susie Sharp's North Carolina Supreme Court. In May 1975, Judge Sharp and friends, refused to even consider the merits of our appeals.

Next move: The Supreme Court of the United States of America. We were knocking on the door of the highest court of the "land of the free, home of the brave," the deliverer of *Dred Scott v. Sandford* in 1857 that long defined our racially inferior status in America, and *Brown v. Board of Education of Topeka* in 1954, that helped to pave our way to liberation over broader avenues to education.

And, of course, as I've already mentioned, the U.S. Supreme Court refused to hear our case. But what we hadn't counted on was that every well publicized step that we and our defense team were taking, the City of Wilmington found itself increasingly associated with us and our case. Rather than being thought of as the lovely port city of plantation mansions, magnolia trees and Spanish moss lining its many, quaint and picturesque streets and broad avenues, it was being thought of as a place where something ugly happened, where blacks and whites violently clashed and justice went undone. Even some North Carolina officials were becoming defensive.

The state's attorney general, Rufus Edmisten, said he was "sick and fed up that North Carolina was being portrayed unfavorably" as national media raised questions in the wake of our trial and appeals. And like any active addict, Edmisten could not see beyond his own needs, in his case, white supremacy and traditional white privilege, to understand how honest and fair-minded people around the world could harbor serious doubts about the way the Wilmington Ten had been convicted and locked away.

Nonetheless, the pressure for our release continued to build.

In February 1978, sixty congressmen signed a petition that urged United States Attorney General Griffin Bell to intervene in the case of the Wilmington Ten. They also petitioned Bell to assist the state of North Carolina in relinquishing its tradition of civil and human rights violations. Some two months later, a Congressional delegation, which included John Conyers, Ron Dellums and Don Edwards, then chairman of the House Judiciary subcommittee of Civil Rights, were to visit us in prison.

Conyers, Dellums, and Edwards, who is white, had also attended our post-conviction hearing, along with Angela Davis whose exposure to our case moved her to label North Carolina at the time the "South Africa of the United States."

Although President Jimmy Carter's stated reluctance to get directly involved in our case, he, at the urging of our supporters in Congress, gave the go ahead for Bell to investigate our case. The investigation looked into the possibility of corruption as well as the possibility that the civil and human rights of the Wilmington Ten had been violated.

Attorney General Bell, in turn, ordered a full-scale investigation by the Justice Department. The results were as explosive, in their way, as the Wilmington's nights of terror and turmoil in February 1971.

What the world learned was that for five years following our conviction, Al Hall had spent his days and nights filled with guilt over the fact that he had lied when he testified against us at trial. The prosecutor's office, under the direction of assistant prosecutor, James T. "Jay" Stroud, had provided Hall, its star witnesses and a convicted felon, with the luxury of a beach cottage on Carolina Beach, just outside Wilmington. When Hall was preparing to testify for the prosecution, he was serving a twelve-year sentence for his confessed role in the February 1971 riots.

And Hall was not alone in his Atlantic coast hideaway some fifteen minutes from Wilmington. Prosecution witness Jerome Mitchell had also been living there on the state's dime. And that dime was being paid to the cottage's owner, G.D. "Tex" Gross, the head of the area Ku Klux Klan. Gross had acknowledged to a reporter from the *Greensboro Daily News* that the cottage was rented from the realty company he owned. He also acknowledged that he went on "service calls" to the cottage while Hall was there and that they "gambled, drank and smoked cigarettes" there while the trial was being held.

There were other Klan connections to the case. Marion W. Millis, testified in 1965 during the House of Representative hearings before the Committee on Un-American Activities Hearings, that he had been involved with the Klan (but to only see what its members were up to). Millis was the New Hanover County Sheriff during the time of our arrest.

It was learned during the post-conviction hearing and confirmed in the federal investigation that followed, that Sherriff Millis, and the trial's chief prosecutor, New Hanover County District Attorney Allan Cobb, worked together in coercing and deceiving Hall. The men persuaded Hall, who was seventeen and developmentally challenged, into falsely testifying that he had participated in the firebombing of Mike's Grocery Store under orders of Ben Chavis.

"Mr. Cobb came upstairs to the county jail, and told me that I could get forty years, for arson," Hall testified during our 1977 post-conviction hearing. He added, under oath, that Sheriff Millis told him that there hadn't been any kind of trouble in Wilmington until Chavis arrived in town. Hall said Millis suggested to him that Ben had also somehow profited from Wilmington's racial troubles, asking if he knew that Ben had come to town in a Volkswagen, and left in a Cadillac Eldorado.

"No, I didn't know it," Hall testified, adding that "they told me that Chavis had threatened my family. So then like they told me what to say in court, because I had gotten mad and I had said that for them to just give me a gun, that I would kill Chavis, you know, and so Stroud said, "no, uh... that the best way to get him is through the law."

"He said the law has so many quirks and turns in it and so like, I went along with that."

For most fair-minded Americans, white or black, it was unconscionable that elected officials would work in collusion with organizations like the KKK, and would then manufacture evidence, and further retard justice by way of bribery and encouraging witnesses to perjure themselves. Hall went on to say that District Attorney Allan Cobb also promised him an early release from prison in exchange for his testimony against us.

And it didn't stop there. Hall exposed several other people who he said assisted Cobb in this conspiracy of manipulating him and manufacturing evidence. Among those he implicated were Bill Walden, an agent of Alcohol, Tobacco, and Firearms, and Wilmington detectives, Charles Fredlaw, W.C. Brown, Ken Hooks, Joe McQueen and Mike Robinson.

"They told me they didn't want me, but they wanted Ben Chavis," Hall testified, adding that it was Walden who showed him how to make and throw firebombs while he occasionally relaxed at another location, the Holiday Inn on Wrightsville Beach, less than ten minutes from downtown Wilmington.

It seemed that Big Al Hall couldn't stop talking once he got started. He went on for days, adding details with testimony that a fire started in the hotel room one day while Walden was teaching him how to make proper firebombs. It was also learned through Hall's testimony that detectives Robinson and McQueen supplied him with alcohol and drugs. Hall also told the hearing, that the law officers would make six-hundred-mile roundtrips to Asheville, NC, shuttling Hall's girlfriend, Deborah Simpson, to the beachfront cottage and hotel room where Hall was continuing to serve his twelve-year sentence.

Apparently, Ms. Simpson had no means of transportation to see her sweetheart, to get to and from the beaches. So some of Wilmington's finest stepped up in the name of romance and cooked up false testimony.

Jerome Mitchell, who was the second witness to testify against us during our 1972 trial, also recanted during our post-conviction hearing. He told the hearing that authorities "told me to cooperate or I could face life in prison." He added that he was reminded that "I had a brother who had just been convicted and that he faced life in prison."

Prior to Mitchell's original testimony five years earlier, he had been facing trial in the brutal slaying of store owner Billy Futch. Following his testimony against us, he was convicted of second-degree murder and armed robbery in Futch's murder. But rather than facing a thirty-year prison sentence for the crimes, Mitchell, who was seventeen at the time of his conviction, was granted youthful offender status following his Wilmington Ten testimony. This meant he would be eligible for parole when he reached twenty-one.

Mitchell told the hearing that he had given false testimony against us during the trial "for myself, because I wanted out of prison." He added that prosecutor Stroud told him that he would "have me out in six or seven months. So, I agreed to testify."

Mitchell also testified that Stroud coached him and Big Al before the 1972 trial. He said that Stroud told him that his role was to corroborate Big Al Hall's testimony. But Mitchell said he had a problem: He wasn't anywhere near the scene of the Mike's Grocery fire when it happened. He testified at the hearing that he knew nothing about what the Wilmington Ten had allegedly done that night.

It wasn't until he was facing thirty years in prison for the robbery-murder, Mitchell told the hearing, that he decided to cooperate with Stroud and lie about us. Tex Gross sweetened the deal, Mitchell testified, by visiting the Carolina Beach cottage often and promising Mitchell that he would protect him after he testified against the Wilmington Ten.

The final key witness, who was thirteen years old when he helped to send all of us to prison, was Eric "Motor Mouse" Junious. He testified at our post-conviction hearing too, and confirmed rumors that he was given a motorbike and a job in exchange for his convicting testimony. According to Wilmington detective, W.C. Brown, the money for the bike was donated by a number of officers who directly participated in the Wilmington Ten case. Brown noted that Stroud was well aware of the mini-bike gift.

"Motor Mouse," who had said he earned his nickname by frequently running from the police, was serving time in a youthful offender prison for three breaking and enterings, and larceny convictions at the time of the Wilmington Ten trial.

While listening to all of this, it struck me how strange it was that all three key witnesses against us had extensive felonious records, while none of the Wilmington Ten had felonious records before we were falsely convicted.

Like his nickname might suggest, Motor Mouse talked and talked at the hearing. He also testified that he had been coached to lie against us at trial. "If I were older, I wouldn't have gone for that really. He conned me out of it," Junious lamented, referring to Stroud.

He testified that he remembered meeting at the Holiday Inn on the beach with Big Al there.

None of this surprised me. This was how (in)justice was practiced when it came to black people in the South. I could have been a character witness for Wilmington's police. When I was doing time in Odom prison, Jackson, I received a visit from detectives Brown and Fredlaw. They indicated to me, Willie Vereen, Reginald Epps, Joe Wright, Jerry Jacobs and James

McKoy that they believed that we were all totally innocent, and shouldn't be behind bars. They told us that it was not us authorities had wanted. It was Ben Chavis.

The detectives tried to convince us that Ben had exploited us for his own gain. They said that Ben had been playing both sides of the fence. That while he portrayed himself as a civil rights leader prior to coming to Wilmington, he had been an FBI informant, something the Black Panther Party had also falsely accused him of being.

Detectives Brown and Fredlaw said that they would be willing to help us if we would help them prove that Ben was guilty. Why hadn't they spoken up at our original trial if they felt so strongly that we were innocent? Why had they allowed us to be indicted in the first place? At that time, I'd felt nothing but contempt and indignation toward these black detectives who had so easily betrayed a group of young, promising black students in hopes of winning concessions from their bosses.

Almost thirty-five years later, my understanding is that they are still waiting for those concessions. There was another black law enforcement officer involved in our case. His name was Joe McQueen, and he was later elected New Hanover County's deputy sheriff. He ran on a promise to keep the black community under control.

The role these officers played in the investigation, trial and conviction of the Wilmington Ten was paramount, although their names were seldom mentioned when the accolades for putting us away were passed out. For years, the mere mention of their names filled me with contempt. My inclusion of them here is merely an attempt to explain how they conspired in the imprisonment of the Wilmington Ten, and how their roles led to a kind of imprisonment of their souls for being willing partners in a racist cabal.

What made it even more troubling is that I'd known Charles Fredlaw for years prior to the Wilmington Ten. I had attended school with his nephew, John, who to this day I consider a friend. At one time, I lived only one block from Detective Fredlaw. When I was twelve years old, I delivered his newspaper.

For years following the conviction of the Wilmington Ten, I held out hope that at least Charles Fredlow would be the one person in the city's police department who would step forward and expose all the official lies and deception surrounding our case. I knew this man. He knew me, and the kind of earnest, young man I was. Once the witness recantations went public, I felt that solid proof of our innocence was in the air. But I still wanted the acknowledgment of that proof from those three detectives who helped to frame us. That admission would be total vindication.

It may sound strange, but I was also concerned about their compromised souls. I thought about the weight of their guilt and misdeeds on their consciences, if they had consciences. They certainly must have known how vicious North Carolina's judicial process was when it had black people in its grip. They must have known about the limitations of Big Al Hall's mental capacity, that he was in no way capable of carrying out the crimes they implicated him in.

All these decades after our conviction, I still cannot understand how these three law men turned such blind eyes and deaf ears to truth and justice in one of the most blatant miscarriages of justice in the history of North Carolina. And these were black men. Is there any wonder why millions of black people still do not trust the police?

Although I have forgiven Hall, Mitchell and Junious, I find it very tough to forgive those detectives. By the summer of 1977, most reasonable people who were familiar with our case had concluded that our prosecution had little to do with truth and justice, and everything to do with exacting vengeance and retribution. But our tormentors had not expected us to become international poster boys for U.S. repression.

In July 1978, Amnesty International declared the Wilmington Ten political prisoners. We were the first group of prison inmates in the country to be officially designated that status; Andrew Young, the American ambassador to the United Nations and prominent veteran of the civil rights movement, acknowledged in Paris that there were "hundreds, perhaps thousands" of political prisoners in the U.S.; and Gary, Indiana Mayor Richard Hatcher, the first black elected mayor of a U.S. city, said political prisoners in American were a fact, and he cited us as a prime example.

But by mid-November 1978, the United States Justice Department filed a petition in Federal Court that it had uncovered evidence that strongly indicated that we were denied a fair trial in 1972. It then petitioned the court to either throw out the state convictions or hold a hearing on the government's findings.

With intense political pressure continuing to mount on North Carolina to do right by us, Governor James Hunt moved, this time commuting our sentences. He reduced our sentences from:

Defendant	Original Sentence	Commuted Sentence
Ben Chavis	25-29 years	17-21 years
Connie Tindall	22-26 years	15-19 years
James Mckoy	20-24 years	14-18 years
Jerry Jacobs	20-24 years	14-18 years
Joe Wright	20-24 years	13-17 years
Marvin "Chili" Patrick	22-26 years	15-19 years
Reggie Epps	20-24 years	14-18 years
Wayne Moore	20-24 years	14-18 years
Willie Vereen	20-24 years	14-18 years

Yet, he clung to his refusal to outright free and pardon us. This made all of us—except for Ben Chavis—immediately eligible for parole.

On September 22, 1978, I was released from Triangle Correctional Center, a minimum-security prison in Raleigh where I had been permitted to resume my studies at Shaw University. The gates were behind me, and this time I didn't look back. My mother gave me a long embrace, one I can still feel to this day. Some friends from college drove me to Shaw where I went to the dean's office, and was assigned a dorm room like the day I had arrived as a freshman, but this time as an upper classman and a free man.

On December 4, 1980, the United States Court of Appeals for the Fourth Circuit, Richmond, Virginia, overturned the convictions of the Wilmington Ten citing *"gross misconduct"* on the part of the prosecution in obtaining our convictions. The year before, Ben Chavis was released from Orange County Correctional Center after completing, on study release, his master's degree in theology from Duke University Divinity School.

The appeals court left open the door for North Carolina to either retry us or dismiss all charges, but it did neither. The state did not act until December 31, New Year's Eve, 2012. Instead, Governor Beverly Perdue, a Democrat, granted us full pardons of innocence less than a week before she was scheduled to leave office. She called the invisible hand that guided our wrongful conviction and imprisonment "naked racism." She also noted that "justice demands that this stain finally be removed. The process in which this case was tried was fundamentally flawed. Therefore, as Governor, I am issuing these pardons of innocence to right this longstanding wrong."

Finally. Finally. Finally.

We were free. But we were hardly free from the tremendous gravity that our ordeal exerted on us. Yet I was then and continue to be today strengthened by my struggle with a blatant miscarriage of justice in much the same way my ancestors struggled against every indignity and hardship that followed them in the bowels of slave ships to American shores. Upon reflection, my own pain has been minimal compared to the centuries of black enslavement, savage destruction of our families, first languages, culture and customs, then the years of lynching and Jim Crow, and all their related agonies.

And still my ancestors, distant and near, survived. And I have survived and have been able to heal the wounds caused by years of being denied justice and respect. It is only because of this experience that I have been able to continue the battle for my people and my own soul, with all the joy of a *Triumphant Warrior.*

EPILOGUE

While attending Shaw University in Raleigh, NC, I had the opportunity to study more than books. One Saturday night in 1975 during my fourth semester there, a classmate and I went to neighboring St. Augustine's College looking for a party. We even ventured into a woman's dorm at the college. Baker Hall. I'll never forget it.

While walking down a hallway not really knowing where I was going, I nearly ran into a young woman who was just minding her business going to her room, I think.

"Hey," she said, at once a little startled and amused to see me standing in her women's-only dormitory.

Her name was Gwendolyn Sue Roberson, and she was beautiful. She looked fit and fashionable, wearing her hair in a huge, Foxy Brown-styled afro. She stood about a foot shorter than my six-foot, three-inch frame. The perfect height difference to reach down to give a warm, affectionate hug and kiss. But that would come much later.

I soon bumped into Gwen again, but this time on campus. And I promptly and properly asked her out. I learned that she was a freshman and a little younger than me because her high school years hadn't been interrupted by participating in a public schools boycott and power struggle for black self-determination like my education had. She came to know me. She thought I was "crazy" and "bold" in all the best of ways.

We fell deeply and divinely in love. For almost the next two years we were inseparable, and only torn apart when the United

States Supreme Court in 1976 refused to hear the Wilmington Ten appeal, a decision that triggered us being sent back to prison. Two months later, while back in prison grays and cellblocks, I received a letter from Gwen. She informed me that she was going to be the mother of our first child. She was pregnant with our daughter, Nasheika.

Three years later, after the case against us was overturned and the Wilmington Ten were freed, I returned to Shaw University in hopes of picking up the pieces of my education. I was determined to graduate, not only for myself, but for my wife and our little girl. But the long, cold shadow of years of cruel and dehumanizing treatment in prison were longer and colder than I had realized. I was also profoundly frustrated and disillusioned by the steadfast refusal of the state of North Carolina to acknowledge our innocence in a case roundly understood as a massive miscarriage of justice.

Soon, I discovered that I had trouble concentrating on my studies and staying true to the right direction. I drifted and found myself squarely on paths of self-destruction; I dipped and dabbed into drugs, at first messing with powdered cocaine, and then stumbling into smoking crack—all of it chased by beer and cheap wine.

Like so many, I thought the drugs and alcohol might heal my wounded spirit. They did not. They only led to me being arrested on drug charges. I went back to prison for that, but luckily, for only a few months.

It took Gwen, a strong and clear-eyed woman, to remind me of where I came from, a long line of men and women who drew great strength from their struggles to survive and thrive. She told me that if I continued to falter, if I allowed racism and injustice to extinguish my fire to succeed, I would be failing not only myself, but all of my people who had come before me.

"We should never allow evil to triumph over good," she told me, adding a most important end note: "You need to be a father and a man."

Words have power and even more so when they have truth and love illuminating them. I heard what Gwen told me with my heart; I actually felt her words. That statement, more than anything else during that period of my life, transcended my turmoil and pulled me back to the road of redeeming my manhood. Gwen deserves so much of the credit. There is nothing like a righteous black woman in counterbalancing the crushing blows of traditional American racism.

With my eyes now clear and my spirit renewed, I decided to leave North Carolina and headed for Michigan in a sort of self-imposed exile. It was August 1983, the same year Gwen and I got married.

There was no love lost between me and my home state. I watched, as much of Wilmington's white power structure took it upon itself to punish members of the Wilmington Ten who went home, and attempted to resume their lives there.

I was extremely fortunate to know, if only barely, the Rev. Herbert Lowe. He was a minister of the United Church of Christ and had worked tirelessly with the Commission for Racial Justice of the United Church of Christ to free the Wilmington Ten. When Rev. Lowe, who insisted that I call him Herb, learned that I was leaving the South, he invited me to stay with him and his family in Ann Arbor, Michigan.

I took him up on his offer, moving there while my family remained behind in Gwen's hometown of Chapel Hill, NC.

The Lowes and I understood that the relocation would be part of a major transition to my new life. He clearly understood how all of the Wilmington Ten that had been badly mistreated by the North Carolina judicial system; and somehow, Herb, a white man, and a Northerner, believed that he had a human obligation to help us rebuild our crumbling lives. Herb's wife, Shirley, and their teenage children, Rob, Kim and Kirsten, along with their eleven-year-old son, all treated me like I was one of the family.

I lived with the Lowe family for six months. White or black, it does not matter. The Lowes are among the best people I have ever encountered. They were diligent in their attempts to understand black America, both socially and culturally. Herb was pastor of a church that was multicultural, multiracial, and unapologetically Christian. I love them dearly.

There are so many factors that tend to separate white and black people in America. Even with the best of intentions, or concerted efforts to ignore the facts of race in this country, it remains a very difficult task to bridge the worlds of masses of black people and their white counterparts. We remain so vastly apart from most white people, socially and culturally and economically.

I enjoyed my talks with the Lowes, even trying to explain something as simple, and yet complex, as the origins and lessons of soul food. For instance, the Lowes still can't fathom how anyone could possibly eat the cooked intestines of livestock—chitterlings. I reminded them that much of the black-American culture and experience grew out of the necessity to make much from very little. It was an enduring element of our strategy of surviving the most horrendous circumstances imaginable.

I told the Lowes that ours is a culture that survived slave ships and the accompanying agonies that might well have destroyed most people; that our culture and traditions evolved into one of poetic beauty and grace. It is a culture that allowed slaves to take leftovers from the master's table transforming the discarded, like pig intestines, into a delicacy. It is all part of a life song of turning trials and tribulations into Negro spirituals, drawing forth the music of blues from the pain and hurt of rejection, blending black and European musical influences and conjuring up jazz, the only truly original, American art form.

I was so comfortable and at peace with the Lowes. And that amazed me most, especially given the fact that I had just jumped from the white-hot, racial frying pan of North Carolina and—in a relative instant—landed into a melting pot of open-minded racial integration while living with a middle-class, white family in Michigan.

But even more amazing things awaited me during that self-imposed exile up North.

I landed my first job at Federal Mogul, a plant that manufactured industrial automobile parts. In less than six months of my arrival in Ann Arbor, I was able to bring Gwen, Nasheika and my three-year-old son, Ashea, to Michigan. Gwen went right to work at a nearby bank. In all, we lived a pretty much normal and uneventful life—until one day in 1985. A routine visit to the doctor revealed that Gwen had cancer. It was a devastating blow. But we kept our faith.

Gwen thought it was best that she and the children move back to Chapel Hill. We agreed that it would be in her best interest if she were in the trusted care of her lifelong physicians at the University of North Carolina-Chapel Hill. A month or so later, after visiting her doctor there, Gwen was told that she was, once again, pregnant.

Needless to say, Gwen experienced a very difficult pregnancy. Our son, Ashard, was born almost a month prematurely. But he was healthy and I was proud, but worried about my young family. I quit my job at Federal Mogul and headed back to North Carolina.

As she lay fading before my eyes, with cancer devouring her body, she exclaimed a single statement: "God is a good God."

Gwen died in Chapel Hill on September 19, 1987. She was thirty-two years old, and I was shattered.

In the days following Gwen's death, I struggled with grief and guilt. I wondered if I had somehow failed her, or whether I had always provided her with the love and support that she needed. I knew the answer all along. I had not.

By the time Gwen breathed her last breath, I had lost my sense of purpose. I was once again without direction. I was thirty-five-years-old and could feel my knees buckling under the dead weight of turmoil and tragedy that life had lain across my shoulders. It just seemed too much to bear at the time.

I was unemployed and unable to care for my children. Ultimately, I left my kids with Gwen's mother, and headed once again for my refuge in the storm: Michigan.

When I arrived in Ann Arbor in August of 1990, my situation was not much different than it had been when I first showed up on the Lowes' doorstep broke and broken. Herb met me at the airport and simply said, "Heard you were struggling."

"Yeah, a little Herb," I answered with just enough breath to make the words.

Herb looked me in the eye and replied, "Don't worry, Wayne. The Church of the Good Shepherd is here to help."

Unfortunately, I was unable to return to my job at Federal Mogul. I did, however, land a job as a janitor with Barfield Building Maintenance, which assigned me to cleaning floors and laboratories at Parke-Davis Pharmaceutical Research Division of Warner-Lambert Company. It was solid, earnest work. One problem: Ann Arbor is an expensive town in which to live and my new job only paid minimum wage.

Herb promised temporary assistance, and I well understood that temporary meant just that. I soon found that temporary would suffice. For all the sheer pain and humiliation I had suffered at the hands of raw racism, I found it strangely ironic that it would be white people who vehemently opposed that same dehumanizing racism, that it would be white people who provided me with life-saving assistance, not only in my quest to redeem myself, but to continue my struggle for justice and equality.

I also soon found that Gwen was right, that God was, indeed, a good God. I turned my gaze inward and found the clarity to rededicate my life to God and my restoration as a man, a man with a mission to battle, once again, for justice and equality. I vowed to never again allow any immoral man or unjust occurrence define my character or worthiness. I would, I told myself, allow Gwen's spirit to live and burn bright in me.

I decided on two things I needed to do if I was going to achieve my dream of bringing my children to Michigan where I could raise them: First, I had to find a decent-paying job; and second, I needed to further my education. Ideally, I could pursue both goals at the same time. But how?

Then there it was an answer.

While listening to the radio one day, I heard a commercial about an electrical apprenticeship program operated by the International Brotherhood of Electrical Workers, Local 252. The ad presented it as an opportunity to work and go to school at the same time. Perfect. The next morning I was at the door of the union hall before it opened. And as soon as that door cracked, I excitedly stepped through it to be met there by a tall, blond-haired guy who introduced himself as John Briston.

I introduced myself and asked about the union's apprenticeship program.

"Have you worked in the industry before?" he asked.

I told him that I had worked for three years on non-union jobs back in North Carolina. Then he asked me if I was licensed. I had to tell him that I wasn't.

"Have you taken any electrical classes or trigonometry classes?" Briston pressed.

Again, I had to tell him, no, I hadn't.

"Well, Wayne, before you apply for our apprenticeship, I will recommend that you go over to Washtenaw Community College and take some math and electrical classes."

He ended our conversation with a kicker: Come back in a year and apply.

I left disappointed, but not defeated. The very next morning, I was at the admissions office at Washtenaw Community College and explaining my dilemma.

"No problem," a young lady in admissions told me. Then she explained that I would have to take a series of placement tests before I could be accepted into the electronics program at the college. I took the test, but scored poorly, very poorly. It seemed I wasn't very good at algebra or trigonometry.

Then the admissions officer sent me, poor scores and all, to talk with the head of the school's electronics department. His name was Larry Kramer and he wasted no words or time telling me that, based on my scores, he didn't think I could make it through his program. He recommended that I try another field. But he did add that Washtenaw had an open-door policy, which meant that no one could prevent me from signing up for classes.

That is exactly what I did, sign up.

I had grown up in the black-American Baptist tradition that taught that "the Lord would make a way, somehow." I knew that somehow I would learn this higher mathematics. The Lord would make a way, somehow. My experience with the Lowe family and the benevolent Christians at the Church of the Good Shepherd should have been affirmation enough. But then there was Marion Morris. She rented me a room in her large home, charging only according to my ability to pay. The Lord at work, again.

When I told Marion about my algebra and trig challenge, she volunteered to teach me. Until I spoke to her about my problem, I had no idea that she had taught algebra, geometry and trigonometry in the state's public school system. When I informed her that I had miserably failed math in high school, she didn't flinch.

"It was not because you couldn't learn to do it," she told me with a smile. "More often than not, teachers are either unable or are unwilling to teach *certain* students."

She didn't have to wink to let me know who those *certain* students were.

Marion could, indeed, teach. She had a way of making math easy and accessible, even practical. To prove it, by the time I finished at Washtenaw two years later, I had taken every electrical course available there, in addition to applied physics. I finished Washtenaw with a 3.96 grade point average out of a possible 4.0. After doing so well, my application for the electrical apprenticeship sailed through the apprenticeship committee.

Five years later, I graduated from the electrical apprenticeship, second in my class with a five-year testing average of 92.5. Yes, Gwen. God is a good God.

As the years passed, I've been blessed to watch my daughter, Nasheika, graduate from the University of North Carolina at Wilmington with a degree in business. My son, Ashea, graduated from Grand Valley State University in Allendale, Michigan, after playing football on a team with two national championships to its name. Ashea now has a promising career as a sales representative for Cintas, a multi-billion-dollar corporation based in Cincinnati. He lives and works in Chicago for the company's first-aid, fire and safety division.

My youngest son, Ashard, went on to Hampton University and studied as an exchange student in Amman, Jordan—a long way from North Carolina.

In the meantime, I've been able to maintain a decent livelihood as a working member of the IBEW, Local 252, where I am known only as Wayne Moore, the hard working electrician. I even had a chance to return to Parke-Davis as an electrician in the construction of one of its new research facilities.

Suffice it to say, I only wanted to be given a chance, an opportunity, not unlike most Americans. But memories and the Wilmington Ten are never far from my thoughts. In 2011, I organized the 40th Anniversary Commemoration of the Wilmington Ten and, in the same year, founded the Wilmington Ten Foundation for Social Justice, Inc.

I still live in Ann Arbor, Michigan, where I completed this memoir.

Where Are They Now?

James McCoy, Marvin Patrick and **Willie Vereen** are living quietly in Wilmington.

Reginald Epps attended Shaw University and graduated from St. Augustine University. He remained in Raleigh, where he still resides and works as a heating and air-conditioning supervisor.

Benjamin F. Chavis, Jr., after his release from prison in December 1979, become Executive Director of the Commission for Racial Justice, then the national president of the NAACP, later still organizer of the 1995 Million Man March. He and pioneering hip-hop mogul, Russell Simmons, founded the Hip-Hop Summit. Ben is presently president of Education Online Services Corporation, which aims to assist historical black colleges and universities in increasing financial sustainability and long-term growth and to move them to the forefront of academic excellence in online learning with the use of twenty-first century technology.

Jerry Jacobs, once one of the top young tennis players in North Carolina, died in 1989 from AIDS-related complications. He was thirty-six-years-old.

Joe Wright, who had been a producer for a Wilmington radio show, died in 1990 of sarcoidosis. He was thirty-seven-years-old. Wright's brother, Thomas, served on the Wilmington City Council and in the North Carolina House of Representatives from 1992 to 2008. He also co-chaired the 1898 Wilmington Race Riot

Commission which closely examined one of the darkest days of white Wilmington's relationships with its black citizens. This commission was begun by the late Senator and supporter of our boycott, Luther Jordan.

Some believe unearthing new details of this incident led to an investigation of Thomas Wright and his eventual expulsion from the legislature for mishandling loans and campaign and charitable contributions. He was convicted of three counts of fraud and was sentenced to seventy- to ninety-five months in prison.

Anne Sheppard, who had relocated to Durham, NC, died in January 2011. She was seventy-three-years-old.

Connie Tindall, one of the most outspoken members of the Wilmington Ten seeking pardons of innocence, died in 2012 from complications of a stroke. He was sixty-two-years-old. Tragically, he didn't live long enough to see those pardons granted on the last day of that year.

All Triumphant Warriors!

REAFFIRMED

That's what I felt deep within, where even the January cold that stalked the National Mall could not touch me as I stood there on Inauguration Day. For so long, frustration and disappointment had taken up residence in the hot, earthen-red marrow of my bones. I reflected on how Michelle Obama must have felt in her husband's maiden run for the White House when she said, "for the first time in my adult life I am proud of my country."

On that Mall with so many others there to witness Barack H. Obama, a *black* man like me, sworn in for his second term as our nation's president, I felt overwhelmed, and like I belonged there. It wasn't just the day's flowery prose and poetry, its soaring songs, festive parades and fluttering flags. It was, for me, the culmination of a realization that the country that I always loved more than it loved me had done right by me—and, along the way, the cause of justice.

In the last hours of 2012, outgoing North Carolina Governor Beverly Perdue issued and signed a Pardon of Innocence for the Wilmington Ten. I was among nine black men and one white woman who were unjustly charged and convicted for the 1971 firebombing of a grocery store in my hometown of Wilmington, NC, during an especially racially tense time following the closing of the city's only black high school. At the time, I was a teenage activist who only wanted, like all ten of us, to see black students treated with some degree of respect and consideration.

For our efforts, the Wilmington Ten were sentenced to a total of more than 280 years in prison. Our case generated widespread condemnation and support, especially following the recantation of the prosecution's three star witnesses. Sixty U.S. Congressmen filed friend-of-the-court briefs with the Fourth Circuit Court of Appeals demanding that it overturn our conviction. The Justice Department found widespread misconduct on the part of prosecutors. President Jimmy Carter even spoke up after Amnesty International declared us political prisoners in 1977.

In 1980, the Fourth Circuit Court of Appeals finally overturned our convictions; we were all released from prison, released but not exonerated. I was free of the degradation of prison life, of physical bondage, but I hardly felt free because every day we spent in North Carolina, we carried the gorilla of injustice on our backs. That heavy weight dogged us for years, following four of the ten to all-too-early graves, and prompting me to try to start a new life in Ann Arbor, MI, where I, now sixty, live and work as an electrician.

But I wasn't thinking about the Great Wrong done to us as I stood at the inauguration, which happened to fall on Martin Luther King, Jr., Day and the one-hundred-fiftieth anniversary year of the Emancipation Proclamation. I was thinking, as I do now during Black History Month, of all the triumphant warriors that came before me. I thought of the strength and courage of Harriet Tubman, Sojourner Truth, Nat Turner, Toussaint L'ouverture, Malcolm X and Dr. King. And Barack Obama.

Being in Washington on that day was an indescribable experience, heavy with the weight of the struggles all Black, Brown, Yellow and Red people have had to wage since we all first set foot on American shores. I give such heartfelt thanks that I could be free, vindicated and live to see a black man stand on the Capitol steps built by slave labor and take the oath of the land's highest office in the same vein as a George Washington and Abraham Lincoln.

I am overjoyed to have received the pardon after forty years of immense pain trying to live without it. However, my greatest joy is found not so much in the fact that I have been exonerated from any culpability in the case, but in the truth that I was able to summon strength through struggle, from all those triumphant warriors who live within me.

My greatest wish is that these kinds of injustices continue to be exposed, so that what happened to the Wilmington Ten won't continue to destroy the hopeful dreams of young black folks, any folks for that matter. A pardon can't give back my life. It does, though, officially bestow upon me the title of Triumphant Warrior.

Earlier that day in DC, I found myself staring up at the great granite likeness of Dr. Martin Luther King, Jr., memorialized on the Mall, as he should be. I couldn't help but think that this tribute was to the same Dr. King who just a little more than forty years ago was the subject of jeers and vilification and hatred. This great monument stood before me in all its majesty, honoring the same man for whom I had heard blaring horns of cars filled with whites cheering his assassination as I strolled through the streets of Wilmington on that awful day in 1968.

But staring up at the stone Dreamer on his January holiday, I wondered if there wasn't a lesson in his turnabout for me, for the remaining six members of the Wilmington Ten. Will history be as kind to us? Could those who water-boarded Lady Justice, and the many who chose to look the other way, to lock us away, ever understand that we were guilty of nothing more than acting like Americans?

I certainly hope so, because if they do, they too will likely find their love and faith in this nation reaffirmed.

TIMELINE

September, 1968. Williston Senior High School, a prominent all-black high school was suddenly closed in order to integrate its eleven-hundred students into the two white high schools. The sudden closing angered many in the black community who felt that while it was inevitable and desegregation was necessary, it did not have to and should not have occurred in the sudden and traumatic manner in which it did.

December 18, 1970. Black students upset over treatment at New Hanover High School, which was one of the newly integrated schools, gather at the nearby Wildcat Café . Seventeen students, all of whom were black, were arrested after reportedly refusing to disperse. Of the seventeen arrested, eleven were expelled following an investigation by Principal John Scott. Scott had previously been labeled a racist by most of the black students.

January 15, 1971. After numerous appeals to school administrators to allow a memorial service for Dr. Martin Luther King Jr., were all rejected, seventy black students stage a sit-in at Hoggard High School's cafeteria. This peaceful protest led the expulsion of fifteen students who were identified as leaders of the protest.

January 26, 1971. Eight students form a boycott committee, which drew up a list of grievances to present directly to Heyward Bellamy, Superintendent of Schools.

January 29, 1971. A white minister Rev. Eugene Templeton invites about one-hundred black students to gather in Gregory Congregational Church (United Church of Christ) to begin a school boycott.

February 1, 1971. Heyward Bellamy meets with students at Gregory Church to discuss grievances.

Rev. Templeton calls Rev. Leon White of the United Church of Christ, Commission for Racial Justice, to ask for assistance for the students in presenting their grievances. White dispatched his field organizer Ben Chavis, to Wilmington.

February 2, 1971. Ben Chavis along with student leaders hold a press conference at Gregory Church to present their grievances, demanding that the expelled students be reinstated immediately.

February 3, 1971. Frustrated by the seeming lack of concern of the part of the Board of Education to provide an acceptable response to the students grievances, the students marched some 500 strong to the Board of Education demanding to speak to Bellamy. Bellamy agrees to meet with Chavis and two of the students. Chavis refuses, saying all the student leaders should be present.

That night Chavis holds a rally at Gregory encouraging the student to continue their struggle for equality in the schools. Students scramble for cover as shots are fired at the church. Later that night several buildings are burned to the ground including L. Swartz Furniture with damages estimated at over $130,000.

February 4, 1971. Certain that there would be bloodshed accompanying the widespread violence, Rev. Templeton calls for curfew. City Manager E.C. Brandon speaking on behalf of Mayor Cromartie and Chief Williamson said afterward, "There was no evidence of any impending racial clashes or violence against the church. Rev. Templeton has nothing to worry about."

Because "the police appear to be on top of the situation," Mayor Cromartie refused to grant a curfew saying that it would be "not only inconvenient but expensive." Responding to that comment, Ben Chavis along with several hundred students march on City Hall to plead to the Mayor to call a curfew. The Mayor refused.

February 5, 1971. About four-hundred blacks march on City Hall demanding better protection for blacks in black neighborhoods, On the steps of City Hall with hundreds of students chanting "We want action!" Chavis demanded that the Mayor and chief of police call a curfew. When the city again refused to declare a curfew Chavis after a phone conversation with a major from the state Highway patrol, said, "I want to publically charge the Mayor and the city council with conspiracy, in setting up the black community for annihilation."

A black minister, Rev. Vaughn, is shot outside of Gregory Church by white vigilantes as he tries to persuade men who were protecting the church to leave the church and go home.

Lum's restaurant burns to the ground and police and firemen responding to another fire at Mike's Grocery Store say they are fired upon by snipers.

February 6, 1971. Mike's Grocery burns to the ground after being torched for a second night. A seventeen-year-old black youth, Steven Corbett, is killed by police who say they were returning sniper fire from the vicinity of Mike's Grocery Store.

February 7, 1971. Harvey Cumber gunned down!

When Harvey Cumber, a fifty-seven-year-old white male, drove through the barricade and began shooting his life came to an abrupt end as someone behind the barricade returned fire. It was then that city officials decided that was time to call a curfew. When Steve had died less than twenty-four hours earlier, Mayor Luther Cromartie had chirped Steve Corbett's death "will serve as a deterrent." A decision to bring in the National Guard was announced at 3:00 p.m. The curfew was announced shortly after 7:00 p.m. It was in effect from 7:30 p.m. Saturday till 6:00 a.m. Monday.

March 6, 1971. North Carolina officials arrested Mr. Chavis on "conspiracy to murder" charges stemming from racial incidents in Wilmington in February 1971 in which Harvey E. Cumber, a fifty-seven-year-old white man, was killed. Other charges placed against Mr. Chavis were: assault on emergency personnel, conspiracy to assault emergency personnel, burning property with an incendiary device, conspiracy to burn property with an incendiary device. Bail for Mr. Chavis was set at $75,000.

The same charges were brought against Marvin Patrick, an associate of Mr. Chavis, and Tommy Atwood. Others were arrested. The eight others were: Connie Tyndall, James McCoy, James Bunting, Michael Peterson, Cornell Flowers, Jerry Jacobs, Willie E. Vereen and Anne Shepard, a white woman. All except Ms. Shepard were charged with arson and conspiracy to assault emergency personnel (firemen and policemen). She was charged with conspiracy to burn property and conspiracy to assault emergency personnel.

March 20, 1971, White student group marches on Hemenway Hall with a list of grievances.

Dr. Hubert Eaton notes that there are only three black classroom teachers at New Hanover High School, though there are others in the vocational department. He went on to say that all black schools (like Williston) are not a solution.

May 30, 1971. Allen Hall charged with burning Mike's Grocery. Signs a statement saying he and Ben Chavis burned store.

April 24, 1972. Joe Wright, Wayne Moore, George Kirby and Reginald Epps arrested on charges of conspiracy to assault emergency personnel and conspiracy to burn property.

May 1, 1972. Trial for Mr. Chavis and the others charged with conspiracy to assault emergency personnel and arson postponed until a federal judge rules on a petition to move the trial to federal court. Attorneys for the defendants had asked for a delay to prepare their case but had been refused by the State of North Carolina. The petition to federal court provided the defense attorneys some additional time to prepare the defense.

June 12, 1972. Mistrial declared for Mr. Chavis and the other defendants charged with conspiracy to assault emergency personnel and arson when the prosecutor becomes "ill." Ten blacks and two whites had been seated in the jury box and accepted by the defense, but the prosecutor had not agreed to accept them.

June 16, 1972. Chavis and twelve other persons charged with offenses in the Wilmington violence released on bail.

October 17, 1972. Chavis and the "Wilmington Nine" convicted on charges of conspiracy to assault emergency personnel and burning with an incendiary device. Anne Shepard convicted on charges of "accessory before the fact" of firebombing. Her original charges had been reduced sometime after the mistrial was declared. Chavis was sentenced to 25-29 years for arson and 4-5 years for conspiracy to assault emergency personnel. The sentences are to run concurrently and therefore total 29 years. Other sentences were: Marvin Patrick and Connie Tyndall, 22-26 years for fire bombing and 4-5 years for conspiracy to assault emergency personnel; Jerry Jacobs, 22-26 years for arson and 3-5 for conspiracy to assault emergency personnel; Willie E. Vereen, Reginald Epps, James McCoy, Joe Wright and Wayne Moore 20-24 years for arson and 3-5 for conspiracy to assault emergency personnel; Anne Shepard, 7-10 years. Bonds for the defendants were: Ms. Shepard, $20,000; all others except Mr. Chavis, $40,000-$45,000; Mr. Chavis, $50,000.

December 1972. UCC Executive Council, complying with promise to support staff arrested in the line of duty, post $50,000 bond for Chavis.

June 17, 1973. Angela Davis holds rally at Antioch Church of God in Christ in support of the Wilmington Ten.

June 1973. UCC General Synod votes to borrow $350,000 bail to free the nine defendants still in prison

December 1974. North Carolina Court of Appeals affirms the convictions.

May 1975. North Carolina Supreme Court refuses to hear the case, orders Ten back to prison.

November 17, 1975. The Hon. Charles B. Rangel enters the Wilmington Ten case into the Congressional Record

January 1976. U.S. Supreme Court refuses to hear the case. Wilmington Ten are jailed.

August 1976. Witness Hall admits he lied in implicating the Ten.

January 1977. A second prosecution witness admits he lied, accusing the Ten in exchange for a mini-bike and job from the prosecutor.

February 1977. The third and only other prosecution witness with knowledge of the crimes indicates serious irregularities in his testimony. May 9, 1977, Civil Rights Activist Angela Davis and U.S Rep. Don Edwards., express support for the Wilmington Ten standing on the Pender County Courthouse steps at Post Conviction hearing.

May 20, 1977. Activist trial lawyer says he sees the Ten case as part of a federal conspiracy launched by the Nixon administration.

May 1977. Despite the recantation of all three key prosecution witnesses, new defense testimony, and the contention of more than two-thousand legal irregularities in the original trial, Superior Court Judge George Fountain finds "no denial "of the constitutional rights of the Ten and denies them a new trial and bail.

January 1978. After a year-long personal review of the case, North Carolina Governor James B. Hunt refuses to pardon or free the Ten and reduces sentences of 20-25 years to 13-17 years. Anne Sheppard had been paroled by that time. The other nine remained in prison.

February 1978. Seventy-five congressmen sign a petition urging U.S. Attorney General Griffin Bell to direct the Justice Department to intervene in Federal Court on behalf of the Wilmington Ten

May 3, 1978. Congressional delegation including John Conyers, Ron Dellums, and Don Edwards visit members of the Wilmington Ten in prison.

July 15, 1978. Speaking in Paris, France, U.N. Ambassador Andrew Young says there are "hundreds, perhaps thousands" of political prisoners in the United States.

July 17, 1978. Gary, Indiana, Mayor Richard Hatcher supports Young's position, saying Young was "telling the truth" and that the presence of political prisoners in U.S. is "a known fact," citing the Wilmington Ten case and the case of Reuben "Hurricane" Carter as examples.

July 31, 1978. Amnesty International declares Wilmington Ten political prisoners.The Wilmington Ten were the first group of prison inmates in the United States of America to be officially declared "political prisoners" by Amnesty International in 1978.

This conclusion by Amnesty International was published and distributed worldwide.

November 15, 1978. U.S. Justice Department files a petition in Federal Court stating that it had uncovered evidence that indicates the Wilmington Ten were denied a fair trial in 1972. It petitioned the court to either throw out the state convictions or hold a hearing on the government's findings.

December 4, 1980. United States Court of Appeals for the Fourth Circuit overturned the convictions of the Wilmington Ten, citing gross misconduct on the part of the prosecution in obtaining convictions.

BEVERLY EAVES PERDUE
GOVERNOR

PARDON OF INNOCENCE
FOR
WAYNE MOORE

WHEREAS, Wayne Moore, at the October 1972 Term of Pender County Superior Court, was convicted of Burning Property With Incendiary Device, Docket Number 72-CR-1676, and by judgment of said Court was sentenced to not less than 20 years nor more than 24 years in the Department of Correction;

WHEREAS, Wayne Moore, at the October 1972 Term of Pender County Superior Court, was convicted of Conspiracy to Assault Emergency Personnel With Dangerous Weapons, Docket Number 72-CR-1674, and by judgment of said Court was sentenced to not less than 3 years nor more than 5 years in the Department of Correction;

WHEREAS, the United States Court of Appeals for the Fourth Circuit issued a ruling in <u>Chavis, et al. v. State of North Carolina</u>, 637 F.2d 213 (4th Cir. 1980), overturning the aforementioned convictions of Wayne Moore;

WHEREAS, it has been made known to me that numerous instances of prosecutorial misconduct and constitutional violations occurred at the trial of Wayne Moore and that the key witnesses, who provided incriminating evidence against him at trial, have recanted their testimony against him; and

WHEREAS, Wayne Moore now seeks a Pardon of Innocence by the State;

NOW, THEREFORE, I, Beverly Eaves Perdue, Governor of the State of North Carolina, in consideration of the above factors, and by virtue of the power and authority vested in me by the Constitution of the State, do by these presents PARDON the said Wayne Moore, it being a Pardon of Innocence.

This Order effective this the 31st day of December, 2012.

Beverly Eaves Perdue
Governor

SELECTED READING

Achebe, Chenua. *Things Fall Apart*. New York: Anchor Books, 1994.

Akbar, Na'im. *Chains and Issues of Psychological Slavery*. New Jersey: New Mind Productions, 1984.

Andrews, F.W. & C.M.. *Journey of a Lady of Quality*. Hartford, Connecticut: Yale University Press, 1922.

Applebome, P. *Dixie Rising*. New York: Random House.

Ayres Alex. *The Wisdom of Martin Luther King Jr*. New York: Meridian. 1993

Angelou, M. *I Know Why A Caged Bird Sings*. New York Random House. 1970.

Betts, R. Dwayne. *A Question of Freedom*. New York: The Penguin Group. 2010.

Brown, Claude. *Manchild in the Promised Land*. New York: Touchstone. 1965. 1999.

Carson, Clayborne . *The Autobiography of Martin Luther King Jr*. New York: Warner Books, Inc. 1998.

Chavis, Benjamin F. Junior Jr. *Psalms from Prison*. New York: Pilgrim Press. 1983.

Cose, Ellis. *The Rage of the Privaledged Class*. New York; HarperCollins Publishers. 1993.

Davis, Kenneth. *Don't Know Much About History*. New York: HarperCollins Publishers.

Douglas, F. .*Narrative of the Life of Frederick Douglas*. New York : Barnes & Noble Classics. (First published in 1845 by the Anti-Slavery Office.) 2003.

Douglas, Frederick. *Two Speeches by Frederick Douglas*. Rochester, N.Y.: O.P. Dewey, Printer, American Office. 1857.

Dubois, W.E.B. .*The Autobiography of W.E.B. Dubois* . Canada: International Publishers Co., Inc. 1968.

Dubois W.E.B. *The Souls of Black Folk*. New York: Random House. (First published in 1903.)

Eaton, H. *Every Man Should Try*. North Carolina: Bonaparte Press. 1984.

Ehle, John. *Trail of Tears, The Rise and Fall of The Cherokee Nation*. New York: Doubleday. 1988.

Forbes, Flores Alexander. *Will You Die with Me? My life in the Black Panther Party*. New York: Washington Square Press. 2006.

Fisher, Louis. *The Essential Gandhi*. New York: Random House. 1962.

Forbes, Flores Alexander. *Will You Die With Me? My Life In The Black Panther Party*. Washington Square Press. 2006.

Franklin, John Hope. *The Free Negro in North Carolina 1790-1860*. New York: Russell & Russell. 1969.

Franklin, J. H. and Moss, A.A. Jr. *From Slavery to Freedom. A History of Negro Americans*. Sixth Edition. New York: Alfred E. Knopf , Inc. 1988

Gibran, Khalil. *The Prophet*. New York : Alfred A. Knopf, Inc. 1927.

Godwin, John. *Black Wilmington and the N.C. Way: Portrait of a Community in the Era of Civil Rights Protest*. Lanham, Md. : University Press of America. 2000.

Grimsley, Wayne. *James B. Hunt: A North Carolina Progressive*. Jefferson, N.C.: McFarland & Company. 2003.

Harrington, Michael. *The Other America*. New York: Touchstone. 1962. 1997.

James, G. G. M. *Stolen Legacy. The Greeks were not the authors of Greek Philosophy, but the people of North Africa, commonly called the Egyptians*. San Francisco: Julian Richardson Associates, Publishers. 1988.

Muhammad, Elijah "Message to the Black in America. Secretarius MEMPS Publications. Phoenix, Arizona. 1965

Myerson, Michael. *Nothing Could Be Finer*. New York: International Press, Inc. 1978.

Newman, Richard. *African American Quotations*. Arizona: Oryx Press. 1998.

Othow, Helen Chavis. *John Chavis, African American Patriot, Teacher, And Mentor (1763-1838)*. Jefferson, North Carolina: McFarland & Company, Inc., Publishers. 2001.

Powell, William S. *Encyclopedia of North Carolina*. Chapel Hill: University of North Carolina Press. 2006.

Prather, H. Leon. *We Have Taken A City*. Wilmington, NC: Nu World Enterprises, Inc. 2006.

Reaves, Bill. *History of Burgaw*. 2006.

Sanchez, Sonya. *Love Poems*. New York: The Third Press, Joseph Okpaku Publishing Co. Inc. 1973.

Smith, Jessie Carney, and Wynn, Linda T. *Freedom Facts and First*. Canton, Michigan: Visible Ink Press. 2009

Smith Robert Samuel, *Race Labor and Civil Rights*. Louisiana State University Press. 2008.

Thomas, Velma Maia. *Lest We Forget*. New York: Crown Publishers, Inc. 1997.

Thomas, Larry Reni. *The True Story of The Wilmington 10 Case*. Khalifah & Associates. 1993.

Tyson, Timothy. *Blood Done Sign My Name*. New York: Three Rivers Press. 2004.

Umfleet, LeRae. *1898 Wilmington Race Riot Report,* May 31, 2006.

Umfleet, LeRae Sikes. *A Day of Blood*. Raleigh: North Carolina: North Carolina Office of Archives and History. 2009.

Washington, James M. *The Essential Writings and Speeches of Martin Luther King, Jr.*

Watson, Alan D. *Wilmington N.C. to 1861*. New York: McFarland & Company. 2003.

Wood, Joe. *Malcom X In Our Own Image*. New York: St. Martin's Press. 1992.

Woodson, Carter G. *Mis-Education of the Negro*.

Wright, Richard, *Native Son*. New York: Harper & Brothers. 1940

WAYNE MOORE

After attending Shaw University following my release from prison, I left North Carolina for Ann Arbor MI. where I joined Local 252 of the International Brotherhood of Electrical Workers. I worked as an inside wireman until my retirement in 2013. In 2010, I organized the Fortieth Anniversary Commemoration of the Wilmington Ten and Founded The Wilmington Ten Foundation for Social Justice. I am a member in good standing of St. Mary's Lodge #4 of the Prince Hall Masons. Also a writer, I am currently residing in Ann Arbor. For more insight and images surrounding the backdrop of this memoir go to *http://triumphantwarriors. ning.com/* and *http://wilmtenfoundation.org/*

31618698R00184

Made in the USA
Charleston, SC
23 July 2014